SO-BRW-163

AMC
River Guide

MAINE

TABLE OF CONTENTS

MAINE WATERSHEDS

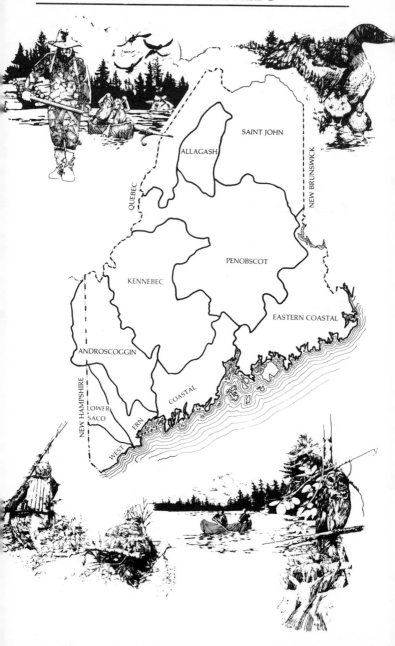

Preface

The first extensive guidebook to New England rivers was *Quickwater and Smooth,* by John C. Phillips and Thomas D. Cabot, published in 1935. This book included only a few Maine rivers, all in the extreme southwestern part, since at that time access to the northern Maine woods was more difficult, and campers were required to be accompanied by a registered Maine guide, who could presumably provide the needed directional information.

In 1965, the Appalachian Mountain Club published its *New England Canoeing Guide.* This was an updated and greatly expanded version of the earlier work, assembled by a committee of volunteers under the direction of Kenneth A. Henderson and Stewart T. Coffin. Revised editions were published in 1968 and 1971.

This book in turn was replaced by the *AMC River Guide* as a result of a decision to adopt a format designed for easier reference. Separate volumes were published for Northeastern and South-Central New England. Updated river descriptions incorporated headings giving important characteristics of each river segment. The volunteer architect of this restructuring was Philip Preston.

Conversations with users disclosed that arbitrary political boundaries had more meaning than the natural watershed boundaries, and the organization of the rivers was changed to reflect that. The second edition was therefore a trilogy: The *Maine River Guide,* the *New Hampshire/Vermont River Guide,* and the *Massachusetts/Connecticut/Rhode Island River Guide.* This is the first volume of the third edition.

This book contains descriptions of more than 3700 miles of canoeing, nearly half of them new or revised for this edition. We thank the following people for providing some river descriptions: David Libby, William Fake, Leonard MacPhee, Terry Trudell, Reg Gilbert, Bill Gerber, Howard Corning, Jerry McCarthy, Zip Kellogg, Bob Roe, Cathy Johnson, George Trudell, and Rick and Elizabeth Burt.

Since both the rivers themselves and the works of man associated with them are changing, no river guidebook is ever complete. We invite the reader to help us along.

AMC Maine River Guide Committee:
Roioli Schweiker, *Editor*
Eric Hendrickson
Philip Preston
Mike Krepner
Jay Spenciner
Jim Chute
Anna McIntyre
Jim Lewis

Introduction

The function of this book is to describe rivers, not to teach canoeing. Many local and national organizations and outfitters offer safety tips, "how-to" books, instruction, and companionship. Take advantage of them.

When the (silver) *AMC Canoeing Guide* was originally written, aluminum canoes were just starting to supplant wood canoes, and many rapids which had previously been carried or cautiously poled were now customarily run. By the first volume of the new *River Guide* series, the proliferation of logging roads had improved access so that "downriver only" trips had replaced the laborious and time-consuming crossing of watersheds to areas otherwise accessible only by floatplane.

Now even more high-tech canoes are being built to deal with the more difficult rapids. Even more former portages have turned into standard runs for experts. The problem of rating rivers, already complicated by variation in water levels, is further compounded by the type of canoe used. A rapid which is an "easy Class III" to an expert in his special-design boat stuffed full of foam may still be a portage to someone else. In *high* water, rapids Class III and above are rated for "heavy-water" boats with extra depth or special design. If you are paddling a small "flatwater" canoe, expect to raise the rating at least one class.

River Descriptions

The river descriptions in this book are arranged by watersheds. The Allagash River, because of its popularity and special status, is treated separately. Rivers that flow to tidewater are described in the last two chapters.

Each of the following chapters, except the Allagash, begins with a map that identifies the rivers described in the text. The principal river is described first and then the tributaries in descending order. In the coastal watersheds the rivers are arranged from west to east.

Format for River Descriptions

The description starts with general information about the river. Each section of river then has a heading which provides significant information about that segment. This is intended to allow rapid "browsing" of the book by people interested in certain types of rivers.

Section subheading   **distance**

Difficulty of the river
  Recommended water levels
  Description of the scenery
    USGS: maps
  Portages:
Campsites:

The detailed write-up appears next, describing the river as the canoeist sees it.

Explanation of Terms

Difficulty of the River

A river is rated by one or more of the following terms. If two or more are used, one of the terms may describe a significantly larger portion of the river. When it does, it appears in bold type.

Lake . . . is used only when the river in a particular section flows through a lake, or when it is necessary to paddle across one to the beginning of a river.

Flatwater . . . is still water, or river with a slow enough current to make upstream paddling equally easy.

Quickwater . . . is fast-moving water. The surface of the river is nearly smooth in high water, apt to be choppy in medium water, and usually shallow in low water.

Marsh, Swamp . . . is water that winds around through, and may be severely obstructed by, vegetation. Route finding may be difficult, and progress is usually slow.

Class . . . refers to the general classification of the rapids (I, II, III, or IV) on the river. There may be one or two more difficult ones noted in the text.

Recommended Water Levels

These ratings apply to the water levels for which the river is best suited. Approximate dates are also given. A river for which high water is recommended may be travelled in medium water, but it is likely to be scratchy with some sections that may have to be waded down. "High water only" implies that much or all of the river is impassable in medium water. The use of the following terms is subject to wide interpretation.

High water . . . occurs when the river is full, with the bases of bushes and trees, especially alders and swamp maples, standing in water.

Medium water . . . occurs when the river extends up to the vegetation on the banks, but few plants are underwater. Marshy areas may be wet. This level is good for gradients of ten to twenty feet per mile, but less than enough for good passage on small rivers with a gradient of over twenty feet per mile.

Low water . . . is acceptable for flatwater paddling and for some rapids on large rivers.

Description of the Scenery

Wild . . . implies long sections of semi-wilderness, with no more than a few isolated camps and only occasional road access. Dirt roads may parallel the river within sight or sound, but they do so only for short distances, and they do not noticeably alter the semi-wilderness character of the trip as a whole. They may, in fact, be closed to the public or impassable altogether.

Forested . . . banks on both sides of the river appear to be densely wooded, but may have a good dirt or tar road running along or near the water. There may be farms and houses nearby, but they are seldom visible from the river.

Rural . . . sections have farms that are visible from the river, and some fields may extend down to the water.

Towns . . . along the river are small and isolated. They are quickly passed, with their presence, other than their effect upon the quality of the water, felt for only a short distance.

Settled . . . areas contain many houses or small buildings within sight or sound of the river.

Urban . . . areas contain multi-storied buildings. The shorelines are frequently unattractive.

USGS Maps

The topographic maps listed with each river description are in either the 7½ minute or the 15 minute series. Titles of the latter are followed by the number "15." The name of a map is in italics if it covers only a very small portion of a route.

Portages

The portages listed include all unavoidable carries (such as dams and waterfalls) and difficult sections where there is usually insufficient water to make them runnable. In addition, some rapids are listed if their difficulty significantly exceeds the rating of that portion of the river. For example,

Portages:	2½ mi	R	**dam**	50 yd
	5 mi	e	**ledge**	
	(11¾ mi	L	**dam**	500 yd)

The first dam is 2½ miles from the start and should be portaged on the right for 50 yards. The ledge at 5 miles from the start can be portaged on either side. The distance will vary with the height of the water and the skill of the paddler. In some cases it might possibly be run, but it is well above the level of difficulty given in the chart above. The parentheses around the dam at 11¾ miles indicate it need not be portaged by those ending their trip there.

Unlisted portages may occur where there are fallen trees, low snowmobile bridges, or carries around rapids you do not wish to run.

Campsites

Information on campsites is listed as follows:

(6) mi	L	**5th St. John Pond** (near canal)—permit
1½ mi	R	**Red Pine Grove** (poor)—NMW $ car

a) Parentheses around the distance indicate that the campsite is located off the route normally followed, and opposite or in line with a point six miles along that route.

b) "L" indicates the left-hand side of Fifth Saint John Pond.

c) The name or location of the campsite is followed by special directions (near canal) or a comment (poor).

d) A fire permit is needed for those sites which are followed by the word "permit." They may be obtained at a Maine Forest Service Ranger Station, including those indicated on the chapter maps.

e) Administering organizations are also noted: Allagash Wilderness Waterway (AWW), Maine Forest Service (MFS), and North Maine Woods (NMW).

f) Fees are charged where the symbol "$" appears, and when a campsite is also accessible by road, the word "car" is written.

There are at present two conflicting theories on camping. The first (required by law on certain rivers) is that all camping should be done at a few developed sites, while the second is that a campsite should never be used more than once to minimize damage to the site. The option selected is usually up to the discretion of the party, but in either case the extensive "improvement" projects described in older campcraft books should be avoided without the specific permission of the landowner. A pamphlet on "Low Impact Camping" may be obtained from the AMC.

Format for Older River Descriptions

WEBB RIVER

USGS:	*Weld*, Dixfield

Some river descriptions have been essentially reprinted from the *New England Canoeing Guide,* with a few minor corrections, and they retain the format used in that book. Recent information on these rivers is especially desired, and should be sent to:

River Guide Committee, c/o AMC, 5 Joy St., Boston MA 02108

Maps

One of the most frequent complaints about the *River Guide* is its lack of detailed maps. Various types have been considered, but all have been ruled out due to their cost in comparison to available alternatives.

Commercial guidebooks that describe relatively few rivers often include strip maps of each run. There are over 3700 miles of river described in the *AMC Maine River Guide,* and to print strip maps at the same scale as USGS 7½-minute quadrangles would require over 1000 pages.

Maine Highway Map: The official highway map of Maine is published by David DeLorme Co., Yarmouth ME 04096.

Maine Atlas: The best single collection of maps of Maine is the DeLorme Maine Atlas and Gazetteer. This is revised frequently and shows all the access roads open to the public, as well as campsites and much other useful information. It is sold at most bookstores and sporting goods stores in the northeast. The scale is ½ inch: 1 mile.

USGS: U.S. Geological Survey maps with contour lines are available at many sporting goods, stationery stores, L. L. Bean, and from the U.S. Geological Survey, Distribution Section, 1200 South Eads St., Arlington VA 22202.

CNTS: Similar maps of Canada are available, which, for

rivers crossing the border, have the additional advantage of also showing the U.S. side. For an index map and information on ordering: Canada Map Office, Dept. of Energy, Mines and Resources, 615 Booth St., Ottawa, Ontario K1A OE9.

NOS: National Ocean Survey charts provided better information on tidal parts of the big coastal rivers than the USGS. National Ocean Survey, Distribution Division (C-44), Riverdale MD 20840.

Tide Tables: These are available in various forms at libraries, marinas, and sporting goods stores, as well as from the NOS address above. Tide information is often given on coastal radio and TV weather reports.

Administering Organizations

Allagash Wilderness Waterway
Bureau of Parks and Recreation, Station 22
Augusta ME 04330
(207-289-3821)

As the popularity of the Allagash has increased, new regulations have been put into effect. To minimize impact, group size is limited and there is a fee for camping. Anyone contemplating a trip on the Allagash should write the Bureau of Parks and Recreation and ask for a map and a copy of the current regulations.

Maine Forest Service
Bureau of Forestry, Ray Building
Augusta ME 04330
(207-289-2791)

In many sections of Maine, the Maine Forest Service has established authorized campsites where fire permits are not needed. However, at many campsites located along the rivers, it is necessary to have a permit in order to build a fire. Information regarding many such sites is given in the individual river descriptions. Fire permits may be obtained at the locations shown on the chapter maps.

Locations of state picnic areas, campsites, and ranger stations are also shown on the DeLorme Maine state highway map.

The Bureau of Forestry's folder, "Forest Campsites," contains a map showing the locations of their campsites and some private ones as well.

North Maine Woods
P.O. Box 382
Ashland ME 04732
(207-435-6213)

North Maine Woods is an organization that was set up to control the access to most of the timberlands north of Baxter State Park and west of Route 11. On behalf of the many landowners of that region, it coordinates the uses of that area by companies engaged in logging operations and by the general public seeking recreation. It maintains checkpoints on the roads which give access to the region and at campsites within.

There is a camping fee to be paid at the checkpoints on arrival. Several flying services are authorized to issue permits, and anyone going in by plane should inquire about this ahead of time. Season registrations are also available.

Since rules and fees are subject to change, write for current information.

Other Information

Paper Industry Information Office
133 State Street
Augusta ME 04330
(207-622-3166)

This organization has information about multiple use on company-owned forest lands, including camping, hiking, and canoeing.

The following outfitters provided assistance and information for the River Guide:

Saco Bound   (603-447-2177)
Box 113
Center Conway NH 03813

Northern Waters   (603-447-2177)
Errol NH 03579

Ed Webb   (207-663-2214)
Wilderness Outfitters
West Forks ME 04985

John Abbott   (207-663-2251)
Kennebec Dories
West Forks ME 04985

James Ernst   (207-672-4814)
Maine Whitewater
Suite 454
Bingham ME 04920

Edwin Pelletier   (207-398-3187)
Box 7
Saint Francis ME 04774

Skitakuk Outfitters   (207-866-4878)
38 Main St.
Orono ME 04473

Smith Hardware Inc.   (207-668-5151)
Box 278
Jackman ME 04945

Eric Hendrickson   (207-455-4096)
Northern River Runners
Box 383—RFD #2
Presque Isle ME 04769

International River Classification

Bear in mind that all ratings are essentially subjective and variable. At low water, a rocky rapid may be trivial for a canoe being poled but totally impossible for an inflatable raft, while the waves at high water will wash the raft right through but fill the canoe with water. All serious rapids should be checked from the shore before running, particularly if the water is unusually high or low.

On small rivers, the greatest safety hazard is often fallen trees. Blind corners should be approached along the inside of the bank if possible. If the current is strong, or obstruction appears likely, the bend should be checked on foot.

Difficult ledges and dams should be checked in advance to find a safe landing spot. Dam-operating personnel should be consulted as to whether there will be water-level fluctuations during the day.

Class I. Very Easy. Waves small, regular; passages clear, sandbanks, artificial difficulties like bridge piers; riffles.

Class II. Easy. Rapids of medium difficulty, with passages clear and wide; low ledges.

Class III. Medium. Waves numerous, high, irregular; rocks; eddies; rapids with passages that are clear though narrow, requiring expertise in maneuver; inspection usually needed.

Class IV. Difficult. Long rapids; waves powerful, irregular; dangerous rocks; boiling eddies; passages difficult to reconnoiter; inspection mandatory first time; powerful and precise maneuvering required.

Class V. Very Difficult. Extremely difficult; long and very violent rapids, following each other almost without interruption; riverbed extremely obstructed; big drops, violent current; very steep gradient; reconnoitering essential but difficult.

Lakes

The text mentions only lakes that would normally be crossed while running a river. Listed below are a few other large lakes which are accessible by car, but which are relatively undeveloped. On each there are established campsites, indicated in the Bureau of Forestry's folder, "Forest Campsites."

Androscoggin Watershed

Aziscohos Lake

> USGS: Second Lake 15, Cupsuptic 15, Errol 15, Oquossoc 15

Mooselookmeguntic & Lower Richardson Lakes

> USGS: Cupsuptic 15, *Old Speck 15,* Oquossoc 15, Rangeley 15

Umbagog Lake

> USGS: Errol 15, Milan 15, *Oquossoc 15*

Kennebec Watershed

Moosehead Lake

> USGS: Brassua Lake 15, Greenville 15, Moosehead Lake 15, North East Carry 15

Eastern Coastal Watersheds

Grand Lake Chain

> USGS: Nicatous Lake 15, Scraggly Lake 15, Springfield 15, Wabassus Lake 15

Spring Water Levels in Maine

The rivers, and the rapids along them, become runnable each spring when warm weather fills them with water from the melting snow and clears them of ice. The length of time for which adequate water is available depends upon the amount of snowfall received during the winter, the rate at which it melts, and the rainfall during April, May, and June. Since many rivers flow through lakes, trips down them must wait until the latter are also ice-free. This frequently occurs in late April to the south, and about a week later farther north.

In the spring, unusual weather conditions may result in floods. Then the rivers are dangerous, and they should be allowed to settle down before you go paddling on them. Sometimes a warm or a dry spring will result in shallow rapids earlier than usual.

The dates given in the river descriptions can be used as a rough guide to the canoeing season. It is usually the case that a river in the north having a large lake in its headwaters provides good canoeing until mid-June if ice-out occurs at the usual time and if the rainfall is about average. By contrast, a river near the coast that does not drain any lakes is likely to be high in mid-April, but low and very likely impassable by early May. Generally, the larger rivers have a longer canoeing season.

If you have doubts about the water level before you set out on a trip, there are three other sources of information which may be of help to you. The first is a local forest warden, the second is a floatplane charter service, and the third is a power company that controls a dam in the area you wish to travel in. A high fire danger is a bad sign, and the local pilots will probably know if the water level is down. And if the discharge from a dam that is used to store water for release later in the year is at a minimum flow, you are in trouble. But do not be surprised if the answers to your questions are not very quantitative.

CHAPTER 1

Lower Saco Watershed

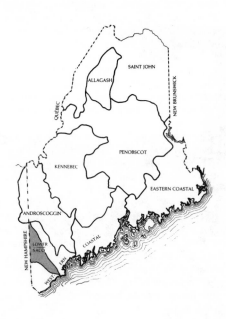

SACO WATERSHED

NH
ME

Cold River

Kezar Lake

Kezar Outlet

Center Conway

Kezar River

Fryeburg

Kezar Pond

Ossipee Lake

Ossipee River

Saco River

Kezar Falls

Hiram

East Limington

Little Ossipee River

Bonny Eagle

Saco River

Biddeford • Saco

Scale in miles

0   5   10   15   20   25   30

SACO RIVER

The Saco is one of New England's most popular rivers. Melting snow and spring rains provide for novice to expert whitewater boating near the headwaters, while below the Maine-New Hampshire border the river is mostly flat and passable at all water levels.

The river begins at Saco Lake just north of Crawford Notch. It drains the southern slopes of the Presidential Range and, in New Hampshire, flows through the Mount Washington Valley of tourist fame. From Conway it winds generally southeast to the ocean south of Portland, Maine.

Although settlement along the Saco began early in the seventeenth century, few towns were located right next to the river, so that it remains to this day a pastoral stream passing through only a few small settlements until it gets almost to the sea. State-supported protection is offered that portion of it in Maine by the Saco River Corridor Commission, which cooperates with local communities in matters relating to zoning and land-use planning.

This book does not include the Saco River or its tributaries in New Hampshire, which are primarily whitewater trips. It also does not include the New Hampshire tributaries of the Ossipee River, which flow into Ossipee Lake and are primarily quickwater. Descriptions of these rivers are available in the companion volume.

The Little Ossipee is a good choice for an overnight trip in the spring. The Saco between Conway and Cornish is very popular for camping trips throughout the canoeing season. (It is, in fact, too popular.)

Spring whitewater is available on the Ossipee and Little Ossipee, while the Saco at Limington Rip can be used all summer. The Saco has a good current and can be run at all water levels. Flatwater is available on lakes and in pools behind dams.

The Saco River: A History and Canoeing Guide by Viola Sheehan, a book about the part of the river in Maine, is available from the Saco River Corridor Association, River Bend Farm, Simpson Road, Saco, Maine 04072. The price is $5.45 postpaid; if sent to a Maine address, $5.70 (incl. tax).

Center Conway—Hiram   43¼ miles

Flatwater, **Quickwater**, Class II
  Passable at all water levels
  Forested, Rural
      USGS: North Conway 15, Ossipee Lake 15,
              Fryeburg, Brownfield, Hiram

Portage:	10 mi	R	**Swan's Falls** 300 yds	
Campsites:	4¼ mi	R	**Sit'n Bull**	commercial $ car
	10 mi	R	**Swan's Falls**	AMC $ car
	14 mi	R	**Canal Bridge (ME-5)**	commercial $ car
	23½ mi	L	**Walker's Falls**	AMC $
	29½ mi	R	**Woodland Acres**	commercial $ car

This is the Sandy Saco, where low water during the summer months exposes miles and miles of beaches. It is a quickwater river in a wide valley of farms and forests. It flows alternately along the edges of fields and through stands of pines and swamp maples. There are a few small towns, but none of them infringe upon the river.

The setting is so peaceful, the water so clean, that the Saco attracts people: hundreds and hundreds of them on a nice summer weekend. Large numbers of them camp along the way, and by late afternoon many of the sandy beaches have been claimed for the night. This kind of high density usage can easily have an impact on the water quality if human wastes are not disposed of properly. The place for them is in a shallow pit dug in the organic layer on the banks away from the river where vegetation and good soil can compost them. Anything buried in the sand bars will soon be in the river, either through leaching or because of erosion.

The river is clearest in the 17½ miles from Center Conway to the confluence with the Old Saco. The current is stronger, the river generally shallower, the banks more open, and the sand bars more numerous. As you approach and pass the Old Saco entering from the north, you will notice that the banks are more heavily forested and the water is darker.

You may park cars at Saco Bound on US-302 between Center Conway and the Maine border, at Swan's Falls (fee), at Canal Bridge on ME-5, at Walker's Bridge on US-302, at the Brownfield bridge on ME-160, and at Saco Valley Garage in Hiram (fee). There is also a public access at the south end of Lovewell Pond that is reached via a road that leaves ME-5/113 southeast of Fryeburg and north of a railroad crossing.

Large-scale canoeing maps of this section of the Saco can be obtained from the AMC Swan's Falls Campground or from Saco Bound ($).

If you build a fire in Maine outside the established campgrounds listed below, you should obtain a permit. In Fryeburg, one can be obtained at Osgood Brothers or at Solari's Store.

Just below the US-302 bridge near Center Conway, the river flows between the abutments of the old covered bridge and soon there are some Class II rips that are bony in low water. The remaining 9 miles to Swan's Falls are mostly quickwater. The main highway approaches the river next to Saco Bound (3¼ mi), then there is Weston Bridge (6¾ mi), and finally Swan's Falls (10 mi), where there is a dam that should be approached cautiously in high water. Portage on the right.

About a mile past Canal Bridge (14 mi) the river swings to the north and a stream enters on the right. The latter can be followed upstream 100 yards or so to Bog Pond, a small and secluded body of water. The next landmark is the Old Saco (17½ mi), which enters on the left.

The **Old Course of the Saco,** as the name implies, used to be the channel of the river. Above the confluence the Saco today follows a canal dug in 1817 for flood control. The western end of the Old Saco is silted in, but the eastern portion of it still drains Kezar Lake.

From the Old Saco (17½ mi) quickwater continues for 6 miles past Walker's Bridge, US-302 (21 mi), and the outlet to Pleasant Pond (23¼ mi) to Walker's Falls (23½ mi) where the short, easy rapids become flooded out at high water. Pleasant Pond is very close to the river, and from it there are good views of the mountains.

Two miles below Walker's Falls the outlet from Lovewell Pond enters on the right. Then the Saco winds somewhat, passing to the west of Brownfield Bog, a major
nesting area for native ducks. Below the ME-160 bridge (29½
mi) there are more meanders for the next 13¾ miles to
Hiram (43¼ mi).

Hiram—Bonny Eagle Dam (ME-35)   25¼ miles

Flatwater, **Quickwater**, Class I–II
    Passable at all levels: *1 dangerous rapid in high water*
    Forested, Rural, Towns
        USGS: Hiram, Cornish, Sebago Lake 15,
            Buxton 15

Portages:	2¾ mi	L	**Great Falls Dam** ¼ mi
	14¾ mi	L	**Steep Falls** 50 yds
	25½ mi	R	**Bonny Eagle Dam** 70 yds
Campsites:	14¾ mi	L	**Steep Falls** (at portage)
	15 mi	R	**Steep Falls** (R turn below old dam)
	19½ mi		**Limington Rips** (island at top)

This portion of the river receives much less use than does
the section preceding it. The water is not as clear as it is near
Fryeburg, but the scenery is comparable. The occasional
rapids are a feature not found on the section from Center
Conway to Hiram.

In the late spring when water levels are generally medium,
a very nice 20¾-mile run can be made by starting at Kezar
Falls and running the Ossipee River to the Saco near Cornish, and then continuing down the Saco to the NH-25
bridge in East Limington.

The Saco has a large watershed, and it is a fairly large
river. The rapids are much more difficult in high water, especially Limington Rips, which generate very large waves.

From Hiram there is flatwater for 2¾ miles to Great Falls
Dam. **Caution!** In high water, go left of an island after a
sweeping left turn. Land on the left above the dam and portage along a trail to a tar road, which leads down to the

river. There is a piped spring below a chain-link fence to the left of the powerhouse.

Two-thirds of a mile below Great Falls Dam there is a Class I rapid at a short left turn. Quickwater continues past the mouth of the Ossipee River (5¾ mi) to the ME-5/117 bridge in Cornish (6¼ mi).

There are riffles just past the Cornish bridge. After 2¾ miles you reach Old Bald Rapid, a short Class II pitch with large waves in high water. There are some more riffles in the remaining 5½ miles to Steep Falls.

Steep Falls (14¾ mi) is a dangerous 7-foot drop, which must be portaged. You are apt to come upon it suddenly, especially in the fast-moving current of high water. Be alert for the sound of falling water, a glimpse of a house on the left bank, or the sighting of a green girder bridge below the falls. When you notice any of them, get quickly to the left bank where there is a short portage. After the falls there is ¼ mile of rapids, Class II in low water, but rougher in high water. They continue under the bridge and past the remains of a dam.

Below Steep Falls, riffles continue intermittently for a mile, followed by almost 3 miles of quickwater to Parkers Rips, a short Class II rapid near a house on the right where the river swings left. In ¾ mile you reach Limington Rips, a ½-mile set of Class II rapids in low water, but Class III with heavy waves in medium water.

The left-hand side of the island requires more maneuvering and is usually used in low water. The drop is steeper on the right, but scouting is easier, and the shore closer in case of mishap. The take-out above the rapid is also on the right to a road immediately adjacent. The hardest section of this rapid is near the end, below the ME-25 bridge (19¾ mi).

Just past Limington Rips the Little Ossipee River enters on the right (20 mi). A deadwater continues for the remaining 5¼ miles to Bonny Eagle Dam (25¼ mi) just below the ME-35 bridge. Take out on the right bank near the powerhouse. If you are continuing down the river, portage beyond the building about 50 yards to a set of steps that lead down past a wellhouse to the river.

Bonny Eagle Dam (ME-35)—Biddeford   19 miles

Lake, Flatwater
  Passable at all water levels
  Forested, Rural, Towns
      USGS: Buxton 15, *Kennebunk 15,* Biddeford
            15, *Portland 15*
  Portages: 1½ mi   L   **dam at West Buxton**
               6¾ mi   R   **dam at Bar Mills**
               10 mi   R   **Skelton Dam**
               (20 mi   **dams)**

More than half of this section consists of deadwaters behind a succession of dams. Near the ME-4A/117 bridge
(8 mi) at Salmon Falls (flooded out), you enter the third
deadwater. As the river opens into the wide lake behind
Skelton Dam at Union Falls (10 mi), head southeast.

A couple of miles after the ME-5 bridge (14½ mi), the
flatwater is broken by a short rapid. Below the Maine Turnpike (18¾ mi) there is a convenient take-out on the right at
Rotary Park (19 mi). There are dams in Biddeford and
Saco, below which the river is tidal.

OLD COURSE OF THE SACO

Kezar Outlet drains Kezar Lake south to the northernmost point of the Old Course of the Saco. The upper (western) portion of the old course is now only a series of
sloughs, its entrance from the Saco unidentifiable. The
lower portion is kept active by the outlets from Kezar Lake,
Charles Pond, and Kezar Pond. Wildlife is abundant; almost every stump and rock is covered with turtles in season.

Kezar Outlet—Saco River   8 miles

Quickwater
  Passable anytime
  Forested
      USGS: Fryeburg 15

The current flows briskly, and vegetation covers the bottom, waving sinuously. Red School Bridge on US-5 (4 mi) and Hemlock Covered Bridge (6½ mi) also allow access.

The outlet from Kezar Pond enters left just above the Covered bridge. The Saco River is another 1½ miles.

KEZAR LAKE OUTLET

This route is popular as an access to the Saco River, making an interesting variation. Swimming is not as desirable as on the main Saco.

Kezar Lake Narrows—Old Course   4½ miles

Lake, Flatwater
  Passable anytime
  Forested
    USGS: Fryeburg 15
    Portage: 4¼ mi   **dam**   10 yds

From the landing at Kezar Narrows, paddle southwest into the lower bay and across it to the outlet (1¾ mi). The lake level is raised by a small dam on the outlet just above the confluence with the Charles River (4½ mi). The wire grating above it must also be lifted over.

Below the dam, the river flows quickly along, passing under a bridge near the confluence. It may be rocky in low water.

CHARLES RIVER

The Charles River is the outlet to Charles Pond, and flows from it to the outlet from Kezar Lake; they meet and flow together into the Old Course of the Saco.

Charles Pond—Kezar Outlet   1½ miles

Flatwater, Quickwater
  Medium Water
  Forested
    USGS: Fryeburg

The Charles River leaves from the east side of Charles Pond. It is rockier and wider than the Cold River, and may require occasional wading to pass when the Cold River is runnable. It passes under a bridge just above the confluence with Kezar Outlet.

COLD RIVER

The Cold River is a small stream that drains the south side of Evans Notch, flowing to Charles Pond, and ultimately to the Saco River. Being a narrow stream with a good watershed, it may be run after summer thunderstorms.

Pine Hill Road—Charles Pond   9 miles

Quickwater
    Medium water: *late spring or after heavy rain*
Forested
        USGS: North Conway 15, Fryeburg 15

Put in from the road to Pine Hill. This Cold River is very small, but flows mostly over a smooth, sandy bottom, with deep pools here and there. The only hazard is an occasional fallen tree. It flows into the north side of Charles Pond, which is about ½ mile in diameter, with the outlet only a few hundred feet to the left.

KEZAR RIVER

This small stream drains the Five Kezar Ponds in Stoneham and flows southwest to the Old Course of the Saco just north of Kezar Pond.

Number Four—Lovell   2¼ miles

This stream can be run from here after a heavy summer rain. It is a canoe-width wide at the start, with overhanging bushes. After 1½ miles it opens up into the flowage from the dam at Lovell, with pond lilies and attractive wooded banks.

Persons continuing can portage right through a culvert under the highway.

Lovell—Old Channel 3½ **miles**

Shortly below the start some old debris obstructs the river. The bottom is sandy where it circles around Smarts Hill. The river enters Swimming Bog about 2 miles from Lovell, and somewhat disappears into it. By keeping to the right-hand channel, one may be able to work through it down to the Old Saco. When the river is up, much of the water overflows into Kezar Pond.

OSSIPEE RIVER

The Ossipee River flows east for 17½ miles from Lake Ossipee, across the Maine border, and into the Saco River near Cornish. It has a dependable flow in the spring, but by summer the water level is too low to run the lower section.

Ossipee Lake—Kezar Falls 10¾ **miles**

Quickwater, Class I–II
  High and medium water: *spring*
  Low water: *passable, some lining required at rapids*
  Forested, Rural, Towns
      USGS: Ossipee Lake 15, Kezar Falls
  Portages: 10½ mi   **1st dam at Kezar Falls**
                  (across island) 30 yds
          10¾ mi R **2nd dam at Kezar Falls**
                        30 yds

Quickwater characterizes this section, although there is one very nice rapid just above the NH-153 bridge in Effingham Falls. There are several more short rapids before Kezar Falls, but for most of the distance the river is smooth. There are vacation cottages along the banks near the beginning, and below East Freedom there are more cottages and houses, with a main highway close by on the left bank for much of the distance. Anyone seeking a paddle in remote surroundings will not find it here.

The dam at the outlet of Ossipee Lake is at the end of a side road ½ mile west of the junction of NH-25 and 153 in Effingham Falls. Put in below the gatehouse and run down the sluiceway to a pool of slackwater. Soon there begins ¼ mile of rapids that are Class II or III, depending on the water level. They are the hardest on the river, and they lead up to the NH-153 bridge (1½ mi).

Then there are 1½ miles of quickwater past the NH-25 bridge (2 mi) to East Freedom, where ¼ mile of Class II rapids leads under a bridge (4½ mi) to the Maine border. The remaining distance to Kezar Falls is mostly quickwater with two short Class II rapids, one before and one after the ME-160 bridge in Porter (7¾ mi).

In Kezar Falls, go to the right of the island and take out at a small bridge (10½ mi). If you are continuing downstream, carry across the island to the foot of the main dam and continue ¼ mile through the town to the second dam (10¾ mi). Take out on the right, carry across the canal, and put in below the dam.

Kezar Falls—Saco River   6¾ miles

Quickwater, Class I–II
  High water: *recommended, early spring*
  Medium water: *late spring*
  Forested, Rural
      USGS: Kezar Falls, Cornish

Below the second dam in Kezar Falls, the Ossipee River takes on a different character. It is a very scenic run past forests and farms almost all the way to the Saco River, with quickwater or rapids for the entire distance.

When the water level is up, the run from Kezar Falls to the ME-5/117 bridge over the Saco can be made in a little over an hour, but if you continue down the Saco for another 14 miles to the ME-25 bridge, you can make a long, scenic trip of mixed flatwater and rapids. Note, however, that Limington Rips, which begin just above the bridge, are very severe rapids in high water.

One-half mile east of the ME-25 bridge in Kezar Falls, turn north onto Garner Avenue and take the first right. Bear left at an old building to reach the dam, or turn right to reach the power station.

Below the dam there are nice Class I and II rapids for 1 mile to Which Way Rips, where the river abruptly divides

around an island. Quickwater and Class I rapids continue to
the first bridge (3½ mi), with more quickwater to the second
(5½ mi). Below the second bridge and past a few cottages,
there are some easy Class II rapids that lead almost to the
Saco River (6¾ mi) only ½ mile above the ME-5/117 bridge
east of Cornish (7¼ mi).

LITTLE OSSIPEE RIVER

The Little Ossipee is a fairly popular trip in southwestern
Maine. It flows east from Balch Pond, a small lake on
the Maine-New Hampshire border, to the Saco River just
downstream from the ME-25 bridge at East Limington.

In high water it is an easy two-day trip of 28¼ miles from
Davis Brook near North Shapleigh to East Limington just
above the confluence with the Saco River. The hardest rapids that are normally run are at Newfield, and they are Class
II. Those at Hardscrabble Falls below ME-117 are so difficult that all but the last hundred yards are usually portaged.
The section below Ledgemere Dam is usually passable
through the summer.

Davis Brook—ME-5   11¼ miles

Flatwater, **Quickwater**, Class I–II
   High water: *recommended, early spring*
   Medium water: *rapids bony, late April to mid-May*
Wild, Forested, Towns
     USGS: Newfield 15

The remotest part of the river is that section above Newfield. Much of the area was burned in 1947, and today it is
covered with scrub growth, predominately gray birch. In
medium water all the rapids are shallow, so high water is
recommended.

ME-11 crosses the Little Ossipee at the Newfield-Shap-
leigh town line. Just south of this point, follow Mann Road
east for 0.9 miles to the double culvert over Davis Brook.

Alternately, a start can be made at the culvert on ME-11.
There are rocks inside that are difficult to dodge in the
darkness. The first mile to Davis Brook contains shallow

rapids, which may be choked with debris and may require short carries.

Davis Brook is a small stream that flows into the Little Ossipee ¼ mile from Mann Road. Then, in the next 4¼ miles, the main river is a mixture of quickwater and short, easy Class I–II rapids. The river flows through some small meadows, and there is at least one beaver dam.

Approaching Newfield, there is a Class II drop over some ledges. Then, beginning just above the bridge (4¾ mi), there is ¼ mile of hard Class II rapids that must be lined in medium water.

Just east of Newfield, ME-11 crosses Chellis Brook. If the depth of the water over the cement brookbed under the bridge is between 1¼ and 1½ feet, the Little Ossipee is probably at medium level. In that case, the recommended start is at Chellis Brook, which joins the main river in 100 yards. If the water under the bridge is less than 8 inches, this section will be scratchy in many places.

Most of the remaining 6¼ miles to ME-5 at Ossipee Mills is quickwater with no significant rapids. About halfway down you pass between the two old abutments of Clark's Bridge.

ME-5—Ledgemere Dam   5¾ miles

Lake
    Forested
        USGS: Newfield 15, Buxton 15
        Portage: (5¾ mi R **Ledgemere Dam**   100
                                      yds)

The flashboards on Ledgemere Dam may not be in place, with the result that the level of the lake may be down a few feet. Ledgemere Flowage, renamed Lake Arrowhead by real estate developers peddling house lots, will then have some sections of shoals and extensive mud flats with exposed stumps. In some places sandy beaches will be exposed. Portions of the lake are attractive; other parts are not. There are a few houses, but most of the shoreline remains undeveloped.

The lake poses navigation problems. The topographic map shows the normal pool elevation, but the lake may not always be full. It may be necessary to use it as a guide to the edge of the forest surrounding the lake. If the water is low, you can detect a current in some of the passages when there is no wind.

Ledgemere Dam—East Limington   11¾ miles

Flatwater, **Quickwater,** Class II
   Passable at all water levels
   Forested
     USGS: Buxton 15

Portage:	4¼ mi	R	**Hardscrabble Falls**	½ mi
	11¼ mi	L	**falls at East Limington** 300 yds	
Campsite:	4¾ mi	R	**Hardscrabble Falls** (end of portage)	

The Little Ossipee is much larger below Ledgemere Flowage than it is above it. The banks are heavily wooded all the way to East Limington, and near the end it flows in a small, narrow valley with steep slopes close to the riverbank. There is a lot of flatwater in this section and almost no easily runnable rapids. The first of the two ledge drops, Hardscrabble Falls, should be portaged, while the second one is just after a logical take-out point near the end of the river.

The current is fast for a mile or so to a short Class I drop. Then it is slow past the ME-117 bridge (1¾ mi) to the second bridge (4¼ mi), which is at the top of Hardscrabble Falls. **Caution!** Stop on the right above the bridge. The falls, which are ½ mile long, begin and end with Class II rapids, but the middle section consists of a steep drop over a series of ledges that will not tempt many canoeists. The portage follows a dirt road close to the right bank, and it makes a sharp right turn after passing a field on the right.

From the end of Hardscrabble Falls (4¾ mi), the river is flat and winding for 6 miles to a short Class II drop within sight of, and ½ mile above, the next bridge. **Caution!** This is the bridge at East Limington located just above the second dangerous pitch. Stop above this bridge (11¼ mi) on the left.

The easiest take-out is just past it on the left, but you should look at the approach, particularly in high water.

Access at East Limington: The bridge above the last portage is about a mile by road from the ME-25 bridge over the Saco River. Heading east from the latter, take the first left.

If you are continuing the last ½ mile to the Saco, portage the falls at East Limington beginning along the road on the left. Another ¼ mile of flatwater brings you to the end of the Little Ossipee. Limington Rips is ¼ mile to the left, and Bonny Eagle Dam is 5¼ miles down the deadwater to the right.

CHAPTER 2

Androscoggin Watershed

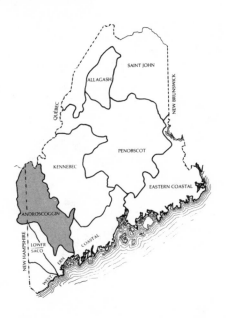

ANDROSCOGGIN WATERSHED

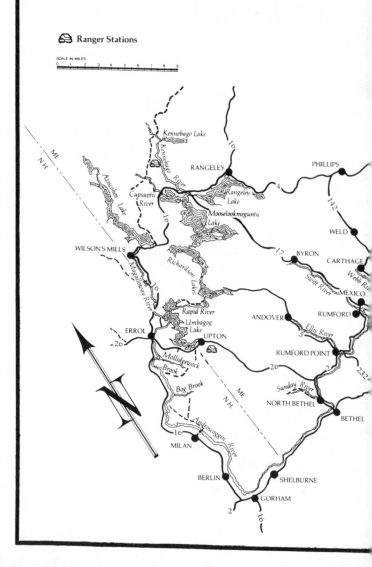

⌂ Ranger Stations

SCALE IN MILES
0 1 2 3 4 5 6 7 8 9

Kennebago Lake
RANGELEY
PHILLIPS
Kennebago River
Azischohos Lake
ME
NH
Cupsuptic River
Rangeley Lake
4
142
Mooselookmeguntic Lake
WELD
WILSON'S MILLS
Richardson Lakes
17 BYRON
CARTHAGE
Webb River
Swift River
MEXICO
Magalloway River
Rapid River
ANDOVER
RUMFORD
Umbagog Lake
Ellis River
ERROL
UPTON
5
26
Mollidgewock Brook
RUMFORD POINT
2
232
Bog Brook
26
Sunday River
ME
NH
NORTH BETHEL
BETHEL
16
Androscoggin River
MILAN
BERLIN
SHELBURNE
GORHAM
2
16

ANDROSCOGGIN RIVER

The river that flows into Berlin clear and almost drink-able becomes severely polluted, like the air above it. From then on, at intervals ranging from twenty to fifty miles, the river picks up additional dosages of paper mill effluent. The water quality improves the farther downstream you get from a paper company, so travel on the river becomes more pleasant, unless of course the wind is blowing upstream from the next mill.

In recent years there has been a letup in the abuse to which the river has been subjected. The Brown Company had its last pulpwood drive on the upper Androscoggin in 1963, and several new treatment plants are either planned, under construction, or operating. A good article on the sub-ject appeared in the March, 1975 issue of *Audubon:* "Of Slime and the River," by Frank Graham, Jr.

The Androscoggin River is formed north of Errol at the confluence of the Magalloway River and the outlet of Um-bagog Lake, which is no longer a clearly defined spot, as the dam at Errol floods many miles up both branches. The lakes in the headwaters form a vast storage area of im-pounded water to run the mills and power stations on the Androscoggin. This is what makes the summer canoeing on the rapids possible.

Lake Umbagog—Berlin   34½ miles

Flatwater, **Quickwater**, Class I–II
  Dam-controlled: *good flow spring through fall*
  Forested, Rural
     USGS: Errol 15, Milan 15, Berlin

Portages:	3¾ mi		**Errol Dam**	
	21¾ mi		**Pontook Dam**	
	(34½ mi		**Berlin Dam**)	
Campsites:	4½ mi	R	**Errol Bridge** car	private $
	8 mi	R	**Mollidgewock** car	private $

This is the clean water section of the Androscoggin. Be-low the Errol and Pontook dams there are whitewater runs all through the summer. Although they are neither long nor difficult, they are very popular because in July and August there are few alternatives in New England.

The valley is an attractive one, though not wild because a main road follows the river closely almost all the way. For this reason, it is rarely, if ever, used for overnight canoe trips, although it might be the end of a long one that begins on the lakes above.

Below Lake Umbagog the river is wide with extensive marshes on both sides. In 3 miles it reaches NH-16, where there is a launching ramp, and ¾ mile beyond is the Errol Dam (3¾ mi), which is portaged on the left.

The section from the Errol Dam to just below the NH-26 bridge, ¾ mile long, consists of a short rapid, a pool, and another ½ mile of easier Class II rapids. Due to the slackwater below where Clear Stream enters on the right, and the proximity of the road, these rapids are not as dangerous as the size and difficulty of the river would normally indicate. If you plan to run this section by itself, the best way to reach it is to park your car beside the pool above Errol and paddle over to the portage on the east bank below the dam.

Below Clear Stream (4¾ mi) there are 3¼ miles of flatwater to Mollidgewock Brook (8 mi), below which there are 3 miles of Class II rapids separated by pools, with mixed smoothwater and riffles for the remaining distance to Pontook Reservoir. There is a bridge (12¾ mi) just above Seven Islands and Bog Brook (16¼ mi) that enters on the left. Portage Pontook Dam (21¾ mi) on the right.

Below the remains of Pontook Dam is the second good whitewater run, 2¼ miles of Class II or III rapids (depending on the water level) that end where the river makes a sharp right turn around some islands. The dam can be reached via a dirt road off NH-16, and at the end there is a take-out point on the right bank at the edge of a large field. You may be able to drive from a turn-out on NH-16 along the edge of the field to the river. Please stay off the field.

The remaining 10½ miles have a good current but no rapids. There is a public access to the river on the left bank (25¼ mi) at the Dummer-Milan town line. There is a bridge in Milan (27¾ mi), and in Berlin you should take out at the playground (34½ mi) located on the left below the first bridge.

Berlin—Shelburne Dam   11½ miles

Flatwater, Quickwater, Class I
  Not recommended: *dams, pollution*
  Urban, Forested
     USGS: Berlin, Shelburne
Portages: **7 dams**

The river valley is very attractive, with views of the Presidential Range to the southwest and lower mountains to the east. Although people do canoe it, and all the dams are supposed to be well marked, this section is not especially recommended. The pollution is distinctly noticeable, parts are unattractive, not to mention the problem of the portages.

Shelburne Dam—Bethel   17¾ miles

Flatwater, Quickwater, Class I
  Dam-controlled: *good flow spring through fall*
  Forested, Rural
     USGS: Shelburne, Gilead, Bethel

Although the water in this section is polluted, the river valley is very attractive, with views of the Presidential Range to the southwest and lower mountains to the east. The river smells somewhat, but more important is the wind direction, which blows ill from Berlin to the west and from Rumford to the east.

Put in below the dam at the bridge on which the Appalachian Trail crosses the river. Two log cribs dominate the view upstream over the dam. There is good current with pleasant riffles for many miles, as the river continually separates around numerous islands.

There is a bridge at 2¾ miles. Above the next bridge near Gilead (8¾ mi) is the most difficult rapid in this section, dropping past rocky outcroppings.

At the site of the old West Bethel ferry landing on the south bank behind the dowel factory is an excellent access to the river. This point is identified on the river by the first visible house in miles and by a small power line across the river.

The current continues slower to Bethel and the ME-26 bridge.

Bethel—Rumford   24½ miles

Flatwater, **Quickwater**, Class I
  Dam controlled: *good flow spring through fall*
  Forested
       USGS: Bethel, Bryant Pond, *East Andover,*
             Rumford
  Portage: (24½ mi   L   **Rumford**   car
                                       recommended)

This is a very beautiful stretch of river, still in the mountains with fine views in every direction. The river flows through open meadows in an open valley, offering many opportunities to enjoy the views, so that were it not for the odor of the water this would be a most enjoyable trip. There are many riffles but no rapids and the current is good. The views toward Grafton Notch are particularly interesting, and birds are abundant. The river is large, and wind can cause considerable trouble.

The best access at Bethel is ¾ mile beyond the ME-26 bridge on the right bank where a road comes close to the river beyond some lumber yards. Here the river turns north; it passes a highway rest area just before the Sunday River enters on the left (4 mi) in North Bethel. Just beyond the rifle at the mouth of the Bear River entering left (6½ mi) at Newry, the river resumes its eastward course. The Ellis River enters on the left (13¾ mi) shortly before the bridge at Rumford Point (14¼ mi).

The remaining 10 miles to Rumford have a good current and are good going all the way.

Take out at the bridge above the first dam at the pull-off on the left, as there are three dams and a major waterfall that make it advisable to carry the whole city in one long portage, cutting across the northward loop of the river where the Swift River enters.

Rumford—Livermore Falls   24 miles

USGS: Rumford, Dixfield, *Worthley Pond,*
          Canton, *East Dixfield,* Wilton,
          Livermore Falls

In this stretch the river is still in mountainous country,
although the higher hills have been left behind. From Rumford it is 4 miles with a good current to Dixfield, where the
Webb River enters on the left. The remaining 20 miles to
Livermore Falls present no problems. For some 7 miles the
river remains in a narrow valley, but then gradually the valley becomes more open and the bottom lands wider and
more rural in aspect. Some 16 miles below Dixfield, Sevenmile Stream enters on the left. There is a big dam at Livermore Falls best carried on the left.

Livermore Falls—Auburn-Lewiston   30 miles

USGS: Livermore Falls, Turner Center,
          Lewiston 15

Once Livermore Falls and its small suburb of Shy Corner
have been left behind, this is a fine stretch of rural Maine. It
is 9 miles of open river with no bridges and only two ferries
to the mouth of the Dead River, which enters on the left,
and then another 2½ miles to the ME-219 bridge at North
Turner. Just below this bridge there is a set of rapids, which
should be looked over before running. In 4 miles more the
mouth of the Nezinscot River is passed on the right, and in
another 2 miles the Turner bridge is reached. From here it is
practically all slackwater for 8 miles down Gulf Island Pond
to the Gulf Island Dam. Many canoeists will want to take
out here, but one can continue 1 mile more to the Deep Rips
Dam, another high dam, and then below that another 2½
miles to the first dam in Auburn-Lewiston, where there is a
long carry around the dam and cascades below.

Auburn-Lewiston—Durham   10 miles

USGS: Lewiston 15, Freeport 15, Bath 15

The river now flows through the rolling country of southern Maine, with less spectacular but still pleasant rural scenery. The Little Androscoggin River enters in Auburn, and the best put-in spot is below this at the southern edge of the city.

Durham—Brunswick   13¼ miles

Flatwater, Quickwater, Class II
   Anytime
   Urban, Rural
      USGS: Freeport 15, Lewiston 15, Bath 15
   Portages: 5¼ mi R **Lisbon Falls** ½ mi
             8¾ mi R **dam at Pejepscot** ¼ mi
          (13¼ mi R **dam at Brunswick**)

It is 2 miles to the mouth of the Sabattus River on the left near Lisbon Center, where there is a Class II rapid by the island. It is then another 2 miles to the dam at Lisbon Falls and another 3½ miles of mostly flatwater to the dam at Pejepscot. Most of the remaining 5 miles are quickwater to Brunswick. It is a long haul from the river to the road on the left side near the I-95 bridge.

There are three bridges in Brunswick. There is no practical way to get off the river below the first one, which is a black truss with the railroad above and a one-lane road underneath. When the river is high there are fair-sized waves under it. Therefore, take out as soon as it is in sight. This is a residential area on US-1. Below the second bridge (suspension footbridge) are Class III–IV rapids and no access before the dam.

Below Brunswick, the Androscoggin River is tidal, and soon flows into Merrymeeting Bay.

MAGALLOWAY RIVER

The Magalloway River is a beautiful, little-used river in western Maine. Many forms of wildlife are abundant. Beginning in the small streams of western Maine, the river runs through Aziscohos Lake, then meanders its way into New Hampshire before joining the outlet of Umbagog Lake to form the Androscoggin River. Above Aziscohos Lake there is no public access.

Aziscohos Lake offers many miles of paddling, with a number of campsites available. Below Aziscohos Dam the Magalloway River offers both whitewater and flatwater trips, which may be run in combination with trips across Umbagog Lake and/or the Androscoggin River.

Camping in the area is uncrowded, but limited to designated areas along the rivers and lakes. Culvert Camps on the Magalloway are administered from Mollidgewock Campground (603-447-2177), 3 miles south of Errol.

Aziscohos Dam—Wilsons Mills   3¼ miles

Class II, III, IV
  Dam-controlled: *good flow*
  Wild, Forested
    USGS: Oquossoc 15, Errol 15

Although it may look tempting, under no circumstances put in just below the dam! Many iron rods are still embedded in the bedrock from logging days and will quickly tear any boat or boater into a multitude of pieces.

One quarter of a mile south of the dam on the east side of ME-16, walk through the state sand/gravel pit toward the river down a steep bank. A rough trail leads 50 yards downstream to a launching below a 10-foot waterfall.

The first few hundred yards are extremely technical, and can be bony at low levels. While usually Class III, this stretch can be Class IV at high levels. Beyond, the rapids are less difficult but still technical. After a mile or so on a left bend a large ledge drop may form a large hole at high levels. A hunting camp may be seen on the right side.

From this point the river decreases in intensity as it nears the NH-16 bridge at Wilsons Mills.

Wilsons Mills—Androscoggin River 16¼ miles

Flatwater, Quickwater
Dam-controlled: *good flow spring through fall*
Forested, Rural
USGS: Errol 15

The lower part of the Magalloway offers a leisurely paddle observing wildlife and picturesque views. The river is narrow at the start, with a 3-mph current, meandering along with views of Aziscohos Mtn. on the east, Halfmoon Mtn. and the spectacular granite cliffs on the sides of the Diamond Peaks and Mt. Dustin off to the west, looping into New Hampshire for a mile. Below the confluence with the Diamond River (6 mi) the Magalloway River begins to widen and in ¾ mile passes under the ME-16 bridge near the Magalloway school house, and back into New Hampshire in another mile. From here on the river wanders extravagantly with many side channels to explore, and pond lilies galore. The Sturtevant Pond outlet enters in a wide culvert from the left. Further down, Culvert Camp is on the right. It is 3 miles on to Umbagog Lake and the Androscoggin River, when the river swings west, away from the highway.

UMBAGOG LAKE

All of the big lakes of western Maine—Rangeley, Mooselookmeguntic, and the Richardson Lakes—drain through the Rapid River into Umbagog Lake and thence to the Androscoggin River. All of these lake levels are artificially raised, creating a very dependable reservoir for power generation. They offer many miles of canoeing, having public launching ramps and campsites.

Umbagog Lake is an irregularly shaped shallow lake, mostly wild, but very accessible. Therefore it is a popular, though expensive, place to camp. Settlement is only at the southern end, along NH-26, where reservations for campsites should be arranged.

Camping at Cedar Stump Campground, at the mouth of the Rapid River, is run by Saco Bound/Northern Waters (603-447-2177), in Errol, who can also arrange shuttle service for the Rapid River.

RAPID RIVER

The Rapid River flows from Lower Richardson Lake to Lake Umbagog, and offers difficult rapids and clean water in a remote setting. The river flow is regulated at Middle Dam on Lower Richardson Lake by the Union Water Power Company for power generation and paper production on the Androscoggin. Sometimes recreational water releases are arranged; a schedule can be obtained from the AMC.

Forest Lodge, the former home of Louise Dickinson Rich, whose book *We Took to the Woods* relates her experiences in this region, is on the tote road below Pond in the River. On the northwest shore of Pond in the River are the remains of the steam tug "Alligator," which was used to winch rafts of logs across the lake. Some of the rocks in the river have been blasted to facilitate log drives, and their sharp edges can be hazardous to boaters.

The Rapid River would be even more popular if the access were less difficult. Middle Dam can be reached by a 3-4 mile paddle across Lower Richardson Lake, while the mouth of the Rapid River can be reached by a 6-7 mile paddle from Errol. A motorboat shuttle is often arranged by whitewater paddlers. A tote road runs from Middle Dam to Sunday Cove on Lake Umbagog, and shuttle service is available through Lakewood Camps at Middle Dam (Andover ME; 207-243-2959) for whitewater paddlers wishing to run the rapids, or for flatwater paddlers wishing to avoid them. It is also possible to hand-carry boats up to run the last section of the rapids.

Middle Dam—Long Pool   3 miles

Lake, Class II, III, IV
   Dam-controlled: *600–2000 cfs runnable*
                        1200–1500 cfs recommended for closed boats
  Wild
      USGS: Oquossoc 15

Put in to the whirlpool below the dam or 50 yards downstream at Harbec Pool. The next ½ mile is Cemetery Rapids, which contains Class III waves with the right side recommended for the upper half and the left side for the lower half. The next 1½ mile is Pond in the River. Lower Dam, at the outlet, is mostly gone, and the 2-foot drop can be run if desired, although some old spikes remain. There is a branch road from the tote road for those wishing to start here.

Then there is 1 mile of Class II–III rapids, scratchy at 600 cfs, to Long Pool, where there is a branch road. People carrying up from downstream should take the turn just after a few houses on the right.

Long Pool—Lake Umbagog   3 miles

Quickwater, Class IV, V
   Dam-controlled: *600–2000 cfs runnable*
                   1200–1500 cfs recommended for closed
                   boats
   Wild
       USGS: Oquossoc 15, Errol 15
   Campsite: 1½ mi   **Cedar Stump**   private $

The first 1½ miles is difficult rapids that should be run only by expert boaters with suitable heavy-water craft. Just below Long Pool the river curves slightly to the right and enters the First Big Pitch, which contains 4–6 foot waves even at lower levels and should be run to the right of center to avoid a large hole to the left. This is followed by several hundred yards of easier rapids to another difficult but shorter pitch, sometimes known as Elephant Rock from the large black rock in the middle. After a short, calmer section at Cold Spring, the Third Big Pitch starts, sometimes called the Staircase, from its appearance when viewed from below, with three steps and a pool below each at the lower water levels. This rapid is longer than the first two, and leads to Smooth Ledge. Here a rock dike extends from the right bank, with a hydraulic and a pool below, a favored spot for lunching and playing.

Next up is an S-turn rapid called Island Rip, which is very intricate at 600 cfs and contains larger waves at higher levels. Then come two hydraulics to the right of center called the Jaws of Death. The upper one is full of air and hard to get out of at 600 cfs, not quite as difficult at 1200 cfs, and becomes a standing wave at 1800 cfs. The lower one should also be avoided.

The Devil's Hopyard is heavy waves studded with boulders for the next mile. The rapids end abruptly, and just below is Cedar Stump, a primitive campsite which can be reached by motorboat from Lake Umbagog. A carry trail up the river connects to the tote road for those desiring to hand-carry. It is about 1½ miles to Long Pool or 2½ miles to Lower Dam.

The last 1½ miles to Lake Umbagog is wide, and the current gradually decreases.

CUPSUPTIC RIVER

The Cupsuptic River rises in a rugged mountain wilderness on the Maine-Quebec border and flows southward into Cupsuptic Lake, one of the Rangeley Lakes. The last 8 miles below Big Falls are relatively flat and offer good canoeing. Access to the start is by private road controlled by the Seven Islands Company.

Big Falls—Cupsuptic Lake   8 miles

Flatwater, Quickwater, Class I
   High water
   Forested
      USGS: Cupsuptic 15
   Portage: 6 mi R **Little Falls** ¼ mi

A start can be made at Lost Brook field, just below Big Falls. The first mile to Portage Brook has fast current, shallow rapids and pools. From there to Little Falls the current becomes more slow moving, and can be canoed either way, as the course becomes more meandering and the balsam banks give way to alder thickets. The river can be reached at the bridge on Lincoln Pond Road. There may be many blowdowns.

Two more miles of slower current bring the canoeist to the bridge at Little Falls. This bridge is readily accessible, and one can put in here to canoe upstream for about 3 miles until blowdowns make further progress impractical. There is a good ¼-mile portage trail on the right around the falls.

If the pitch is just right, an expert canoeist *might* lift over the small log dam at the bridge and run the falls. A mass of downed trees for 200 yards below the falls makes a carry imperative. There is a portage trail on the right. Below here are 2 miles more of slackwater to ME-16 and Cupsuptic Lake.

KENNEBAGO RIVER

The Kennebago River rises just east of the high peaks on the Maine-Quebec border and flows south to drain the rugged mountain area north of the Rangeley Lakes. It enters Mooselookmeguntic Lake close to the outlet of Rangeley River from Rangeley Lake. The dirt road which follows up the river is not open to the public.

The upper and lower sections are relatively quiet, but the middle section is an expert whitewater run in the early spring.

Bear Brook—Kennebago	**8 miles**

Pond, **Flatwater**, Quickwater, Class I
  Medium water-rapids: high water
  Wild
       USGS: Cupsuptic 15
       Portage: (8 mi   **power dams)**

At high water it is possible to put in at the Bear Brook bridge, reached by permission through a Boise Cascade gate. Shallow rapids lead for a while to Little Kennebago Lake, which is a mile across to the outlet at the south end, where there is a launching ramp, reached via Lincoln Pond Road from ME-16, east of Aziscohos Lake, or from Tim Pond Road from ME-27, north of Estis. One can paddle upstream a ways from this point. The river meanders 3 miles to the outlet of Kennebago Lake, and it is another mile down the river past the former settlement of Kennebago to the first of two power dams.

Kennebago—Bridge   6 miles

Class III, IV
  High water
  Wild
        USGS: Cupsuptic 15, Oquossoc 15

Permission is needed to drive in a private road opposite the Cupsuptic MFS. Put in below the lower dam at the old settlement of Kennebago. The rapids are continuous and difficult, the lower part being harder.

Bridge—Mooselookmeguntic Lake   7 miles

Flatwater, **Quickwater**, Class I, II
  Medium water
  Wild, Forested
        USGS: Oquossoc 15

The first mile below here is easy rapids, probably scratchy in mid-summer. This is followed by a good current for the next 2 miles to Kamankeag Brook, which can be reached by driving up the old railroad grade on the east side of the river. The current becomes slower and the river more winding for the final 4 miles to the ME-16 bridge and Mooselookmeguntic Lake, passing a camp on the left bank partway down. Moose are often seen along the river.

RANGELEY RIVER

The Rangeley River is the connecting link between the two lakes. It starts at the ME-16 bridge at the northwest edge of Rangeley Lake, where it looks like a continuation of the lake.

Rangeley Lake—Mooselookmeguntic Lake
                                        1½ miles

Lift over the screens and paddle 200 yards to the dam, which can be carried left, as there are fish ladders on the other side.

Below the dam are fairly continuous Class II rapids to Mooselookmeguntic Lake. These can be quite thin in summer with a loaded canoe.

See USGS Oquossoc 15 map.

WILD RIVER

The Wild River drains the Carter and the Baldface-Royce ranges in the White Mountains, flowing northeast to Hastings, where it is joined by Evans Brook from Evans Notch, and then flowing north into the Androscoggin River at Gilead, Maine.

Hastings—Gilead	**3 miles**

Class II, III, IV
  High water: *mid-April*
  Forested
    USGS: Bethel

Put in where the Wild River approaches ME-113. About a mile below the start the river turns away from the road just below a large gravel turn-out. From here past the next right-hand turn is the heaviest water on the trip, Class IV. The last mile above the US-2 bridge is easier, Class II. A few inches more or less water changes the run from dangerously heavy to bony.

PLEASANT RIVER

The Pleasant River rises in the mountains in the southern part of Mason and flows north to the Androscoggin near West Bethel.

Second Bridge—Androscoggin River	**4½ miles**

Flatwater, Quickwater, Marsh
  Medium high to medium low
  Rural
    USGS: Bethel

At the bridge on the second side road south of US-2 the Pleasant River is a tiny stream. It slithers down a flat valley with the usual obstructions. Below the next bridge (1½ mi) it is slightly larger, but still has many beaver dams and deadfalls. Below the US-2 bridge it is ¾ mile to the Androscoggin.

SUNDAY RIVER

The Sunday River rises in the northern Mahoosuc Range and flows southeast into the Androscoggin River at North Bethel. It enjoys a beautiful setting in a small, peaceful valley with the Mahoosucs rising impressively in the background. The waters are crystal clear.

Above the Pool   ¼ mile

Put in ¼ mile above the pool (2¾ miles above the covered bridge) after asking permission, as it is private property. High water is needed, so the best time is usually around the end of April.

The rapids are Class III at the start. Where the river splits into three branches, stop and scout. Currently most of the water is in the center and left; the run in the center is more difficult than the left. Where the branches come together is a small, river-wide hydraulic.

Pool—Androscoggin River   7¾ miles

Quickwater, Class I, II, III
   High water: *late April, early May*
   Forested, Rural
      USGS: Gilead, Bethel

Below the pool is an easy Class III rapid, then the rapids are mostly Class II the rest of the way to the covered bridge, with a few slightly harder. Watch carefully for downed trees.

Below the covered bridge there is another mile of easy rapids, and then the current gradually slows to the Androscoggin. The easiest take-out is from a side road on the right upstream of the US-2 bridge (7½ mi).

BEAR RIVER

The Bear River drains the south side of Grafton Notch. Most of this section is easy rapids, but there are three widely separated Class III ledges.

North Newry—Newry   6¾ miles

Quickwater, Class I, II, III
   High water: *April*
   Forested, Rural
         USGS: Old Speck Mt. 15, *Bethel 7½*

Put in at the Devil's Horseshoe, which is ¼ mile north of the tiny settlement of North Newry on ME-26. The Horseshoe is a geologic feature that looks so much like a breached dam that you'll question whether its origin was entirely natural. Kayakers may be tempted to run the heavy 4-foot drop through the break.

Busy Class II water starts immediately and lasts for about ¾ mile to where Branch Brook comes in from under ME-26 on the left. Here there is a 3-foot sloping ledge with a tiny bit of a slot in it. The setup for the slot is a fast "S"-turn, Class III when the water is high.

Fast current and scattered rocks continue for ¼ mile to a sudden but straightforward drop over a 2-foot ledge. The river then runs fast and fairly unobstructed for another mile to a 2- to 3-foot ledge, which produces a strong roller and some haystacks.

The remaining 4 miles to US-2 are mostly fast current with occasional rocks or tight corners, none of which rate more than Class II at average mid-April flows. The Androscoggin River is 100 yards downstream of the US-2 bridge.

ELLIS RIVER

The Ellis River rises in Ellis Pond and flows westward through the hills into the Andover intervale, where it meets the West Branch of the Ellis River. Above South Andover, it is too shallow to canoe in low water. Unlike the other rivers in this region, it is a stillwater stream offering an easy trip in very enjoyable surroundings.

Andover—Rumford Point   **17 miles**

Flatwater, Quickwater
  Medium water
  Rural
        USGS: Old Speck Mountain 15, Ellis Pond,
              East Andover

One can put in at the crossing of ME-5 over the West
Branch of the Ellis River just below the turn to South Arm.
It is a small meadow brook here, winding through the intervale for 2 miles to the junction with the main river. It then
becomes larger but continues its winding course another 2½
miles to the bridge at South Andover. For the next 8½ miles
the river writhes and twists through the flat valley bottoms
to the bridge at North Rumford School. The meanders continue, but with a somewhat less tortuous course for the final
4 miles to the US-2 bridge, only 200 yards above the junction with the Androscoggin River.

SWIFT RIVER

The Swift River rises in one of the unincorporated townships south of Rangeley and flows south through Byron,
Roxbury, and Mexico to the Androscoggin River at Rumford. For the most part it is too steep to canoe. It is perhaps
best known as a popular place to pan for gold, although
more aluminum than gold is now to be found on some
rocks. The river rises and falls quickly, so that it is difficult
to tell the best time for canoeing. It is impassable when low
and dangerous in spots at high water. At medium water it is
canoeable from below the gorge at Byron.

Byron—Mexico   **13 miles**

Quickwater, Class I, II, III
  Medium water
  Forested, Towns
        USGS: Ellis Pond 15, Roxbury 15, Rumford 15
      Portage: 10 mi   R   **dam and ledge**   ½ mi

Put in just below the gorge. There are some very sharp drops in the first mile, then easier going for 3 miles (Class I to II) to Roxbury. One mile below here the river steepens, with some drops that may require lining down in the remaining 3 miles to Frye. There are 3 miles of quickwater and Class I rapids to Hale, where there is an easy Class II ledge just above the bridge and a heavy Class II–III chute underneath it. Next, an impassable pitch and a dam require a rather long portage. About 1 mile of Class II water brings the canoeist to "Tubbs," and an "S"-turn drop that is harder than it looks (Class III at high water). The rapids diminish and disappear in the 2 miles to Mexico and the US-2 bridge 100 yards above the junction with the Androscoggin.

WEBB RIVER

USGS: *Weld,* Dixfield

The Webb River rises in Lake Webb in Weld, from whence it flows south through Carthage to form the boundary between Mexico and Dixfield, finally emptying into the Androscoggin River at Dixfield. The upper part between Lake Webb and Carthage is steep and rapid, suitable only for early spring canoeing by experts, but below Carthage there are many miles of pleasant paddling, mostly smoothwater and usable in all but a dry season.

Carthage—Dixfield   9 miles

Put in at the ME-142 bridge at Carthage. There are 2 miles of meadow paddling, then 2 miles more through woodlands to the falls, where a short carry should be made. Below there are another 4 miles of marshy woodlands to a bridge at the beginning of a 100-yard-long rapid near the northern edge of Dixfield. In the next mile to the Androscoggin River there is an impassable waterfall before the US-2 bridge is visible.

SEVENMILE STREAM

USGS: East Dixfield, Wilton

Sevenmile Stream rises in Carthage and flows east and then south to the Androscoggin River in Jay. Its upper stretches are too steep to canoe, but below East Dixfield it has a few miles of good canoeable sections. It is a relatively small stream and should be canoed early in the season when the snows are still melting on Saddleback Mountain. This is mountainous country and the views are good.

East Dixfield—Androscoggin River   8 miles

Put in at East Dixfield from a side road off ME-17. The first 2½ miles are all rapid but not difficult. The going is almost all through open meadow lands, but by the time Birchland Cemetery is reached, the river has become much more quiet, and from there to the Androscoggin River the going is all smoothwater with a fair current. Take out at the US-2 bridge less than 100 yards above the Androscoggin River.

DEAD RIVER

USGS: Norridgewock 15, Augusta 15, Farmington Falls, Fayette, Wayne, Turner Center

---

The Dead River is the outlet from Androscoggin Lake to the Androscoggin River. It should not be confused with the Dead River in Somerset County, a tributary of the Kennebec and a fine whitewater run. It is only 7 miles long, but it drains a series of lakes that can offer many miles of pleasant canoeing. Both the lakes and the river are flatwater paddling and can be done at any season. From the head of Flying Pond in Vienna it is possible to obtain some 18 miles of lake and river paddling to the Dead River and another 7 miles of easy going down the river to the Androscoggin, or some 25 miles in all.

Flying Pond   2½ miles

One can put in at Vienna, from which it is only 1 mile to the cove on the east shore where the outlet is located. There is a long arm of the lake to the south of this, however. The outlet runs through a series of ponds, the last one 1 mile long behind the dam at Mount Vernon. The dam must be carried into Minnehonk Lake.

Minnehonk Lake   1¼ miles

From Mount Vernon at the northern end of the lake it is only a short way to Hopkins Stream at the southern end.

Hopkins Stream   3 miles

There are 200 yards of brook to Horseshoe Pond, the outlet of which takes off just to the right of the inlet. It is then 3 miles down an easy stream of smoothwater to the dam at West Mount Vernon, where a short carry brings one into Crotched Pond.

Alternative start via
Parker Pond   3¾ miles

It is possible to put in at the north end of the pond where the stream from Whittier Pond crosses under the road at the shore in Vienna. Only the northern end of the pond is in Vienna; the rest of it is in Fayette, although most of the shores are in Chesterfield and Mount Vernon. The outlet is at the southeast corner where a short river takes off. After ½ mile there is a dam and then 100 yards more to the millpond behind the dam at West Mount Vernon, which is ½ mile farther on. This point can also be reached from Flying Pond in Vienna and Minnehonk Lake in Mount Vernon by coming down Hopkins Stream from the latter. Below this is Crotched Pond.

Crotched Pond   3¾ miles

This pond is sometimes called Echo Lake. Although the outlet is at Fayette on the west bay, where there is a small dam, there is an equally long east bay, which also provides pleasant canoeing.

Lovejoy Pond   2½ miles

It is only 2 miles from Fayette to the outlet at North Wayne, but there is also a northeast arm inviting exploration by the paddler. About ¼ mile down the outlet river, at North Wayne, there is a dam that must be carried.

Pickerel Pond and Pocasset Lake   3 miles

Just below the dam at North Wayne, Pickerel Pond begins. It is only 1 mile from the inlet at the northeast end to the outlet at the northwest end, but a large bay to the south offers access to marshes. Pocasset Lake is 2 miles long and wider than some of the upper lakes. The outlet river takes off at Wayne, west of the peninsula jutting into the lake from the south. There are two dams here a short distance apart.

Androscoggin Lake   2½ miles

This is the largest lake in this chain. Although it is only 2 miles from the inlet to the outlet, the Dead River, which takes off near the tip on the north side of the peninsula jutting into the west side of the lake, there are many miles of canoeing in the large southern and western bays.

Androscoggin Lake—Androscoggin River   7 miles

Flatwater (motor boats)
  Anytime
  Forested, Cottages
     USGS: Wayne, Turner Center
    Portage: 5½ mi   **dam**

The Dead River starts on the north side and near the tip of the peninsula extending nearly 2 miles into the lake. It is nearly 2 miles down the river to the village of Dead River and the highway bridge. The river then winds and twists for another 3 miles to the next bridge, below which are 2 miles more of river to the Androscoggin River, with an easy lift around a low dam. One may take out at a farm on the left bank just below the mouth, or go on down the Androscoggin 3 miles to the ME-219 bridge.

NEZINSCOT RIVER

The Nezinscot River rises in the high hills of Sumner, its East Branch forming the boundary between Sumner and Hartford. The two branches meet just below Buckfield and the main river flows east to the Androscoggin River at Turner. The East Branch below East Sumner is small and quite rocky even in high water. The main river is more placid and can be canoed in any but dry seasons. The river runs through pleasant valleys with open meadows and woodlands.

Buckfield—Androscoggin River   15 miles

Flatwater, **Quickwater**, Class I, II
  Medium water
  Forested, Rural
      USGS: Worthley Pond, West Sumner-
          Buckfield, Poland 15, Turner Center
  Portages: 8 mi   **dam at Turner**
               (14½ mi   **dam at Keens Mills)**

Put in at the ME-117 bridge south and east of Buckfield. The next 8 miles to the dam at Turner are flat river through open meadows and woodlands with the river making several big loops a few miles above Turner. Below the dam at Turner there is ¼ mile of Class II rapids over and around low ledges. Three miles of quickwater and Class I rips bring one to the first of two ME-117 bridges at Turner Center; there is a strong Class II rapid just below this bridge. The second bridge is 1 mile below. It is then 3 miles more to the dam at Keens Mills, where most canoeists will decide to take out rather than going the additional ¼ mile to the Androscoggin River.

WEST BRANCH NEZINSCOT RIVER

The West Branch of the Nezinscot flows from West Sumner to the main river at Buckfield. The dirt road that follows and crosses the river may be impassable for all but four-wheel-drive vehicles in the spring when the river is usually run. The first mile of river below the ME-219 bridge is heavily obstructed by alders and is not recommended.

West Sumner—Nezinscot River   10¾ miles

Flatwater, **Quickwater**, Class I, II
  High water
  Forested, Rural
      USGS: West Sumner, Buckfield
      Portage: 9¾ mi   **dam in Buckfield**

The best spot to start is the bridge a mile south of West
Sumner. Take a dirt road south from West Sumner, and in
¼ mile take the left fork. This road follows close along the
river to North Buckfield.

In a short distance, the rapids begin, Class I with
stretches of quickwater between. There is a drop of 1½ feet,
which is easily run. All of the drops are runnable, in no spot
becoming more difficult than Class II. There are a few small
islands that can be run on either side, and an occasional
fallen tree, which will not hinder progress much. The stream
banks are quite pretty, and the woods mostly hardwood and
quite open.

There is a short stretch of flatwater, and then as North
Buckfield is approached, the gradient becomes steeper and a
little more effort and quickness is required to maneuver
around the rocks. The stream is not very strong, and flow
rates in the neighborhood of 100 to 150 cfs provide the best
running. One can take out downstream on the right at the
North Buckfield bridge, but parking is limited. There are a
few hundred feet of rapid left, and then the river becomes
flat and meandering through meadows with occasional
woods. Approaching Buckfield, the stream becomes quite
steep and rocks are numerous. The dam in Buckfield spills
water, and the pool above it is not very long or still.

It is awkward to reach the river below the dam. After a
short rapid, it runs into a meadow, meandering until it joins
the East Branch to form the Nezinscot about a mile below
Buckfield.

LITTLE ANDROSCOGGIN RIVER

The Little Androscoggin is one of the larger tributaries
of the Androscoggin. It rises in Bryant Pond southeast of

Bethel, flows southeast to West Paris, and then south through Paris to Oxford where it turns easterly to flow through Mechanic Falls and join the Androscoggin at Auburn. The first 4 miles below Bryant Pond are too steep and rapid to canoe, but from Tubbs School in Greenwood it can be canoed all the way to the mouth, although there are a number of dams to be carried in some of the towns. Because of the pond at its head, it can be canoed fairly late in the spring, but except in the lower part it is apt to be too low in the summer. Outside of the few large towns, the scenery is very attractive, although not spectacular.

Third Bridge—South Paris   12 miles

Flatwater, Quickwater, Class I, II
  Medium water: *April, May*
  Forested, Towns
    USGS: Greenwood, West Paris
  Portages: 2 mi   e   **4-ft dam**   carry across
                                        road
              4½ mi e   **Snows Falls**   (difficult)
                                        100 yds
              6 mi   R   **Bisco Falls**   20 yds
             (12 mi   **dam)**

Put in at the third ME-219 bridge upstream of West Paris at a stream junction. The stream is small, with easy rapids halfway to West Paris, and then quickwater to the dam in the center of town below a bridge on a side road. Take out upstream of the bridge and carry across the road.

The rapids below the bridge are more difficult than those above, for ½ mile. Then it is smooth to Snows Falls at a highway rest area on ME-26. Rapids and small ledges extend for ¼ mile, then quickwater to Bisco Falls, an 8-foot dam at a natural ledge. Access is difficult.

Rapids continue below the falls, gradually diminishing.

Below there is a long stretch of smoothwater with meanders, 5 miles to South Paris. One can take out where the river comes close to the road 2½ miles below the falls, the ME-26 bridge, or 1 mile farther down at the ME-117 bridge.

South Paris—Mechanic Falls   20 miles

USGS: Greenwood, West Paris, Norway 15,
       Poland 15, Lewiston 15

This is largely flatwater through meadows and woodlands
with many meanders. Put in just below the ME-117 bridge
in South Paris. The stream meanders for 2 miles in a southwesterly direction to a point below Norway, where the
stream from Penneseewassee Lake joins on the right. The
river now becomes very winding for the next 7 miles
through meadows and woodlands to Oxford, where it
passes under the ME-121 bridge. Just below the bridge the
stream from Thompson Lake enters on the right. The river
becomes very twisty, with numerous oxbows for the next 2
miles to the dam at Welchville. The following 8 miles to
Mechanic Falls are largely through meadows and woodlands, with many meanders and oxbows. It is best to take
out at the ME-11 bridge just west of town, as there are a
large dam and many mills in Mechanic Falls, which make
the carry difficult.

Mechanic Falls—Auburn   13 miles

This section is all flatwater. Put in below the dam at
Mechanic Falls. From here to the next dam at Hackett Mills
there are 4 miles of winding river through meadows, some
now overgrown with bushes and trees. From Hackett Mills
to the next dam at Minot is 1 mile of paddling. The next 7
miles to Auburn are through meadows. The river does not
wind and twist quite as much as above. There is a gauging
station at the bridge 4 miles downstream. It is best to take
out several miles below this bridge on a side road on the
right bank before entering Auburn, as there are several
dams and an impassable rapid before the Little Androscoggin enters the Androscoggin River in the middle of Auburn.

SABATTUS RIVER

USGS: Lewiston 15

The Sabattus River drains Sabattus Pond through Lisbon to the Androscoggin River. It is only 9 miles long, and the lower part below the dam at Lisbon Center cannot be run, but above there are a number of miles of good canoeing, much of it through woods and some open pastureland. It can be canoed almost any time during the week when the mills are operating, but on weekends spring would be better.

Sabattus—Lisbon Center   8 miles

There are three dams at Sabattus, so that it is best to put in at the ME-126 bridge below all three. The river is a quiet, meandering stream that passes under a bridge in 1 mile and the Maine Turnpike in 1 mile more. Below this there are 1½ miles with quite large meanders to the dam near Robinson Corner. From here it is 3 miles to the first dam in Lisbon, where many canoeists will probably elect to take out. There is another dam ¼ mile below and then 1 mile of easy canoeing to the dam at Lisbon Center, which marks the end of navigation, as the 1 mile below the dam to the Androscoggin River is too steep for canoeing.

CHAPTER 3

Kennebec Watershed

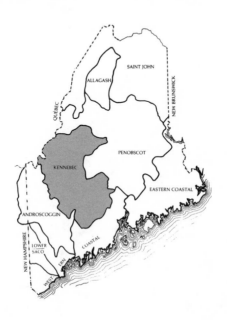

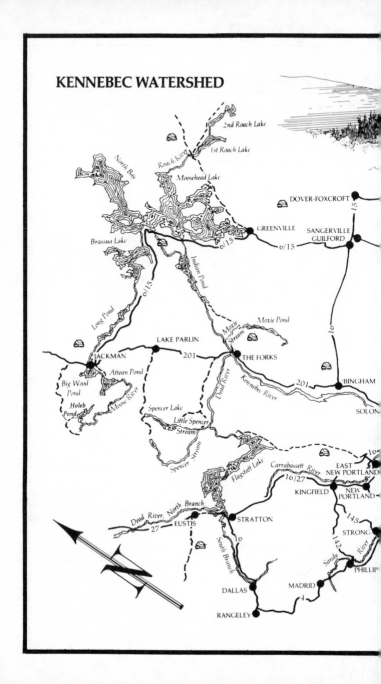

KENNEBEC WATERSHED

2nd Roach Lake

1st Roach Lake

Roach River

North Bay

Moosehead Lake

DOVER-FOXCROFT

GREENVILLE

SANGERVILLE
GUILFORD

Brassua Lake

o/15

o/15

Indian Pond

Moxie Pond

Long Pond

o/15

Moxie Stream

LAKE PARLIN

15

JACKMAN

201

THE FORKS

201

BINGHAM

Attean Pond

Big Wood Pond

Holeb Pond

Moose River

Spencer Lake

Dead River

Kennebec River

SOLON

Little Spencer Stream

Spencer Stream

Flagstaff Lake

Carrabassett River

EAST NEW PORTLAND

16/27

NEW PORTLAND

Dead River, North Branch

KINGFIELD

145

27

EUSTIS

STRATTON

16

142

STRONG

South Branch

Sandy River

PHILLIP

DALLAS

MADRID

4

RANGELEY

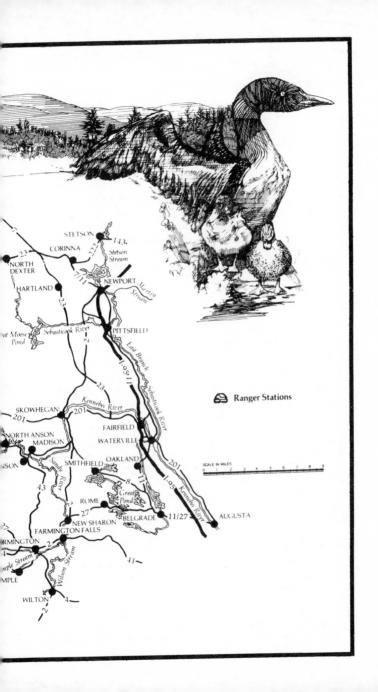

STETSON
CORINNA
NORTH DEXTER
HARTLAND
143.
Stetson Stream
Martin Stream
NEWPORT
PITTSFIELD
Sebasticook River
East Branch
Sebasticook River
rit Moose Pond
I-95 11
SKOWHEGAN
Kennebec River
201
201
NORTH ANSON
MADISON
FAIRFIELD
WATERVILLE
SMITHFIELD
OAKLAND
NSON
Sandy River
8
ROME
Great Pond
I-95 Kennebec River
43
NEW SHARON
BELGRADE
11/27
AUGUSTA
27
FARMINGTON FALLS
RMINGTON
mple Stream
Wilson Stream
41
MPLE
WILTON
4
2

Ranger Stations

SCALE IN MILES
0 1 2 3 4 5 6 7 8 9

KENNEBEC RIVER

The Kennebec River is one of the largest rivers of Maine. It flows from Moosehead Lake southwest to the sea below Bath, having received the waters of the Androscoggin River at Merrymeeting Bay just above Bath. It has been largely harnessed for power so that most of the river is smooth paddling. The upper part above The Forks is rapid and should be run by experienced canoeists only. This river was the route of Benedict Arnold's abortive invasion of Canada in the fall of 1775, when he ascended the river to Carrying Place Stream about 25 miles above the present site of Anson, and then crossed through the three Carry Ponds to Bog Brook on the Dead River, a spot now flooded by Flagstaff Lake, and followed the North Branch of that river into Quebec. His tiny force of 1100 men suffered severe privations and numerous losses on the journey. As the flow of the river is controlled for power purposes, it may be run at any time.

Moosehead Lake—Harris Station

Moosehead Lake drains by two outlets into Indian Pond. They provide quite different types of canoeing. The West Outlet, which leaves the lake 2 miles below Rockwood, halfway up the lake on the west shore, carries relatively little flow of water and consists almost entirely of a series of ponds. It is probably passable with some carries. It is some 9 miles long and is followed most of the way by a dirt road. The East Outlet, which leaves the lake at the village of Moosehead one quarter of the way up the lake on the west shore, is only 3½ miles long, with heavy and continuous rapids, suitable for experts only. Its flow, which is controlled for power generation, is fairly constant and usually very heavy.

via West Outlet—Indian Pond   10 miles

Lake, Quickwater, Class I
   Dam-controlled
   Forested
         USGS: Moosehead Lake 15, Brassua Lake 15
      Portage: 5½ mi   **liftover**

When this route has water it is an easy run through rather wild country. From ME-15, just below the small dam, 1¾ miles down a pond leads to Class I rapids between Long Pond and the next pond. If these are runnable, all should be. From here to Churchill Stream each pond is followed by rapids. A dirt road on the right is not obtrusive.

Just beyond a railroad bridge is a very low bridge that may have to be carried on left. Just beyond Churchill Stream is a slightly harder rapid, then a mile of quickwater and another rapid to Round Pond. The outlet is straight across the pond.

After another smooth mile ½ mile of rapids ends in the backwater of Indian Pond. Keep to the left around islands for another mile to the main body of the lake. A boat ramp is a mile directly across the lake to the south. It may also be possible to drive to the lake at a campsite ½ mile to the north.

via East Outlet—Indian Pond   3½ miles

Quickwater, Class II, III, IV
  Dam-controlled
  Wild
      USGS: Moosehead Lake 15, Brassua Lake 15

The rapids on this run are separated by sections of quickwater. At low flow (below 2000 cfs), they are mostly Class II–III; at higher flows they are Class III–IV.

The dam at the lake is followed by a gauging station, a railroad bridge, and the ME-15 bridge. In ½ mile is a narrow chute with a long ramp and cliff on the right. Scout from the left. The next 2 miles alternate fast current and rapids, which are usually spread out, but there are a few large boulders. A dirt road, which follows high on the left bank, descends here to river's edge. At 3 miles the flowage from Indian Pond comes into view, but just before reaching the pond there is a heavy drop over a ledge not easily seen from above. Land on right and scout. The far left has an insignificant drop; the right is all Class III–IV and can be run in more than one place. Below here is a quiet pool and a picnic site on the right.

Indian Pond   9 miles

Indian Pond is an artificial lake, long and thin, with rather unattractive shores. It is 9 miles from either approach to a boat ramp at the south end. There are campsites near the north end, one on an island at the West Outlet and one at the East Outlet, both of which are inclined to be insect-infested. There are also two others halfway down, one on each side. There are excellent mountain views and few buildings or powerboats.

Take out at the landing and picnic areas to the left of the 155-foot-high Harris Dam, maintained for the public by the Central Maine Power Company.

Harris Station—Carry Brook   3¾ miles

Class III, IV, V
    Dam-controlled: under 1000 cfs: not recommended
                         1000–2300 cfs: open boats class III, IV
                         over 2300 cfs: expert covered boaters
                         only
    Wild
        USGS: The Forks 15

Below Harris Station, the Kennebec flows through a wild gorge that is among the most impressive in size and beauty in New England. Because of its dependable water flow and continuous difficulty, it is the finest decked-boat whitewater run in Maine. However, the canyon walls rising sheer from the turbulent river that give the gorge its incomparable attraction compound its navigational difficulties. Scouting is difficult, and the most severe drops are not feasible to portage, line, or evade. This run is only for boaters of proven skill; others may find themselves in over their heads with no retreat possible. Most people prefer to enjoy the gorge from a commercial raft trip.

The flow in the Kennebec is most inconvenient for canoeing this section of river. When the generators at the Harris Station are shut down, there is practically no water in the river, and then it must be run from Carry Brook Eddy by poling or lining down the shallow rapids. The generators are often started up in mid-morning on weekdays, with the result that the river rises several feet in a few minutes. With all three generators going, the flow is 6500–8000 cubic feet/second. Spring is the best time for high water on weekends.

To get the water release from Harris Station for the day or the following day, telephone Central Maine Power Company, Augusta, (207) 622-5861, and ask for the dispatcher.

At the radio-controlled gate to Harris Station ¼ mile from put-in, use the speaker to identify yourself. A road leads down to the river to the left of the power station.

The river is extremely narrow, and because of the cliffs can be a long, bad swim. The size of the waves varies with the water level in an unpredictable manner, dependent also on whether the river is rising or falling. At 1000 to 2300 cfs the current is moderate, and it is possible to eddy and scout the rapids. Above this level the current is very fast, and stopping is difficult.

Just out of sight of the put-in, the rapids begin, build up to Class IV within ½ mile, and continue uninterrupted for 2 miles. At levels above 2300 cfs the first notable spot is Three Sisters, 1 mile from the start, and 100 yards below a bare slide on the right, site of a former log chute. Here the current funnels to the right of center into a series of powerful standing waves that vary in number and shape with flow. Turbulence generated by flows around 6500 cfs is particularly awesome, and has flipped 22-foot rafts.

The next mile is the narrowest part of the gorge, characterized by continuous, impressive, and choppy standing waves. The river makes a series of bends where the water can push a boat against the cliffs on the outside.

The upper gorge ends at Cathedral Eddy, where the river makes a sharp right turn marking the first corner of a "Z"-turn. After ¼ mile of quickwater, the river makes the second bend left in the "Z"-turn, where Chase Brook enters on the right. The eddy on the left point of the "Z" is an excellent spot for decked boats to play. The bend is followed by 100 yards of Class III. Magic Rapid (Class V) begins in another ¼ mile. It can be seen ahead, where the river disappears from sight, dropping about 25 feet in 250 yards. A trail on the left makes the mandatory scouting easy. Prominent features are two holes. At the beginning on the left, by shore, is Magic (Rock) Falls. Fifty yards below and just to the right of center is an even worse hole called

Witchcraft, which is a real keeper. The rest of the drop is
large waves and smaller holes.

In another mile Dead Stream enters on the right, dropping over a series of pretty falls. Carry Brook Rapid starts
immediately, ending at Carry Brook Eddy.

Carry Brook—The Forks   8½ miles

Quickwater, Class I, II, III, IV
  Dam-controlled, anytime
  Wild
      USGS: The Forks

Although most of this section is just an easy float, Black
Brook rapids are ½ mile long, and unfeasible to line or portage, so the boater putting in here should be prepared to
deal with them directly. At open boat levels under 3000 cfs
they are Class III, above 3000 cfs they are Class IV.

The put-in at Carry Brook can be reached by taking a
road that leaves the Indian Pond Road at an old shack ½
mile north of the Black Brook Bridge. The cable that used
to facilitate launching down the steep cliff has been removed and may not be there any more (bring carabiners and
a track line).

Black Brook Rapids start just below the confluence of
Carry Brook with the Kennebec, which is a mile from the
start at Carry Brook Eddy. They are continuous for ½ mile,
with one easier spot in the middle, and cliffs on each side
that prevent lining or portaging. Halfway down, and 100
yards above where the river bends to the right, a wide, dangerous hole at levels below 5000 cfs is in the center of the
river; stay to either side. For the next 7 miles to The Forks
the rapids are nearly continuous but easier, Class I and II.

Two miles above The Forks, Moxie Stream enters on the
left. It is ½ mile up the trail on the left bank to Moxie Falls,
a 90-foot cascade believed to be the highest in New England. It can also be reached by taking a steep dirt road that
leaves the Moxie Pond Road 2 miles above The Forks. The
trail to the top of the falls leaves this road ½ mile from the
main road.

Take out at the ballpark on the right above the bridge, or on the left at the confluence.

The Forks to Caratunk 9 miles

Flatwater, Quickwater, Class I
    Anytime (dam-controlled on both branches)
    Scratchy in low water
    Forested, Occasional Cottages
        USGS: The Forks 15, Bingham 15

Below the confluence with the Dead, the Kennebec becomes more gentle, offering a pleasant, easy paddle, which, though not remote like the rivers above, is away from the road most of the distance, and attractive.

There is a pull-off just at the confluence on the left that makes a good spot to launch. The rapids are continuous, but easy. In 3 miles Gilroy Island is passed, with a good channel on either side, and Class II rapids below. It is possible to take out at the Appalachian Trail crossing.

Caratunk to Wyman Dam 12 miles

The current gradually diminishes somewhere around 5 miles to the backwater from Wyman Dam, an attractive lake with steep, wooded hills rising above it. A public boat landing near the head of the lake offers access. The 140-foot-high Wyman Dam in Moscow is the second of the big power dams of the Central Maine Power Company. Carry on the west end near the powerhouse.

Wyman Dam—Skowhegan 30 miles

Flatwater, Quickwater, Class I
    Anytime
    Forested, Rural, Towns
        USGS: Bingham 15, Anson 15, Norridgewock
            15, Skowhegan 15
    Portages: 5 mi L **Solon Dam** 200 yds
              18 mi R **2 dams in Madison** 1 mi
            (30 mi L **2 dams in Skowhegan**
                                1½ mi)

The river now becomes considerably more settled and the banks more open. In 1 mile below the Wyman Dam one passes Bingham on the left and in another 5 miles reaches Caratunk Falls and Solon Dam, portaged by a 200-yard carry on the east bank. It is then 8 miles to the mouth of the Carrabassett River at North Anson. In another 5 miles, mostly through open meadowlands, the twin towns of Anson and Madison are reached. Here there are two dams ½ mile apart, between which the river loops to the east. The portage is on the west bank. There is a rapid below the lower dam for a short distance and then a short rip ½ mile below. It is then 2 miles to the confluence with the Sandy River at some open fields on the right bank. The next 4 miles to Norridgewock offer no obstructions. Another 5 miles largely through open fields brings one to Skowhegan, where there are two dams. Here the river divides into two channels around an island: the North Channel and the South Channel. The best take-out spot is about 200 yards above the North Channel Dam on the left. One then carries along Elm, Russell, and Water streets to the Great Eddy below the gorge. This avoids the difficult scramble down into the gorge below the dams. This gorge can only be run by experts. If conditions are right experienced canoeists may take out on the island between the dams and put in below to run the gorge, 1 mile (Class III–IV), to the Great Eddy.

Skowhegan—Waterville   20 miles

Flatwater, Quickwater
   Anytime
   Rural, Urban
      USGS: Skowhegan 15, Waterville 15
  Portages: 13½ mi R **dam at Shawmut**
            19 mi R **dam at Waterville**
         (20 mi L **Ticonic Falls**)

This stretch has no obstructions, and the river runs through rolling country with fairly open banks, a fair and pleasant landscape for 13 miles to the dam at Shawmut in the town of Fairfield, where the carry is on the right bank. There is a bit of quickwater below the dam, then 3 miles more of pleasant country at least as far as Fairfield 3 miles above Waterville, where the urbanization starts. There are two dams across the river in Waterville. The first dam is best carried on the right or Waterville side. The second dam, 1 mile down at Ticonic Falls, is more easily portaged on the left or Winslow side.

Waterville—Augusta   20 miles

Flatwater, Quickwater
   Anytime
   Rural
      USGS: Vassalboro 15, Augusta 15
   Portage: (20 mi   **dam at Augusta)**

There are no obstructions in this section of river. Below the dam 1 mile the Sebasticook River enters on the left and 1½ miles farther down Messalonskee Stream enters on the right. There is then only pleasant paddling through open country to the dam at Augusta, which is near the northern end of town. Below Augusta the river is tidal.

Augusta—Bath   30½ miles

This section is tidal, and past some large cities, most of which have public launching ramps. High water at Augusta is 3 hours 54 minutes later than Portland; tidal range is 4–5 feet. It is 6 miles to Gardiner and another 11 miles to Richmond and the head of Swan Island.

From the ramp in Richmond it is a 9-mile circuit of Swan Island. The Western channel has the most flow. At low tide, mud flats extend ½ mile south of the island.

From Richmond it is 8½ miles through Merrymeeting Bay to the Chops into Goose Bay. The east side of Lines Island has less current and more interest in terms of scenery and water conditions. There is a public ramp on the west side at the north end of Bath, and a public float above the bridge.

MOOSE RIVER

The Moose River rises in the mountains along the Canadian border in western Maine and flows east to Moosehead

Lake. West of Jackman on US-201, 23¾ miles of the river
are a part of the Bow Trip, one of the best rivers for canoe-
camping in Maine.

Bow Trip   34 miles

For many reasons this is one of Maine's most popular
trips, especially for groups. It can be done in three days,
and at any time of the year when the water is not frozen.
There is only a token amount of whitewater, and even that
is readily portaged if necessary or desirable. It is a circuit
trip, so there is no shuttling of cars. And the scenery is some
of the best Maine canoeing has to offer, with only isolated
development on the two lakes and almost none on the river.

But for all these benefits, there is a price: the river is
heavily traveled in the summer and on long weekends in the
spring and fall.

For those who do not wish to build their character by taking the 1¼-mile portage between Attean and Holeb ponds, it
is possible to drive to Holeb Pond from US-201 north of
Jackman near the MFS Ranger Station.

Lakes, **Flatwater,** Class I
  Passable at all water levels
  Wild
        USGS: Attean 15, Long Pond 15
  Portages: 4¼ mi   **Attean Pond–Holeb
                             Pond**   1¼ mi
              19¼ mi   L   **Holeb Falls**
              30¼ mi   L   **then R Attean Falls**
  Campsites: 1¼ mi   R   **Attean Pond** (N shore)
                             permit
               4¾ mi   **long portage** (E end)
                             permit
                6 mi   **long portage** (W end)
                             permit
               (9) mi   R   **Turner Brook** (N end,
                             Holeb Pond)   permit
              19¼ mi   **Holeb Falls** (end of
                             portage)   permit
              22¾ mi   L   **Spencer Rips**   permit
              30¾ mi   L   **Attean Falls**   permit

The road to Attean Pond leaves US-201 0.6 miles south of the railroad crossing in Jackman to a monitored parking area where a fee is charged. Paddle west for 4¾ miles down the long arm of Attean Lake to the portage. At least three trails lead more or less west from this point. Locating the correct one is not hard for experienced route-finders, but causes problems to some because it is poorly signed. The middle trail, just left of the campsite, is the correct one. If you do not cross the railroad tracks in a mile, you are too far south.

There is a 3¼-mile paddle the length of Holeb Pond to the outlet (9¼ mi). In 1 mile Holeb Stream meets the Moose River (10¼ mi).

The alternate put-in at Holeb Pond may be reached using a four-wheel-drive vehicle by turning left off US-201 3¼ miles north of the bridge over the Moose River at Jackman. Follow the well-traveled gravel road for 10 miles. At a point where the road turns right sharply a small, rough dirt road runs to the pond and intersects it at a point just south of the outlet of Turner Brook.

All of the Moose River in this section is flat, except where specifically noted. From Holeb Stream it is 3¾ miles to a minor drop over a ledge at Camel Rips (14 mi).

The start to the Holeb Falls portage, 4½ miles further on, is easily identified by the high rocky ledge on the right and the colossal boulders in the river. The river divides just above McNair's Landing, although the left fork is much smaller and appears to be a tributary. Take the left branch and then immediately turn right, because a tributary does in fact enter the left branch at this point. Follow this branch past two short drops with rock ledges on both banks. At a point ½ mile from the turn-off to the left branch, turn left again into a narrow inlet. The portage around Holeb Falls begins at this point. **Caution!** Watch carefully for the last turn-off to the portage. There are several quick, Class II drops after the turn-off and before the falls. Once in these rapids it is a difficult carry back along the bank to the turn. The first two turns show clearly on the Attean Quadrangle.

The river wanders for 11 miles from Holeb Falls to Attean Falls (30¼ mi), with two short drops: Mosquito Rips (19¾ mi) and Spencer Rips (23¾ mi). Attean Falls consists of two rapids, Class I or II depending on the water level. There are two portages: on the left for the upper rapids, on the right for the lower ones. Attean Pond is ¾ mile below the falls, and 2¾ miles across the lake to the north is the landing (34 mi).

Attean Landing—Long Pond   19 miles

Lakes, Quickwater
  Medium water
  Forested
        USGS: Attean 15, Long Pond 15

The west shore of Wood Pond at Jackman is built up, but east of US-201 the river and lakes along it are mostly wild. Long Pond has an alder- and willow-lined shore that is evidence of a dam long since washed out. The shore line of Brassua Lake typifies that of a flooded lake: dry-ki, a few exposed sand banks, and green trees with dead limbs that died when these trees were within a forest, not along a lake. Both lakes are for the most part undeveloped.

From the landing on Attean Pond there is ¾ mile of flatwater on the river and another 2½ miles across Wood Pond to the outlet. On the short river segment between Attean and Wood ponds, there are the remains of a steamboat and barge rotting away on the left. At Wood Pond, there is an excellent campsite on the left. Access at Jackman is from a public landing on Wood Pond or at the US-201 bridge.

Except for the riffle under the bridge, it is 6½ miles of smooth and somewhat winding river to Long Pond (11 mi), an 8-mile paddle with two narrow guts between the three separate sections. The river at the outlet is reached by a dirt road leading north off ME-6/15 just west of the Long Pond-Sandwich town line. At the east end of the clearing by the railroad tracks, follow a well-worn path to the river.

Long Pond—Moosehead Lake   **15½ miles**

Lakes, Quickwater, Class **I, II,** III, IV
   Passable at all water levels
   Forested, Cottages
      USGS: Long Pond 15, Brassua Lake 15
  Portages: 2½ mi L **Ledge/Falls** 200 yds
             12½ mi R **Brassua Dam**   200 yds
  Campsite: 5 mi L **Brassua Lake** (on point
                               where lake opens up)

Between Long Pond and Brassua Lake the Moose River
drops steadily through wooded hills. Here there are several
miles of challenging rapids when the water is high, but since
this is a large river, these rapids are passable in lower water when they are easier to negotiate and when the harder
pitches can be lined.

Below Long Pond the intermittent rapids of Class I and II
extend for 2½ miles to a bridge at the site of the former
Long Pond Dam on a well-used logging road that comes in
from ME-6/15. **Caution!** Under the bridge is a ledge, which
should be scouted. Landing on the left to scout, line, or
carry may be difficult as the current is fast. One can also
take out here. A short distance below is a low waterfall that
can also be portaged or lined on the left.

Below these two ledges, there are nearly continuous rapids for 1¾ miles. At the start they are Class III, but soon
they moderate to Class II. One-half mile from the bridge
there is a sharp left turn followed by a short stretch of
quickwater. Soon there are more Class II rapids and one
more, larger section of quickwater. Then more Class II and
another Class III section, which starts just above a quick
"S"-turn that begins to the right. Intermittent Class II rapids continue to slackwater, which soon opens into Brassua
Lake (5 mi).

It is 7½ miles across Brassua Lake to the dam (12½ mi), the
road to which may be closed. Portage on the left. Below the
dam there are Class I rapids and quickwater for 1 mile. The
last 2 miles to Moosehead Lake (15½ mi) are flat, highly
developed, and most of it is close to the highway.

ROACH RIVER

The headwaters of the Roach River consist of a complex of mountain ponds east of Moosehead Lake, of which it is the largest tributary. It combines a variety of lake and whitewater paddling with good views of mountains that range from 2500 to 3500 feet.

Access is via a private road that leads from Kokad-jo along the north shore of First Roach Pond, across the dam at the foot of Second and along the latter's south shore, and across the Roach River at the inlet. About 2 miles beyond, a road to the right leads to Third Roach Pond. Spencer Bay on Moosehead Lake is accessible by car from Kokad-jo on both sides of the river.

Third Roach Pond—Kokad-jo   12½ miles

Lakes, Class I, II
  High water: *mid-May to mid-June*
  Forested
      USGS: Jo-Mary Mountain 15, First Roach
           Pond 15
     Portage: (12½ mi   **Dam)**

The Roach River begins ¾ mile from the road access to Third Roach Pond. Some scouting of rapids may be necessary in the 1½ miles to Second Roach Pond, where dry-ki is apt to be a problem.

From the outlet of Second Roach Pond (5¾ mi), the river flows for 1¾ miles, with rapids that may have to be scouted, and more dry-ki waiting for you when you reach the north inlet of First Roach Pond (7½ mi). It is a 5-mile paddle down the lake to the outlet at Kokad-jo (12½ mi).

Kokad-jo—Moosehead Lake   6½ **miles**

Class II, III
  High water: *mid-May to mid-June*
  Wild
      USGS: First Roach Pond 15, Moosehead Lake
            15
  Campsites: 6½ mi   R   **high bluff**   MFS
               6½ mi   L   **small island**   MFS

One mile below the dam Lazy Tom Stream enters on the
right. Below this point, the rapids are continuous, Class II
and III all the way to Spencer Bay on Moosehead Lake. The
drop in this section is almost 200 feet. There are no dangerous falls or drops, but neither are there any sections of
slackwater.

DEAD RIVER

The not-so-Dead River flows from Flagstaff Lake to the
upper Kennebec River. It is one of New England's most outstanding whitewater rivers, and you can run it in whichever
season you wish. For hour after hour you paddle through
nearly continuous rapids along a 15-mile section of wild
river where the gradient averages 29 feet per mile.

The river takes its name from the flatwater section that
now lies beneath Flagstaff Lake. Long Falls Dam, at the
northeast end, normally releases only a minimum flow on
weekends, but arrangements are made each year with the
Central Maine Power Company (207-623-3521) to release an
optimum water flow on selected weekends throughout the
summer. This schedule of release dates is made available to
whitewater groups in New England, and it can be obtained
from the AMC and from the Penobscot Paddle and Chow-
der Society, Box 121, Stillwater, Maine 04489.

The head of the rapids at the mouth of Spencer Stream
can be reached by turning west off US-201 about 3 miles
north of West Forks and following rough roads for approximately 17 miles. Webb's General Store, West Forks, Maine
04985 (207-663-2214) will provide transportation along these
roads.

Above Grand Falls, the Dead River flows slowly through meadows where there are good views looking back at the Bigelow Range. Below Grand Falls, a spectacular drop of about 30 feet, the narrow river valley is very attractive, although you will spend most of your time looking at the river. At medium water level, 1000 cfs, it takes 2½–3 hours to reach Spencer Stream from Big Eddy, and 3–4 hours to run the rapids to The Forks.

Flagstaff Lake   18 miles

Flagstaff Lake is formed by a dam that floods the "dead" part of Dead River and backs up the North and South branches. The lake is 18 miles long. The shores are wild, and the views of the jagged peaks of the Bigelow Mountains half a mile above are spectacular.

The first half has enough points and islands to break the wind, but a strong wind would be troublesome on the wide last half. Take the north channel around the high island a couple of miles east of Jim Eaton Hill.

Over the years stumps of the old forest have pulled free of the bottom and been stranded in coves and shallows. The end of the south channel around the island is blocked by thick rafts of stumps from shore to shore.

At Flagstaff Dam, land as close to the left as possible. Either drag across the stumps and dam or use a short, faint trail cut around them. Carry ¾ mile much on a good road accessible by a paved road from New Portland.

Big Eddy—Spencer Stream   7¾ miles

Flatwater, Class I, II
  Dam-controlled
  Wild
        USGS: Little Bigelow Mountain 15
      Portage: 7 mi   L   **Grand Falls**   ½ mi
   Campsites: ½ mi   R   **Big Eddy**   MFS car
                 7¾ mi   L   **Spencer Stream**   permit
                                         car

On the west side of the river at the foot of Long Falls, there is an observation point below the road to Spring Lake.

A boat can be lowered to the river here for ½ mile of easy Class II rapids that extend under the bridge to Big Eddy Campsite.

Below Big Eddy (½ mi) there is flatwater for 6½ miles to Dead River Dam. The portage around Grand Falls begins on the left bank above the washed-out dam, following a dirt road, and turning right onto another in about ¼ mile. The portage ends at a pool, below and out of sight of the falls.

Below the end of the portage, the current is strong as it passes an island at the mouth of Spencer Stream (7¾ mi).

Spencer Stream—The Forks 16 miles

Class II–III
   High water (over 1500 cfs): *very difficult and dangerous*
   Medium water (1000–1200 cfs): *recommended*
   Low water (below 800 cfs): *not recommended*
   Dam-controlled: *good flow in spring and intermittently through fall*
Wild
   USGS: Pierce Pond 15, The Forks 15
   Campsite: 15½ mi L **Webb's Store** private $
                                       car

This is the classic "Dead River" run. Shortly below Spencer Stream, the fun begins at Spencer Rips, the first set of rapids, with a short, difficult section at the end, best run on the extreme right. Unless you go with someone familiar with the river, it will seem to be an indistinguishable succession of Class II and III rapids, broken infrequently by pools and easier drops. An old log chute (2½ mi) high on the right is seen at a big, deep pool just above Hayden's Landing, marked by some log cribwork on the right. The Basin, 3½ miles from the start, is a long section of quickwater.

The river is generally wide and boulder-strewn, offering many routes from which to choose. At frequent intervals there are steeper rapids that require expert handling and are dangerous in high water. Normally the depth is two to three feet. The hardest section is Poplar Hill Falls, the last difficult rapids of the trip (12 mi), a tough Class III run, especially in high water. They are easily located on a map because there was a bridge just below them, but unless the rapids are pointed out to you, you may be in them before you realize it.

By the time you reach the site of the washed-out bridge, the rapids have moderated considerably, and most of the remaining distance to US-201 (15¼ mi) and the Kennebec River (16 mi) is Class I.

South Branch, DEAD RIVER

The South Branch of the Dead River flows out of Saddleback Lake on the north side of Saddleback Mountain northwards for some miles and then turns northeast through an open valley with many farms to Flagstaff Lake, which it reaches at its southwest corner near the town of Stratton. It offers a fine variety of canoeing: a steep and difficult gorge, a long stretch of mostly smoothwater, and a fine whitewater run. All these are in a beautiful setting between the Saddleback Range on the one side and East Kennebago Mountain on the other, much of it through a green farming country offering fine views to the river traveler. It is a small river and the water runs off quickly after the snow is gone. Most of the rapids, therefore, are apt to be very shallow after the middle of May.

Dallas School—Langtown Mill   5¾ miles

Quickwater, Class II, III, IV
   High water: *April*
   Forested
      USGS: Kennebago Lake 15, Rangeley 15, Quill
      Hill, *Tim Mountain,* Stratton 15

The first 3 miles of this run are not recommended except for experts. Put in at the ME-16 bridge at Dallas School. There are 2 miles of smoothwater, then a few small rapids near a state picnic area. Below this the river enters a deep gorge, a portion of which can be seen from the highway. This gorge is difficult to scout, but it *must* be scouted. Usually it can only be run when there is snow on the ground. If the level of the water is just right, this can be run by an expert canoeist, but there are at least two drops that must be lifted around. It is not feasible to take out here because of the steep bank up to the highway. Therefore, those not wishing to make this portion of the run should take out at the state picnic area. After 1 mile of very hard going (Class IV), the river comes near the road, where those wishing to avoid the difficulties of the gorge above will probably choose to put in. The rapids for the next 3 miles to Langtown Mill gradually become easier (Class II).

Langtown Mill—Green Farm Bridge 6½ miles

Flatwater, Quickwater
  High water: *April*
  Forested, Rural
    USGS: Kennebago Lake 15

Below Langtown Mill the river flows slowly, with many meanders and views of Bigelow and East Kennebago mountains.

Green Farm Bridge—
Flagstaff Lake (ME-27) 7½ miles

Lake, **Quickwater,** Class II, III
  High water: *May*
  Forested, Rural
    USGS: Quill Hill, Stratton 15

This bridge is about 1 mile off ME-16 on a gravel road that leaves the highway at Green Farm, and it makes a good put-in spot for the lower section of the river. The first 4 miles below the bridge are quickwater with frequent Class I rapids. Most of the boulders in the riverbed were dynamited years ago for log runs. About 1 mile above Lutton Brook the rapids begin abruptly and for the next 1½ miles to Nash Stream are continuous and fairly difficult (Class III).

As the river burrows into the bedrock the scenery becomes outstanding: ragged cliffs, rocky portals, sunlight slanting through the hemlocks. The riverbed is mostly shallow ledge with a few deep pools. The last 1½ miles of rapids below Nash Stream are not so difficult. About ⅓ mile below Nash Stream the river doubles around a rock spine with a little beach shelving into a deep pool.

As the river nears Flagstaff Lake the current tapers off. After entering Flagstaff Lake a dirt road on the right is passable to 4-wheel-drive vehicles. The last mile across flowed lands has views of Bigelow Mountain. When the lake is full the ME-27 bridge is too low to pass under, but boats can be slid through a culvert on the right.

Stratton is another mile.

DEAD RIVER, North Branch

Much of the waterway up which Benedict Arnold and his men struggled on their way to Canada in the fall of 1775 has been flooded, and little remains of the wilderness through which they traveled. It was on the North Branch of the Dead that his party was beset by floods late in October 1775. The story of that journey is told in *Arundel,* an historical novel by Kenneth Roberts (Doubleday, 1945).

Today, this river still flows relatively free in a rugged setting. The river is followed by ME-27, but only occasionally is the highway close enough to be visible from the water. Except for a few cabins, there is hardly a building above Eustis. From the head of Chain Lakes, the narrow valley frames a view of the Bigelow Range.

The North Branch has some challenging rapids, but most of it is flat; over 17 miles of the route described here is canoeable in all but low water.

Chain Lakes—Eustis   **19 miles**

Lakes, **Flatwater, Quickwater,** Class II–III
  High water: *mid to late May*
  Medium water: *June*
  Forested
    USGS: Chain of Ponds, Jim Pond, Tim
        Mountain, Stratton 15

Portages:	5 mi	L	**Chain Lakes Dam**	10
			yds	
	7¼ mi	R	**Sarampus Falls**	15 yds
	(19 mi		**dam at Eustis)**	
Campsites:	0 mi		**Chain Lakes** (NW end)	
			? car	
	13½ mi	R	**Alder Stream** (upstream ½	
			mi) MFS car	
	21½ mi	R	**Cathedral Pines**	
			private $ car	

The dam (5 mi) at the outlet of Chain Lakes should be portaged on the left. The North Branch begins with ¾ mile of quickwater, which slackens at an abrupt left turn just above the ME-27 bridge (5¾ mi). Then there are 1½ miles of good current to Sarampus Falls (7¼ mi), a short ledge drop beside a roadside picnic area. It usually must be lifted around.

Little Sarampus Falls, just around the next right turn, is a shorter drop, and it is followed by 4¼ miles of flatwater to Shadagee Falls (11¾ mi). The latter is flanked on both banks by low ledges, and it should be scouted. Beyond, flatwater continues for another 4¼ miles to Upper Ledge Falls Dam.

The washed-out log-driving dam (16 mi) is usually run on the left, and it is followed by 150 yards of Class II rapids. Then, after about 300 yards of flatwater, you reach Ledge Falls, a Class III set of rapids, roughly 300 yards long, that begin with a sharp drop by a large boulder on the left. They should be scouted before running. Flatwater continues for 2¼ miles to the dam at Eustis (19 mi).

When the water level in Flagstaff Lake is low, there are a few riffles below the dam, and the river banks are exposed for several miles. There is a bridge and a causeway 2 miles

south of Eustis. At the northeast end of the lake, the Dead
River begins below Long Falls Dam (40 mi).

SPENCER STREAM

Spencer Stream rises on the slopes of Kibby Mountain
just east of the boundary range and flows south and west to
the Dead River below Flagstaff Lake. It passes through
some beautiful and wild country, but each year sees more
roads in the area. The stream is usually too low for canoeing by the end of June, but it will come up after heavy rains.
It is difficult to reach the headwaters of the river, and the
old access road to Baker Pond is flooded out by beavers.
Flying in is presently the only option, but check with Ed
Webb for new roads.

Baker Pond—logging bridge   13¾ miles

Pond, **Quickwater,** Class I
  High Water
  Wild
        USGS: Spencer Lake 15, Pierce Pond 15

From the inlet it is a 1½-mile paddle down the pond to
the outlet at the south end and then 1½ miles down Baker
Stream to Spencer Stream. Baker Stream is small, with
many shallow rapids, which may have to be lifted over.
From the mouth of Baker Stream there are 2 miles of pleasant quickwater in Spencer Stream followed by 3 miles of
slackwater to Spencer Dam (7¼ mi), a logging dam of which
only the foundation remains. Below the dam are 4½ miles of
continuous rapids to a logging road bridge that offers access
on weekdays but is gated on weekends.

Logging bridge—Dead River   7½ miles

Class I, II, III
  High water
  Wild
        USGS: Pierce Pond 15
    Portage: 4½ mi   L   **falls**

Below the bridge are more Class I rapids to Spencer Gut (4¼ mi), which is a ½-mile gorge with high rock walls, down which the stream plunges in a series of falls and pools. The portage is on the left bank over a high ridge. On the right is the grave of a logger drowned in the gut in 1905. Below the gut are sporty rapids past smaller cliffs. Heavy rapids continue for 1 mile to the mouth of Little Spencer Stream (5¼ mi), while below that there are 2 miles of Class I rapids to the Dead River.

LITTLE SPENCER STREAM

Little Spencer Stream flows out of Spencer Lake south to Spencer Stream some 2 miles from its confluence with the Dead River. It provides an alternate route to Spencer Stream and the Dead River. In high water it is a pretty stream to pole down, but usually it is low and the canoe must be lifted over the shallow places.

Whipple Pond—Fish Pond   5½ miles

This is a chain of wilderness ponds separated by short pitches that are too small and steep to run. The scenery, especially on Hall Pond, is outstanding.

Put in from the jeep road from US-201 to Spencer Rips on Moose River, at the east end of Whipple Pond. Follow its narrow arm west to the rocky outlet, where an old trail is blazed to Hall Pond. The glacier dropped great boulders in clumps and rows, nearly blocking the pond at one point. The remains of an old logging dam mark the start of a short rocky pitch to the next pond. Drag and paddle through several more ponds to the marsh above Fish Pond.

Fish Pond—Spencer Stream   12¾ miles

Lake, Quickwater, Class I, II
   High water
   Medium water: scratchy
   Wild
      USGS: Spencer Lake 15, Pierce Pond 15

The Spencer Lake-Rock Pond road crosses Clark Stream, the inlet to Fish Pond, one mile of narrow, winding stream above the pond. With a high clearance vehicle, one can drive to Fish Pond, passing through a beautiful stand of white pine ¼ mile before the inlet. It is 1½ miles down Fish Pond to the narrows, 400 feet into Spencer Lake, which is 5¼ miles to the south end. The old dam (7¾ mi) at the outlet was burned; lift over.

Little Spencer Stream is a delightful paddle with intermittent rapids in a narrow stream for the 5 miles to the confluence with Spencer Stream. Since Spencer Stream is wider, it will be too low when it is still possible to paddle Little Spencer Stream, in which case one can take out at the confluence.

CARRABASSETT RIVER

The Carrabassett River rises in the mountains of northwestern Maine on the north side of Sugarloaf Mountain. It is a wild and tumultuous mountain brook above Carrabassett village and uncanoeable, but from there down it offers some fine whitewater canoeing and in its lower stretches some smoothwater travel. The valley is sparsely settled, and the stream is rocky and clear. The river rises and falls quickly after rains. The best time for running is probably early in May when the snows are still melting on Sugarloaf.

Carrabassett—Kingfield   10 miles

Class II, III
  High Water: *April, early May*
  Forested, Towns
      USGS: Little Bigelow Mountain 15
  Portage: 10 mi R **dam**

If the water is high enough, a start can be made at Valley Crossing, but the usual start is at Packards Pool, at a 1-lane bridge on a side road ½ mile below Valley Crossing.

The rapids are almost continuous to Kingfield, alternating between long, easy stretches and short, difficult pitches around boulders and over ledges. The road parallels the river all the way. Take out ½ mile above Kingfield at the

State Highway Garage on the right. One can also take out at either side of the dam at Kingfield, but it is best carried on the right.

Kingfield—New Portland   6½ miles

Class I, II
   High water: *early May*
   Forested
         USGS: Little Bigelow Mountain 15, Kingfield
               15

This is an attractive stretch; the river is wider, and the rapids not as difficult as the section above. The valley is more open. Take out at the wire bridge in New Portland.

New Portland—North Anson   13½ miles

Flatwater, Quickwater
   Almost anytime: wet summers
   Forested, Rural, Towns
      USGS: Kingfield 15
   Portages: 5½ mi   **ledge**
               9½ mi   L **Cleveland Rips**
               (13½ mi   **falls)**

The views improve as East New Portland is reached. The canoeist should take out above town, as there is an impassable drop under the bridge.

Put in on the right bank below the drop. This section is mostly quickwater, but halfway down is Cleveland Rips. There is some open pastureland, but mostly woods until close to North Anson. Take out above the village of North Anson, as there is an impassable falls in town. It is then another mile to the Kennebec River.

SANDY RIVER

The Sandy River rises in the Sandy River Ponds a few miles south of Rangeley and flows east to the Kennebec River, which it reaches a few miles south of Anson. Its

upper reaches are a tumultuous mountain torrent and uncanoeable until Smalls Falls, about 4 miles above Madrid. In
the 52 miles from here to the junction with the Kennebec,
the river drops 700 feet and offers a variety of canoeing for
all tastes. Because of the many dams, canoeing on weekdays
will be better, for there will be more water in the river and
the season will be prolonged, even into the summer. For
weekend canoeing the spring will be better, when the snows
are still providing water from the melting on Saddleback
and Mt. Abraham.

Smalls Falls—South Branch   5½ miles

Class II, III, IV
  High water, medium water
  Forested, Towns
    USGS: Rangeley 15
     Inspect: 3 mi   R   **ledges**
                3½ mi   R   **ledge**
                4½ mi   e   **falls**
                4¾ mi   e   **falls**

The Sandy River is very small here, but it can rise quickly
when the snows are melting in the mountains. Then the rapids become very heavy. In high water it is an interesting
kayak run; in medium water it can be run by open canoes.
Four ledges are particularly difficult. Action taken at them
depends on the water level.

Put in below Small Falls from a track on the left bank.
The first mile is continuously difficult, with some fallen
trees, especially at a sharp "S"-curve. Below the first US-4
bridge the going is easy away from the road. As the river
turns back toward the road, and just below a long island, a
series of four ledges starts, with the last one being the highest. These are best scouted/lined on the right and run on the
left. These are more ledgy compared to the rounded boulders above. The rapids become easier as they follow the
road to the bridge in Madrid (3½ mi).

The second ledge below the bridge should be scouted as it
is full of sharp rocks. The river swings away from the road
and ¼ mile above the second US-4 bridge is a small gorge,

which should be inspected in advance. Below the second US-4 bridge is another falls, the steepest of all, with a large boulder below, making an island in the gorge. The rapids gradually ease to the third ME-4 bridge, just above the confluence with the South Branch.

South Branch—Phillips   5¾ miles

Class II, III
  High water: *early May*
  Forested, Rural
    USGS: Phillips 15
    Portage: (8½ mi L **falls**)

This is a somewhat less difficult run than the section above but it should still be attempted only by those with a fair amount of experience, as there are a number of Class III rapids to be encountered. From the ME-4 bridge 2 miles south of Madrid, it is only 200 yards to the confluence of the South Branch. About 1 mile below here Orbeton Stream, which flows out of Redington Pond on the east flank of Saddleback, enters on the left. The junction is a fine lunch spot. The brawling mountain stream is left behind here, and below one travels on a wide river with the open pastures providing many fine views of the mountains to the north and west. The rapids are nearly continuous although not difficult, but at nearly every bend there are heavy waves, which must be avoided. Take out on the left a mile upstream of Phillips at Davenport Flats where the road comes close to the river.

Through Phillips   2½ miles

Both the ME-142 and the ME-149 bridges have "unrunnable" gorges above them. Persons attempting the gorge above ME-142 should scout carefully from above and below, as the height is deceptive. The best approach is from directly upstream through a 3-foot-wide chute on the left of the rock island. It is possible to take out at a railroad park on the left bank, a mile above the next waterfall.

Phillips—Fairbanks Bridge   17¼ miles

Quickwater, Class I, II
  High water, medium high water
  Forested, Rural
      USGS: Phillips 15, Kingfield 15

Below the ME-149 bridge put in on left to run the Class III rapid within sight downstream, and another Class III rapid ¼ mile downstream where the river makes a sharp turn to the right. Or put in on the left below these. The remainder of the 8 miles to Strong is quickwater and riffles, with lovely mountain views.

A half mile above Strong is a Class II rapid that runs for ¼ mile. A ballpark on the right below the bridge in Strong offers good access.

At Strong the river turns south; several Class II rapids occur. The river is constantly changing in depth from shoal water to deep pools. A mile above the Fairbanks Bridge, ME-4, an easy ledge drop can make things "sporty." Access is downstream on the right.

Fairbanks Bridge—Farmington Falls   10¼ miles

Flatwater, Quickwater
  Medium water, low water
  Rural, Towns
      USGS: Kingfield 15, Farmington

The river is smooth the remaining 3½ miles to Farmington. A ½ mile below Farmington Temple Stream enters on the right. Another ½ mile brings an interesting ledge drop, and then the river is smooth and winding for the next 6 miles to Farmington Falls. Just above the ME-156 bridge Wilson Stream enters on the right. Persons wishing to avoid whitewater should take out well above the bridge, or a mile further upstream where the river comes close to the road on the right.

Farmington Falls—New Sharon   6 miles

Quickwater, Class I, II, III
  Medium water
  Rural
      USGS: Farmington, New Sharon, Farmington
            Falls

The remains of a washed-out dam are visible above the bridge as the river begins to pitch for 200 yards of Class I–II water. Then the river smooths out and winds through farm country to the town of New Sharon. Here the river turns sharply to the left and under the US-2 bridge.

Rapids start well above the bridge, increasing in intensity to a sharp right-hand turn that generates "5-foot" waves. These should be avoided except by experts in high water and scouted carefully in medium water. The rapids end in ¾ mile where a campground is on the left bank.

New Sharon—Kennebec River   20¼ miles

Flatwater, Quickwater
  Medium water, low water
  Forested, Rural
      USGS: New Sharon, Norridgewock 15, Anson
            15
  Portage: 16 mi   **dam**

The river flows smoothly with good current below the rapids in New Sharon. There is a gauging station on the right bank near Witham Corner and in 5 miles there is a dam below Sandy River. Below the dam are 3½ miles of winding river to the junction with the Kennebec River. Take out a mile downstream on the left bank or 5¾ miles downstream at Norridgewock where there is a boat ramp.

SANDY RIVER, South Branch

The South Branch is a very small stream that can be run in medium water as an alternate start to the Sandy River. It has been run from above the confluence of the branches 2.7

miles above ME-4 on Number Six Road, but this is too small and obstructed to recommend. A better start is 1.5 miles where the river comes close to the road. It is a fast Class II to an abutment on a private road a mile above ME-4, where the difficulty gradually diminishes.

TEMPLE STREAM

Temple Stream rises in Avon and flows southeast to the Sandy River at West Farmington. It is small, there are several dams, and the running is mixed smooth and rapids.

Drury Pond—Sandy River   8½ miles

Flatwater, Quickwater, Class I, II, III
  High water: *early spring*
  Forested, Rural, Towns
     USGS: Farmington
    Portage: 1½ mi   **dam at Temple**
             7½ mi   **dam at W. Farmington**

If the water level is high enough, it is possible to put in just below the outlet of Drury Pond north of Temple. The first 2 miles to the dam are all smooth. The next 2½ miles below the dam to the first bridge have Class II rapids. The next 1½ miles to the millpond the rapids become steeper, Class III. Then it is 1½ miles down the pond to the dam at West Farmington. Below the dam the river is mostly smooth for the remaining mile to the Sandy River, a mile below Farmington.

WILSON STREAM

Wilson Stream rises on the north side of Saddleback Mountain but does not become canoeable until Wilson Pond in Wilton. The 15 miles from there to the junction with Sandy River at Farmington Falls offers a variety of rapid and smoothwater with only two dams to carry.

There is a sharp rapid through the town for ¾ mile to the lower dam, so that it is well to put in below this dam. In another ¾ mile there is a fall that requires a carry, so that most canoeists will decide to put in below this fall.

Wilton—East Wilton   3½ miles

Class II
  High water
  Forested
      USGS: Wilton
      Portage: (3½ mi   L   **dam East Wilton)**

Put in below the lower dam in a parking lot on the right just below the bridge, 1½ miles below Wilton. From here to East Wilton the river is mostly Class II rapids. In East Wilton take out on the left above a broken dam. Carry on the road across the bridge and put in on the right.

East Wilton—North Chesterville   10 miles

Quickwater
  Medium water: *May*
  Forested, Towns
      USGS: Wilton, Farmington Falls
      Portages: 1 mi   **low dam**   lift over
                    (11 mi   **broken dam**   North
                                Chesterville)

After a short Class II rapid below the dam, it is mostly quickwater to the dam at North Chesterville. A small dam 1 mile below the start may be lifted over.

North Chesterville—Farmington Falls   4 miles

There is a short rapid below the dam. The following 4 miles to Farmington Falls and the junction with the Sandy River at Farmington Falls are all smoothwater.

SEBASTICOOK RIVER

USGS: Guilford 15, Skowhegan 15, Pittsfield
15, Burnham 15, Waterville 15

The Sebasticook River rises in North Dexter and flows south for a long distance, paralleling the Kennebec before finally joining that river at Winslow, opposite Waterville. As most of the drops have been dammed for power purposes, it offers a long river run even in the summer through a section of rural Maine in which industrialization and urbanization have hardly begun. The upper section should probably be run in the spring, when there is plenty of water.

North Dexter—Great Moose Pond   22 miles

Put in at North Dexter from ME-23, or if the water is low, from a side road that leaves the main road south of North Dexter and reaches the river ½ mile lower down, where it is somewhat larger. This section of river is still somewhat small and best run at high water. It is mostly smooth and the only rapid can be lined or carried. It runs through a mountainous country with fine views in all directions. For 13 miles from the start the river runs through marshes in a general southwesterly direction to Mainstream Pond. There are then 3 miles of paddling to its southwest end and the town of Mainstream. Below the town there is ½ mile of rapids followed by 1 mile of easy river to Lake Como. The outlet leaves the lake at its southwest corner, and in ¼ mile there is a sharp rapid, after which the river is easy for 1 mile to Great Moose Pond. One can take out at Castle Harmony just before entering the lake or continue southeast across the lake 3 miles to the outlet at Wildwood.

Great Moose Pond—Pittsfield   10 miles

From Wildwood at the outlet of Great Moose Pond it is only 2 miles to the first dam at Hartland. There are two dams here, and it is best to make a ½-mile carry and go around both dams and the rapid below the lower dam. There is a tannery here, which adds pollution, making the river unattractive. This situation clears up, however, in about 2 miles so the river is again quite clean 4 miles down at the beginning of Douglas Pond just below the West Palmyra bridge. Another 2 miles down Douglas Pond brings the canoeist to the dam at Waverley just above Pittsfield. It is 1 mile below here to the dam at Pittsfield.

Pittsfield—Winslow   **30 miles**

From Pittsfield it is 3 miles to the junction with the East Branch of the Sebasticook River and 1 mile more to Peltoma Bridge on Horseback Road. Another 3 miles of river and 2 miles of deadwater bring the canoeist to the dam between Pittsfield and Burnham. There is ½ mile of quickwater below the dam to the gauging station on the right bank, and then easy going for the 11 miles to Clinton through open rolling country with mostly wooded banks but some open meadowland. At Clinton the current quickens and about 3 miles down the river drops 1½ feet over a ledge. A channel in the middle offers the only route through, but the waves at the end are high and can easily swamp a canoe. The pitch should be scouted before running. Some 2 miles farther down at Benton Falls, there is a series of ledges running diagonally across the river. There are also two concrete piles in the river that are difficult to avoid. This section should be looked over before running. The best route is generally close to the left shore. The bad drops at the end may be impossible, so one may have to take out after running part of the rapid and carry around the drops. It is then another 5 miles to the dam at Winslow, best carried on the left, only ¼ mile above the junction with the Kennebec River.

SEBASTICOOK RIVER, East Branch

USGS: Pittsfield 15

The East Branch of the Sebasticook River rises in Martin Bog in the southern part of Dexter, but is hardly canoeable until it reaches Corinna. From here it provides an alternative and somewhat shorter start for the trip down the main Sebasticook River. It flows through open, rolling country in which the banks are largely wooded. It has the advantage that there are a number of spots at which access can be had, so that the trip can be matched to the stage of water. It can probably be run in any but a dry summer.

Moody—Newport   11 miles

It should usually be possible to put in at the bridge on the side road off ME-7 in the northern part of the town of Corinna. This bridge is just west of Moody and below a dam on the river. The river is small for a few hundred yards and then opens up to a wider stream for the 3 miles to the millpond above Corinna, passing a bridge at Lincoln Mills 2 miles down which is an alternative starting point. There is then 1 mile of deadwater to the dam at Corinna. Below this dam there is ¼ mile of millpond to the second dam, then ½ mile of millpond to the third dam. Below this dam there are 3 miles of river to the entrance to Sebasticook Lake, then 3 miles across the lake to the town of Newport at the southwest corner, where the river flows out.

Newport—Sebasticook River   9 miles

There are two dams at Newport, the first at the lake and the second ½ mile below across the millpond. Canoeists starting here will probably put in, therefore, below these dams. There are then 9 miles of good current, the last half through a large bog to the main Sebasticook River 3 miles below Pittsfield. Those not wishing to go farther can take out 1 mile down that river at the Peltoma Bridge on Horseback Road.

STETSON STREAM

USGS: Stetson 15, Pittsfield 15

Stetson Stream is the outlet of Pleasant Lake in Stetson and flows west to Sebasticook Lake, thus providing an alternate means of access to the East Branch of the Sebasticook River. It runs largely through swamps and is sluggish, losing most of its altitude at the dam at Stetson. It may be run in the summer if not too low, but is better in the spring.

Pleasant Lake—Newport   12 miles

One can put in at the east end of Pleasant Lake from a side road off ME-222. It is then 2 miles west across the lake to the outlet, which is located in a bay on the north side near the western end. Some 1½ miles of travel down the river through a swamp brings the canoeist to the ME-143 bridge and the dam at Stetson. There are then 2½ miles of river, again largely through swamp, to Sebasticook Lake, 1 mile down the arm of which one passes under Durham Bridge into the main lake. Some may wish to take out here. It is then 5 miles across the lake to the town of Newport at the southwest corner, where the East Branch of the Sebasticook flows out.

MARTIN STREAM

Martin Stream rises in Troy and Thorndike, and flows north and west into the East Branch of the Sebasticook a mile below Newport. It becomes canoeable in Dixmont, and is a pleasant trip on a small stream with good current through relatively wild country.

The spring migration of suckers up Martin Stream is most impressive, sometimes carpeting the bottom with masses of fish.

Dixmont—Newport   16 miles

Lake, Flatwater, **Quickwater,** Swamp, Class I, II
   High water: *spring*
   Wild, Forested, Rural
      USGS: Dixmont, Plymouth, Newport
   Portages: 1½ mi R **Dixmont Falls** 20 yd
            9¾ mi R **Plymouth dam** 150 yd

Put in at Mitchell Road just west of ME-7 between Dixmont and North Dixmont. The stream is small. It is 1½ miles to Dixmont Falls, then 150 yards to the ME-7 bridge in North Dixmont. After ½ mile, the river enters an alder jungle thick enough to impede all but the most determined.

At around 7 miles the flowage from the dam in Plymouth is reached with a paddle down the lake to the dam and falls in Plymouth (9¾ mi). Just below is a nice Class II rapid.

About 13 miles there is a sharp ledge drop to look over. The bridge at Ridge Road in Newport is 14½ miles, the last before the confluence with the East Branch (16 mi).

BELGRADE LAKES TRIP

USGS: Norridgewock 15, Augusta 15,
        Waterville 15

The Belgrade Lakes offer a variety of trips. The usual trip
is a circular one starting from East Pond and ending at
Messalonskee Lake only 3 miles from the starting place.
One can then return to the start or descend Messalonskee
Stream to the Kennebec River at Waterville.

East Pond   2½ miles

This is the highest of the chain and the usual starting
point. There is access at a public picnic spot off East Pond
Road, just south of "Alden's Camp."

The Serpentine   2 miles

This is the outlet of East Pond. It is wide and smooth. In
1½ miles there is a sharp left turn. The channel to the right
can be explored but is only the outlet of Sucker Brook. Just
beyond on the right is a lunch site. In another ½ mile the
dam at Smithfield is reached. This can either be carried, if
there is enough water in the brook below, or the canoe
taken 300 yards to the beach at North Pond.

North Pond   2 miles

From Smithfield on the east shore it is only 2 miles to the
outlet, Great Meadow Stream, which takes off at the center
of the south shore, but there are many more miles of lake to
explore, including a possible trip into Little Pond through
the Narrows at the southern end of the west shore.

Great Meadow Stream   4 miles

This is the outlet of North Pond and leaves that pond
near the center of the south shore. It twists and turns its way
for 4 miles to Great Pond, marking the boundary between
Rome on the right and Smithfield and Belgrade on the left.

Great Pond   5 miles

This is located in Belgrade, although the north and part of the west shores are in Rome. It is a very large lake, and one should be on the alert for sudden squalls. There are public campsites on Crooked and Oak islands. It is only 5 miles southwesterly across the lake to the outlet at Belgrade Lakes on the west shore, but there are many bays and inlets to explore. The outlet is really only an extension of the lake for ½ mile to the dam. Here one should take out at the cement bridge and carry 50 yards around the dam and into Long Pond.

Long Pond   6 miles

Although the northern end of the pond in Rome is worth exploring, the usual route crosses the pond to the west shore, where it turns south and passes under the bridge at Castle Island in 2 miles. Another 4 miles of southward paddling brings the canoeist through a constantly narrowing pond to the outlet, Belgrade Stream. About 1 mile above the outlet Ingham Stream enters on the right.

Belgrade Stream   9 miles

It is 2 miles down the stream to Wings Mills. After going under the bridge, keep to the right to avoid the sluiceway on the left. Canoes can be hauled over the old fish ladder on the right. It is then only 6 miles more to Belgrade and another 1 mile to Messalonskee Lake.

Messalonskee Lake   8 miles

This is an Abenaki name meaning Snow Pond. The lake is long and narrow and provides an 8-mile paddle to its northern end, where at Oakland one is only 3 miles from the starting place at East Pond. One can terminate the trip here or continue on down Messalonskee Stream to the Kennebec River.

Messalonskee Stream   9 miles

This is the outlet from the Belgrade Lakes and consequently the water level holds up well and it can be run in the summer. The banks are a mixture of wooded and open

land, and the river flows in a pleasant valley. There are
three dams and an impassable cascade in Oakland, so that
one cannot go directly into the river from Messalonskee
Lake. It is best to make a 2-mile carry around all these
obstructions and put in at the pond below town. Below
Oakland 1½ miles is a dam where a ½-mile carry is necessary,
as most of the water flows through a penstock to the reservoir ½ mile below. The carry is on the right. It is then 4 miles
to the first dam in Waterville and then 1 mile of backwater
to the second dam. From this dam it is 1 mile to the Kennebec River.

COBBOSSEECONTEE STREAM

The upper Cobbosseecontee Stream is a series of lakes
and streams, starting with Torsey Lake in Mount Vernon
and descending through Maranacook Lake and Lake Annabessacook to Cobbosseecontee Lake, from which Cobbosseecontee Stream flows to the Kennebec River at Gardiner.
The trip can be made in either direction, as most of the
way is lakes or backwater from dams, with easy paddling
through gentle, rolling country. Only the ⅛ mile of rapids
between the dams below Cobbossee Dam requires high
water. The trip can be extended for many miles of additional paddling on the lakes.

Torsey Lake—Gardiner   40½ miles

Lakes, Flatwater
   Passable at all water levels
   Cottages, Forested
       USGS: Augusta 15, Gardiner 15
   Portages: Numerous on connecting streams—
               see text below.

Torsey Lake   3½ miles

One can put in at the north end of the lake from a side
road about 1 mile off Cobbs Hills Road (ME-41) in Mount
Vernon, or at the south end at the very tip of the lake. The
lake is long and narrow, twisting about in its course southward.

Torsey Lake outlet   2 miles 3 dams

There is a dam at the outlet, and then 1 mile of millpond to Readfield, where there are two dams. It is best to carry these both together. The final 1 mile to Maranacook Lake is a meandering meadow brook. If the water in this stream is too low for a canoe, the entire 2 miles can be easily carried by road.

Maranacook Lake   5½ miles

From the inlet stream, crossed by ME-41 almost at the lake shore, it is 5 miles down the lake, passing the town of Maranacook halfway, to Winthrop where there is a public launch area at Norcross Point with toilets and water. At Winthrop the outlet is Mill Stream.

Mill Stream   ¾ mile 1 dam

This provides the connection from Maranacook Lake to Lake Annabessacook or vice versa. At the Maranacook Lake end, enter the stream under Memorial Drive, lift over the small dam at the other side of the bridge, and descend to the Main Street bridge. Here the canoes must be carried across the street 100 yards to the water just beyond the Carlson Woolen Mill. It is then possible to paddle the remainder of the distance and enter Lake Annabessacook through a large culvert under US-202.

Lake Annabessacook   4 miles

It is 4 miles down this lake to the outlet stream. It is about 2 miles to the narrows, and from here one should head for the southeast corner where the outlet is located.

It is possible to paddle up the outlet stream to Lower Narrows Pond, if the season is not too dry, passing under a road and through a culvert.

Juggernot Stream   1¼ miles 1 dam

This is the outlet of Lake Annabessacook and provides unobstructed travel to Cobbosseecontee Lake, except for a short carry over the outlet dam.

Cobbosseecontee Lake   6½ miles

Cobbosseecontee means Sturgeon Lake in the Abenaki language, "contee" meaning "lake." Rightfully one should not repeat the word "lake," but as so few people know the Indian tongues, the usage will probably continue. The dam at the outlet raised the level of the lake 9 feet, enlarging the lake area but reducing the size of some of the islands. Although it is only 6 miles north up Cobbosseecontee Lake to the outlet, Cobbosseecontee Stream, on the east side, there is another 3 miles to the head of the lake at East-Winthrop, and 2 miles from the inlet to the south end of the lake at Dismal Swamp in Monmouth. There are many islands inviting exploration.

Cobbosseecontee Stream   11 miles 2 dams

It is only ¼ mile from the bridge near the lake shore to the outlet dam, which must be carried on the west end. There is a ⅛ mile set of Class II rapids at high water, but they must be carried when it is low, on the west side. The Collins Mill Dam is another short portage (on the west) 2½ miles below Cobbossee Outlet dam. Some 6 miles below the dam Oxbow Pond is reached, and in another mile Horseshoe Pond. The river is wide all the way to Pleasant Pond, after the Collins Mill Dam.

Pleasant Pond   2 miles

Although it is only 2 miles down Pleasant Pond from the inlet to the outlet, Cobbosseecontee Stream, at the north end, one can paddle some 4 miles to the south into Upper Pleasant Pond and enjoy a considerable mileage of lake travel.

Cobbosseecontee Stream—Gardiner   4 miles

From Pleasant Pond it is an easy paddle for the 4 miles to Gardiner. Take out above the first dam, for in the last mile and a half to the Kennebec River there are three more dams and some difficult Class III-IV rapids, with some sewage and paper mill effluent mixed in.

CHAPTER 4

Penobscot Watershed

PENOBSCOT WATERSHED

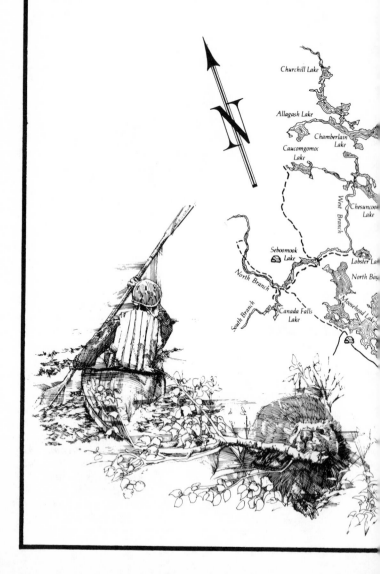

Churchill Lake

Allagash Lake

Chamberlain Lake

Caucomgomoc Lake

West Branch

Chesuncook Lake

Seboomook Lake

Lobster Lake

North Branch

North Bay

Moosehead Lake

South Branch

Canada Falls Lake

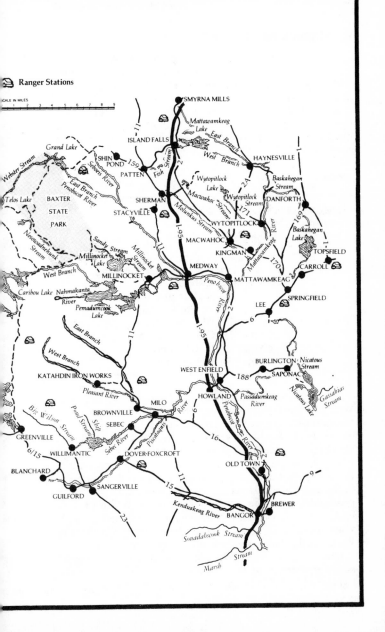

Ranger Stations

SCALE IN MILES
1 2 3 4 5 6 7 8 9

SMYRNA MILLS

Mattawamkeag Lake
East Branch

ISLAND FALLS

West Branch
HAYNESVILLE

Grand Lake
SHIN POND
159
PATTEN
Fish Stream
2
2A
Baskahegan Stream

Webster Stream
East Branch Penobscot River
Seboeis River
Wytopitlock Lake
Macwahoc Stream
Wytopitlock Stream
DANFORTH
171
169

Telos Lake
BAXTER
STATE
PARK
SHERMAN
STACYVILLE
WYTOPITLOCK

Baskahegan Lake

Neosowadnehunk Stream
Sandy Stream
Molunkus Stream
MACWAHOC
KINGMAN
TOPSFIELD
1

Millinocket Lake
Millinocket Stream
11
I-95
MEDWAY
170
CARROLL
2

Caribou Lake
Nahmakanta River
MILLINOCKET
Penobscot River
MATTAWAMKEAG
Mattawamkeag River
SPRINGFIELD

West Branch
Pemadumcook Lake
LEE
6
2

East Branch
11

West Branch

KATAHDIN IRON WORKS
BURLINGTON
Nicatous Stream
SAPONAC

WEST ENFIELD
188

Pleasant River
MILO
HOWLAND
Passadumkeag River
Nicatous Lake
Gassabias Stream

BROWNVILLE
SEBEC
Ship Pond Stream
Piscataquis River
6
16
Penobscot River

Big Wilson Stream
GREENVILLE
6/15
WILLIMANTIC
Sebec River
DOVER-FOXCROFT
OLD TOWN
9

BLANCHARD
SANGERVILLE
15
11

GUILFORD
23
Kenduskeag River
BANGOR
BREWER

Souadabscook Stream

Marsh Stream

PENOBSCOT RIVER

This is a large river paralleled by highways, often on both sides, and bordered by a mixture of forests and farms, cities and towns. It is quite different from the East and West branches, which join to form it.

Since most of the drops have been harnessed for power, this river consists primarily of smoothwater with some quickwater. In many sections it is more like a long, thin lake than a river.

Medway—Bangor   70 miles

Flatwater, Quickwater, Class I, II
    Passable at all water levels
    Dam controlled: *adequate flow all year*
    Forested, Rural, Towns
        USGS: Millinocket 15, Mattawamkeag 15,
            Winn 15, Lincoln 15, Passadumkeag
            15, Orono 15, Bangor 15

Portages:	7 mi	L	**Mattaseunk dam**
	36 mi	R	**W. Enfield dam**
	60 mi	L	**Old Town dam**
	61 mi	L	**Old Town dam**
	67 mi	L	**Veazie dam**
	(70 mi	R	**Bangor dam)**

From Nicatou Island at the confluence of the East and West branches, the Penobscot River flows for 7 miles to Mattaseunk Dam, carried left. From there it is 4½ miles to the mouth of the Mattawamkeag River (11½ mi) at Mattawamkeag. In another 1¾ miles is the beginning of Five Island Rapids, which are ½ mile long. They are easy Class II, and the principal drop, frequently bony in low water, is at the end of the islands as Winn is approached. Flatwater predominates for the next 16 miles past the North Lincoln bridge (20 mi) to Mohawk rapids, a ¾ mile section with some rocks and a good current. In another 5½ miles the West Enfield Dam is reached and carried right.

Below the West Enfield Dam (36 mi) the Penobscot passes the mouth of the Piscataquis River (37 mi) on the right, the ME-6/155 bridge (37¼ mi), and the Passadumkeag

River (41¼ mi) on the left. In the next 18¾ miles to Old Town, the river flows through somewhat wider bottom lands and spreads into several channels with many islands.

About two miles above the first dam at Old Town, one should take the left channel if one wishes the most direct route. On the right the Stillwater River (actually a western channel of the Penobscot) leaves, headed northwesterly.

The first dam at Old Town (60 mi) is located upstream of the highway bridge connecting Old Town with Milford. It is carried left. One flatwater mile downstream (61 mi) is the second dam at Old Town, also carried left. There is a Class II rapid below this dam. Two miles downstream, where the Stillwater rejoins the Penobscot, there is a Class III rapid, the most difficult on the lower river. Scouting from the right side may be warranted for those with loaded canoes. On the right there is an easier passage. Four miles below (all Class I) one comes to the Veazie Dam (67 mi), carried left. Three miles downstream one encounters the remains of the Bangor Dam (70 mi). As of this writing there is a section of the dam missing on the Brewer (southeast) side. If the tide at Bangor is high or nearly high, one can canoe through this breach. Otherwise, avoid its powerful currents. As further deterioration of this dam is imminent, scouting is recommended.

Bangor—Bucksport   21 miles

The Penobscot is tidal below Bangor, and a large river. Canoeists should take note of tide and weather. A number of launching ramps are available.

The section below the breached Bangor Dam, 1½ miles upstream of the mouth of the Kenduskeag River, is very urban and has strong currents when the water level in the river is high. From East Hampton to South Orrington the river is generally quite scenic and flat except when wind and tide are opposed. The river then opens up and becomes over a mile wide in places.

It is possible for experienced canoeists to go down the main (west) channel from Bucksport and then back up East Channel for an 11-mile circuit of Verona Island. The combination of ebbing tide and upstream wind can create large rolling waves in the main channel. Current patterns near the north end of the island can also be confusing.

The tidal range at Bangor is 13 feet; high water is 4 minutes later than at Portland.

HEADWATERS OF THE PENOBSCOT

The Penobscot River has two major tributaries, the East Branch and the West Branch, which offer a variety of canoe trips through a vast semi-wilderness area of Maine. The West Branch is itself formed by the confluence of the North Branch and the South Branch, two small streams that drain a wild and densely forested area that is accessible only via private logging roads.

The North Branch was formerly the principal means of access to the headwaters of the Saint John River. Carry trails to Fifth Saint John Pond and Baker lake were popular routes before modern logging roads and airplanes, but they have become completely overgrown.

The West Branch from Seboomook Lake to Millinocket is a large river with good canoeing throughout the summer. However, during spring run-off, the high water can cause dangerous conditions in some places. The West Branch is one of the most scenic sections of the Penobscot. Its banks are heavily forested, with little evidence of civilization, and the spectacular views of Mount Katahdin along the lower section add to its wilderness character. Roads from Greenville and Millinocket allow easy access at several points along the river.

The East Branch of the Penobscot flows from Grand Lake Matagamon at the northeast corner of Baxter State Park to Medway, where it joins the West Branch, forming the main river. The East Branch, although not as large as the West Branch, offers good canoeing throughout most of the season, and, like its western sister, affords good views of the mountains of Baxter State Park. Webster Stream, a tributary of the East Branch, flows from Telos Lake to Grand Lake.

PENOBSCOT RIVER, West Branch

The West Branch of the Penobscot is formed by the junction of the North and the South branches at the west end of Seboomook Lake. It flows generally east for 108 miles through well-wooded valleys and unpopulated lakes to Medway, where it joins the East Branch.

Its upper waters were formerly the most traveled waterways in Maine because they were the access not only to the West Branch itself, but also to the East Branch, the Allagash, and the Saint John. Today, private logging roads provide easy access to many points along the river.

The river is large enough so that it can be run at any season, but some of the more difficult rapids must be carried at high water.

Pittston Farm—Roll Dam Campsite   16 miles

Lakes, Flatwater, Class I
  Spring, summer, fall
  Wild
      USGS: Seboomook Lake 15, North East Carry
           15
  Portages: 12½ mi   L   **Seboomook Dam**
              (13¼ mi   R   **Ledges**   3 mi)
  Campsites: 12 mi   R   **Seboomook Dam** $ car,
                                   BPR permit
              (16 mi   R   **Ledges** $ car, BPR
                                   permit)

Seboomook Dam is 12½ miles from Pittston Farm, and it must be portaged on the left. Below the dam, the river is mixed smooth and rapid for 7¾ miles to North East Carry. Only ¾ mile from Seboomook Dam, you reach the first of a series of low ledges, many of which are unrunnable for any but the most experienced canoeist. A carry trail on the right side beside a large boulder about 40 yards above the first drop leads to a gravel road. This road can be followed to the BPR campsite on the river bank beside the last pitch.

Campsite—Ripogenus Dam   43½ miles

Lakes, Flatwater, Class I
Spring, summer, fall
Wild

USGS:		North East Carry 15, Caucomgomoc Lake 15, Chesuncook 15, Ragged Lake 15, Harrington Lake 15	
Portage:	(43½ mi	R	**Ripogenus Dam** 2½ miles (by car))
Campsites:	six sites		**between Ledges and Pine Stream** BPR permit
	21 mi	R	**Pine Stream** BPR permit
	24 mi	R	**Boom House** BPR permit
	three sites		**on Chesuncook Lake** BPR permit
	41½ mi	R	**Chesuncook Dam** $ car, BPR permit

This is the smoothwater section of the West Branch. The ledges below Seboomook Dam are generally considered unrunnable, so canoe trips frequently begin at the BPR Roll Dam Campsite. Below, the river continues with moderate current to North East Carry (4¼ mi).

Lobster Stream enters on the right in 2½ miles. Sometimes it flows backwards into Lobster Lake when the West Branch is rising.

Lobster Lake, which has several attractive campsites, makes a good side trip. The lake is an easy 2-mile paddle via Lobster Stream. The bridge for the private road from Northeast Carry crosses Lobster Stream just above the confluence with the West Branch.

In the remaining 17¼ miles there are a variety of campsites, some of which are listed above. The current slows, becoming flowage from the lake for the last several miles. The bridge on the Ragmuff/Caucogomoc private road crosses at 11 miles. At Boom House campsite (24 mi) the river opens up into Chesuncook Lake.

Chesuncook Dam (41½ mi) near the southeast end is a convenient take-out point. There is no dam there; it is just the site of a dam flooded out by the present Ripogenus Dam (43½ mi) 3 miles to the east at the end of Ripogenus Lake.

If you are continuing down the West Branch, you must portage 2½ miles along the road on the south bank from Rip Dam to Big Eddy because Ripogenus Gorge is impassable to loaded canoes.

Ripogenus Gorge—McKay Station   1½ miles

Class III, IV
    Dam controlled: *recommended level 800 to 2000 cfs only*
    Wild
        USGS: Harrington Lake 15

This run begins just below the dam with a short but exceedingly difficult portage. This is a run for experienced decked boaters only after thorough and complete scouting. The most difficult drop is the last one.

McKay Station—Big Eddy   2½ miles

Class IV, V
    Dam controlled: *below 1000 cfs—very dangerous*
                   1500–2000 cfs—recommended
                   2500–3500 cfs—rapids become "pushy"
                   above 4500 cfs approaches class VI
    Wild
        USGS: Harrington Lake 15

This is a world-class whitewater run for expert boaters only. Beware! (A good motto for this section would be *Eschew Obfuscation* or *!!!)*

Entering the gorge the boater runs into standing waves of about a meter in height for about 200 meters with an eddy on the left. This eddy is your last chance to see Exterminator, Class IV, a set of very large waves, then a hole. From here you enter Staircase Rapid, Class IV +, a series of four very large holes. Leaving the Staircase is an eddy below which you have a choice. On river right you have the Little

Heater, a Class IV cascade 3 meters high, while on the left is the Big Heater, Class III. Shortly, you leave the gorge and enter Little Eddy with take-out or put-in on the left.

Below Little Eddy is a Class II–III rapid about 200 meters in length. Here there is an excellent view of the Katahdin skyline. In about 300 meters you come to Trouble-maker Rapid, Class IV, which contains several small holes and a very strong breaking standing wave. Then you enter 200 meters of Class II rapid before an eddy that is the last eddy before Cribwork Rapid.

Cribwork Rapid is about 600 meters in length, very strong, Class V, with no way to stop in the middle. This must be scouted. (Watch someone else run it first if possi-ble.) As you pass under the bridge, pass Telos Hole, which guards the rapid. From here is a wild and rocky rapid drop-ping better than 8 meters.

Less than 20 meters after Cribwork you enter Bone Cruncher (2 mi), Class IV, with large holes and waves. The remaining distance is Class I to Big Eddy Rapid, Class III.

Big Eddy—Spencer Cove   22¼ miles

Lakes, Flatwater, Class II–V
  High water (over 3000 cfs): *dangerous*
  Medium water (2000–3000 cfs): *recommended*
  Low water (under 2000 cfs): *recommended*
  Dam-controlled: *good flow spring through fall*
  Forested

USGS:	Harrington Lake 15, Katahdin 15, Norcross 15		
Portages:	2¼ mi	R	**Big Ambejackmockamus Falls**
	6 mi	L	**Sourdnahunk Falls**
	11 mi	R	**Pockwockomus Falls**
	13¾ mi	C	**Debsconeag Falls**
Campsite:	0 mi		**Big Eddy** private $ car many additional campsites

---

This section is one of the most scenic along the Penob-scot's many branches. It also contains some heavy rapids. The Great Northern Paper Company generates electricity at

Ripogenus Dam, and the river downstream has a good flow all year.

The regular text is for boaters who wish to only run rapids up to Class III. The text in italics is for experts in heavy-water boats.

It is 1 mile to Little Ambejackmockamus Falls, a Class II or III drop depending on the water level. One mile beyond, and past some rapids, take out on the right where the road is close to the river at a sharp left turn (2¼ mi) in order to carry round Big Ambejackmockamus Falls.

Big Ambejackmockamus Falls: 400 meters of standing waves to a Class IV drop with a very large, dangerous keeper in the center. At the second drop run right or left as there is a hole in the center. The third drop has a large wave with a pool at the bottom. Each drop should be scouted on the left.

A short distance below the falls, the Horserace begins, a long rocky Class II–III rapid with pine-lined banks. If the water stage is not right, or the canoeist inexperienced, it is necessary to carry 1½ miles around both Big Ambejackmockamus Falls and the Horserace to Sourdnahunk Deadwater.

After 2 miles of deadwater, take out above the ledge on the left and carry Sourdnahunk Falls (6 mi).

Nesourdnahunk Falls, Class IV: As you turn left in Class III rapids the river goes over a falls with a 4-meter vertical drop. The right is very rocky. The left is a very heavy run over the drop into a large hole with about 10 standing waves below, followed by 300 meters of Class II.

At the end of the carry is the 3-mile Abol Deadwater, which extends to some Class I rips under the Abol bridge ½ mile above Abol Falls. There is easy Class II above Abol Falls (10 mi). Stay along the right bank; the portage begins at a small beach right after a large one, and close to the falls. Follow the roads and take a left. A cabin faces the falls, which is visible from above.

Abol Falls, Class IV: The falls is 250 meters long and full of very large rocks and waves. It is best run on the right, which is also the best place to scout. The run behind the island on the right is very narrow with large rocks.

Quickwater continues for ½ mile, then easy Class II to a cabin on the right marking Pockwockamus Falls (11 mi).

Portage along the road on the right, then take the third left
to the bottom of the falls. A shorter trail begins very close
to the top of Pockwockamus Falls.

*Big Pockwockamus Falls, Class IV: Large rocks and
many standing waves. Scout from the right watching carefully for a hole on the right about 100 meters into the
rapids.*

Pockwockamus deadwater extends for 2½ miles to Debsconeag Falls (13¾ mi), which can be portaged on either
side. The portage on the left begins 100 yards above the falls
in a small cove, length ½ mile. The portage on the right is
below a large island in a tiny clearing where the bank is
steep but only 3 feet high. The portage is 620 yards up a hill
and down to the end of the falls.

*Debsconeag Falls is a very dangerous Class V rapid with
several river-wide keepers. This is the hardest rapid in this
section of the river, and if run it should be scouted from the
left and run in several sections.*

There is a drop with a big wave; then it is a 3-mile paddle
across Debsconeag Deadwater to Passamagamet Falls (17
mi), a Class III drop, rocky with two chutes.

In 1¾ miles you reach Ambejejus Falls, though high water
in the lake below may flood them out. The river soon opens
into Ambejejus Lake (19 mi).

In Spencer Cove 3¼ miles to the east, the road to Baxter
State Park comes close to the lake (22¼ mi).

Spencer Cove—ME-11 (Quakish Lake)   11 miles

Lakes
  Anytime
  Forested, Scattered Cottages
      USGS: Norcross 15, Millinocket 15

From Spencer Cove it is 4 miles across Ambejejus Lake
and the end of Pemadumcook Lake to Nicks Gut, where the
canoeist passes into North Twin Lake, and an additional 5
miles down that to Elbow Lake. One can make a detour
here if desired into South Twin Lake, which is about the
same size. It is 1 mile across Elbow Lake to the dam, which
must be carried. There is then 1 mile of river, passing under
ME-11 halfway down, to Quakish Lake.

ME-11—Shad Pond, via West Branch   6½ miles

Flatwater, Class III, IV
  Water diverted by dam: *seldom possible*
  Forested, Settled
    USGS: Millinocket
    Portage: 2 mi   **Quakish Dam**

From the boat launching ramp at ME-11 to Quakish Dam is 2 miles. The dam diverts most of the water to power plants, but during spring run-off this stretch is sometimes possible. This historic stretch contains Blue Rock Pitch and Grand Falls, 3 miles below the dam, and runs into Shad Pond.

Quakish Dam—Shad Pond   3½ miles
(alternate route via Millinocket Stream)

For through travelers, when there is no water in the West Branch it may be possible to paddle the mile to the outlet of Ferguson Pond, and portage through the Great Northern Paper Company mill to Millinocket Stream, which is followed for 2¼ miles to Shad Pond.

Shad Pond—East Branch Penobscot   5½ miles

Flatwater, Quickwater
  Anytime
  Settled, Unattractive
    USGS: Millinocket
    Portages: 1¾ mi   **60 foot dam**
                3½ mi   **dam at East**
                           Millinocket
                5 mi   **dam at Bethel Church**

One can put in or take out at Rice Farm on the left, at the entrance to Dolby Flowage, at the end of which is a 60-foot high dam. In another 1½ miles the somewhat lower dam at East Millinocket is reached. It is then only 1½ miles more to the last dam at Bethel Church, below which ½ mile the West Branch meets the East Branch to form the main Penobscot River.

PENOBSCOT RIVER, South Branch

The South Branch flows from the border mountains northwest of Jackman to Seboomook Lake. Its upper part is too steep and too small for canoeing even in high water. The lower part, below Canada Falls Dam, has a series of ledges so that a portage along the road to Pittston Farm is recommended. Although the middle section provides a fast run in high water, it is not really worth the effort of getting to the put-in point, especially since there are better and more accessible rivers in the same general area. The upper part of the watershed contains only a few ponds, so the water level drops rapidly after spring run-off.

Bridge—Canada Falls Dam   17½ miles

Lake, Class I, II
  High water only: *May*
  Wild
        USGS: Sandy Bay 15 (for access), Penobscot
              Lake 15, Seboomook Lake 15
  Portage: 17½ mi   **ledges**   3 mi (by car)
  Campsite: 17½ mi   L **Canada Falls Dam**   MFS
                        $ car

A private road from US-201 about 12 miles northwest of Jackman follows the south bank of the South Branch for 8 miles until it crosses the river 3 miles downstream from Little Canada Falls.

There are shallow rapids for about 2 miles to Kellher Falls, a sharp ledge drop that cannot be run and is difficult to line. This section can be carried on the left.

The next 9½ miles to Canada Falls Lake (11½ mi) are mostly good current with shallow rapids. It is 6 miles across the lake to Canada Falls Dam (17½ mi) at the end of the northeast arm.

The remaining 3½ miles to Seboomook Lake contain several severe ledge drops that cannot be run or lined through. It is recommended that this section be portaged using the road from the campsite at the dam at Pittston Farm on Seboomook Lake.

PENOBSCOT RIVER, North Branch

The North Branch flows from Big Bog South to Seboomook Lake, where it joins the South Branch to form the West Branch. Since there are few lakes and swamps to provide headwater storage, this section can only be run during early spring run-off. The lower portion contains broad sandbars, and usually after May low water makes canoeing impossible.

Access to Big Bog is by a private logging road from Pittston Farm on Seboomook Lake.

Big Bog Dam—Pittston Farm   20¾ miles

Class I, II
  High water only: *May*
  Wild
      USGS: Norris Brook 15, Penobscot Lake 15,
            Seboomook Lake 15

Most of this river has good current with shallow rapids. There is a bridge 4½ miles below the put-in point at Big Bog Dam, and in 4¼ miles you reach the mouth of Dole Brook (8¾ mi). There are easy rapids and smoothwater for the 7¼ miles to Leadbetter Falls (16 mi), a short rapid under a bridge, which can be run in medium water, but which is difficult in high water. In 4 miles the river opens into a bay at the end of Seboomook Lake (20 mi), with Pittston Farm beyond on the right (20¾ mi).

It is a 12¾-mile paddle down Seboomook Lake from the mouth of the North Branch to Seboomook Dam (32¾ mi).

NESOWADNEHUNK STREAM

Nesowadnehunk Stream, locally spelled Sourdnahunk and pronounced 'sourdihunk,' originates in Little Nesowadnehunk Lake on the Penobscot side of the divide south of Telos Lake and in a steep mile of travel runs into Nesowadnehunk Lake. Below this lake, enlarged by the lumbermen to run logs down the river below, the stream flows south for some 17 miles to the West Branch of the

Penobscot about ½ mile below the Sourdnahunk Falls, in the Abol Deadwater. Because the water level is controlled at the dam it can be run almost anytime down to the Daicey Pond brook, about 13 miles, but the authorities at Baxter State Park discourage running more than the first 5 miles down to Campground 5 at Sourdnahunk Field. The lower end of the stream is a tumultuous descent over falls and cascades to the Penobscot, unrunnable but well worth a visit on foot.

Nesowadnehunk Lake—Campground 5   5 miles

Quickwater, Class I, II
  Medium water
  Wild
      USGS: Telos Lake 15

Nesowadnehunk Lake is a large body of water some 5 miles long and 1½ miles wide. The Sourdnahunk Tote Road from Baxter Park reaches the lake at the outlet dam. There is also a sporting camp 1½ miles up the lake. One can put in below the dam and enjoy a fine 5-mile run down easy water, mostly Class I and II rapids with numerous pools in between, to Sourdnahunk Fields where the road from Ripogenus Dam crosses. This is a delightful and easy run offering fine views of Mt. Veto and Doubletop on the right and Katahdin with its satellites on the left.

Campground 5—Daicey Pond Brook   8 miles

Class I, II, III
  Medium water
  Wild
      USGS: Harrington Lake 15
      Portage: 2 mi   L   **Ledge Falls**   100 yds
                          From various points—
                          lower river impassable

This is a considerably more difficult section and should be undertaken by experts only, as the river drops sharply with pools in between the drops. Ledge Falls is a natural rock falls. Then it is Class I-II for 1¾ miles to Slide Dam, which has been washed out for many years, leaving 250 yards of Class III; scout from the left. The river is then easier for the 2 miles to the road crossing for the Kidney Pond Camps. This is an easy spot to take out. About 2 miles below here is the Appalachian Trail crossing, about ¼ mile above the Daicey Pond brook. One can take out here and carry a short distance to the Daicey Pond Camp road. River travel is possible for another 1 mile, but there is no way to take out except by poling back upstream. The old toll dam there marks the beginning of the wild plunge down to the Penobscot.

NAHMAKANTA STREAM via DEBSCONEAG LAKES

Nahmakanta Stream is a tributary of the Penobscot River, West Branch, at Pemadumcook Lake. It flows from Nahmakanta Lake, a medium-sized lake situated among the low mountains southwest of Baxter State Park. The beginning of this stream can be reached from Debsconeag Deadwater on the West Branch via the Debsconeag Lakes.

A circuit trip from Spencer Cove on Ambejejus Lake, up the West Branch, through the Debsconeag Lakes, and down Nahmakanta Stream to Pemadumcook Lake is a three- or four-day trip through relatively isolated country. The Debsconeag Lakes are clear and in rugged settings, but there are several long portages on this approach to Nahmakanta Lake. Nahmakanta Stream provides a short but enjoyable run in May.

Penobscot River, West Branch—
Nahmakanta Lake   **10¼ miles**

Lakes
  Wild
      USGS: Katahdin 15, Harrington Lake 15,
            Jo-Mary Mountain 15
  Portages: 2½ mi   L   **into Second Debsconeag**
                                  Lake   ¾ mi
               4¾ mi   L   **towards Third**
                                  Debsconeag Lake   400
                                  yds
                5 mi   **into third Debsconeag**
                                  Lake   30 yds
               7½ mi   R   **into Fourth Debsconeag**
                                  Lake   ½ mi
                9 mi   R   **into Nahmakanta Lake**
                                  1¼ mi
  Campsite: ½ mi   R   **First Debsconeag Lake**
                                  (beach at east
                                  end)   permit

Keep to the west of the island that encloses the north end
of Debsconeag Deadwater and follow the short passage
westward into First Debsconeag Lake. The latter is 2 miles
long, and at the west end (2½ mi) a ¾-mile portage leads to
Second Debsconeag Lake. (The portage trail forks near the
middle; go right.)

On the south shore of Second Debsconeag Lake near the
west end, a small brook enters the lake. The portage (4¾ mi)
begins just east of this brook and ends at a small pool above
an abandoned driving dam. A 100-yard paddle leads to the
third portage, a 30-yard scramble into Third Debsconeag
Lake.

Third Debsconeag Lake (5 mi) is the largest of these
lakes. It is horseshoe-shaped, and the portage to Fourth
Debsconeag Lake leaves a short distance before the end of a
narrow, west arm.

The portages between the West Branch and Fourth Debsconeag Lake follow a snowmobile trail, but the last, from
Fourth Debsconeag Lake to Nahmakanta Lake, follows a

dirt road to a bridge at the beginning of Nahmakanta
Stream. Begin this portage at a landing on the west shore a
short distance from the southwest end of the lake.

NAHMAKANTA STREAM

Nahmakanta Lake—
Pemadumcook Lake   **5¼ miles**

Quickwater, Class I, II
  High water: *May*
  Wild
      USGS: Harrington Lake 15, Jo-Mary Mountain
            15, Norcross 15

Campsites:	0 mi	R	**Shelter on Appalachian Trail**
	5 mi	R	
	7¾ mi	L	**2 sites**
	9½ mi	R	
	12 mi	R	**Pemadumcook Lake** car

Nahmakanta Stream begins at the southeast end of Nahmakanta Lake. At the right-hand bend below the bridge
there is a narrow 200-yard Class III rapid that can be
scouted or portaged most easily on the right bank. Following a ¼-mile deadwater, there is a succession of short easy
Class I and II rapids, which are all separated by pools.
These extend for about a mile.

Then you reach a second ¼-mile section of flatwater (1½
mi), followed by more short rapids and a nice ½-mile Class
II rapid that extends through about half-a-dozen bends in
the river before it ends at a pool (2¾ mi). Then there is
another mile of short, easy Class I and II rapids with pools
or quickwater between them. The last 1½ miles are mostly
quickwater with a few easy rapids.

From the mouth of Nahmakanta stream (5¼ mi), it is 10¼
miles down Pemadumcook Lake and across Ambejejus
Lake to Spencer Cove (15½ mi) on the road from Millinocket to Baxter State Park.

MILLINOCKET STREAM

USGS: Katahdin 15, Stacyville 15, Norcross
15, Millinocket 15

Millinocket Stream is the outlet of Millinocket Lake and
flows south from that lake to the West Branch of the
Penobscot at Shad Pond, south of Millinocket.

The dam at the outlet can be reached from the south via a
road that leaves the Millinocket-Spencer Cove road 1½ miles
north of Millinocket.

The Class II rapids at the start give way to easier rapids
and quickwater to the bridge in Millinocket.

Below the factories (access to river from a dirt road on
the east bank), the rapids are heavy, over crunchy, sharp
ledges to Shad Pond, where it joins the East Branch. There
is no access at Shad Pond, but a mile downstream a road
comes close to the left bank.

SANDY STREAM

Millinocket Lake has one major tributary: Sandy Stream.
It drains the southeastern flank of Mount Katahdin. The
upper sections of Sandy Stream are too steep to canoe, but
the lower part, reachable via Togue stream, is runnable.
These streams are very remote, and they are only occasionally run. Access to Togue Stream is possible only after the
ice has gone out of Lower Togue Pond, and that usually
occurs in early May.

The first mile of Togue Stream is the hardest. Where
there are drops in elevation—you cannot really call them
rapids—there is a combination of large rocks, overhanging
trees, and jackstrawed logs that requires that you line the
canoe. Portaging is not a very easy alternative, so you must
resign yourself to working the canoe slowly downstream,
snaking around some obstructions here and sawing some
logs there. Improvements made one year are likely to be
undone in high water the next. Patience, determination, and
about 2 hours will bring you to a large beaver pond. From
that point, the river is virtually unobstructed, and for the

next 2 miles you will find yourself in a very wild section of Baxter State Park.

The flow in Sandy Stream is subject to rapid fluctuations because of the steepness of the upper watershed. There are only a few ponds and swamps in its headwaters, so the water level is very responsive to a heavy rainfall or a rapid melting of the snow.

Lower Togue Pond—Millinocket Lake   10½ miles

Lakes, Quickwater, Class I, II
  High water: *dependent upon heavy rain or rapid snow melting*
  Medium water: *May*
  Wild
        USGS: Katahdin 15, Norcross 15, Millinocket 15
  Campsite: 10½ mi   L   **mouth of Sandy Stream** permit

Lower Togue Pond lies just outside of the southern boundary of Baxter State Park, and the road from Millinocket to the park goes along the western shore. The entrance of Togue Stream (1¼ mi) is on the northeast shore of the pond, but the exact location is difficult to see unless you are close to it.

In the first 100 yards of Togue Stream is a short, linable drop, in the middle of which is an old, rotting bridge that can just be sneaked under in medium water. For most of the next mile, short navigable sections alternate with others where lining and some clearing is necessary. After a couple of hours of slow progress, you reach a large beaver pond (2¼ mi) that is several hundred yards long. It is located along the northernmost portion of the stream.

For the next 2¾ miles, there is a mixture of flatwater, quickwater, and Class I rapids. Then there is a 50-yard, Class II rapid immediately above the confluence with Sandy Stream (5 mi).

Sandy Stream is much larger than Togue Stream. The first half of it consists mostly of quickwater over small stones with gravel bars and wide, sweeping turns. An occa-

sional overhanging tree constitutes the primary hazard of
Sandy Stream. There is also a large log jam where the river
splits to go around an island.

In 3 miles you reach a 50-yard, Class II rapid that begins
at a washed-out driving dam (8 mi). Then after 1 mile of
flatwater, you come to Red Pine Rapids (9 mi), a ¼-mile
pitch that is Class II in medium water and Class III in high
water. It extends through an "S"-turn, and it may be easily
scouted from or portaged along the left bank. The final 1¼
miles to Millinocket Lake (10½ mi) are smooth.

There are two places to take out, both 4½ miles from the
mouth of Sandy Stream. One is at Millinocket Dam (15 mi)
to the southeast, and the other is to the southwest at the
dike between Millinocket Lake and Spencer Cove on Ambejejus Lake (15 mi).

PENOBSCOT RIVER, East Branch

The East Branch drains the region north and northeast of
Mount Katahdin. It has also been the recipient of part of
the Allagash drainage since the construction of Telos Dam
in 1841. In that year, three other dams were constructed
along the Allagash, making it possible to drive logs from the
upper Allagash region down the East Branch rather than
north to the Saint John River. Today, Telos and Grand
Lake Matagamon Dams are used to store water for use in
power generation farther downstream.

Generally there is sufficient water in Webster Stream
through early June. The East Branch is canoeable for much
of the season. The lakes are usually drawn down from mid-
September to mid-October, providing a good flow at that
time.

You can travel by canoe from the West Branch to the
East Branch using the two access routes described in Chapter 5, "Allagash Wilderness Waterway."

Grand Lake Dam—Medway   47½ miles

Flatwater, Class I, II, III
  High water: *difficult*
  Medium water: *recommended*
  Low water: *passable but thin*
  Dam-controlled: *good flow spring and early fall*
  Wild
      USGS: Traveler Mountain 15, Shin Pond 15,
             Stacyville 15, Millinocket 15
Many portages depending on water level
Campsites: ¾ mi   L   **Grand Lake Road**
                            (bridge)   private $ car
               9¾ mi   L   **Grand Pitch**   permit
              23½ mi   L   **Lunksoos Camp**   MFS
                            car
              27¼ mi   L   **Whetstone Falls**
                            (between rapids)   MFS
                            car

From just below Grand Lake Road bridge, where there are a few rapids, there is smoothwater for 4½ miles to Stair Falls (5¼ mi), a series of shallow ledges. They are best run on the left if water level permits; if it does not, there is also a portage on the left. Then for 1¼ miles there is quickwater to Haskell Deadwater, below which is Haskell Rock Pitch (7 mi), the first of four falls on the East Branch. (The USGS Traveler Mountain Sheet shows Haskell Rock Pitch in the wrong location.) There is a ½-mile portage on the right. There are three sets of rapids in the next mile to Pond Pitch (7¾ mi), the second falls. There is a portage on the left.

Below Pond Pitch, in ¾ mile, you reach Grand Pitch (9¾ mi), the third and most spectacular of the Grand Falls of the East Branch. The portage is on the left. About ½ mile beyond is Hulling Machine Pitch, the fourth falls. Stop above the rapids just above the falls and portage on the right. Less than a mile below these falls is Bowline Falls, a short Class II rapid. If you run it, a starting on the far right is recommended. Mostly smoothwater continues for the remaining 9 miles to the mouth of Sebeois River (21 mi).

Flatwater continues for the next 6 miles to Whetstone Falls (27 mi). These consist of two sets of rapids separated by fastwater. The upper section, Class III, can be run by experienced canoeists in medium water. The lower part is easier in medium water, but it should be scouted first. It may be difficult in high water. At Lunksoos Camp (23½ mi), as well as above the bridge at Lower Whetstone Falls, the MFS campsites offer good access to the river.

The next rapids are in 9 miles at Crowfoot Falls, Class II or III depending on the water level. After another 2¼ miles, below a railroad bridge, is Grindstone Falls. This is a Class III–IV rapid, which should be run empty. The first drop is best run on the left, the remainder, about ½ mile of heavy rapids even at medium water, is runnable between the shore and the main current.

The last 9 miles to the confluence with the West Branch (47½ mi) in Medway are mostly smooth, except for Meadowbrook Rips (40½ mi) and Ledge Falls (45 mi). The latter are difficult in high water. You pass under the ME-157 bridge (47 mi) ½ mile before reaching the West Branch.

WEBSTER STREAM

Webster Stream flows from Telos Lake through a man-made canal to Webster Lake and then on to Grand Lake Matagamon. Since most of the stream and much of Grand Lake lies within the boundaries of Baxter State Park, campsites must be arranged and paid for in advance with the park office in Millinocket.

Telos Landing—Grand Lake Dam   24 miles

Lakes, Class I, II, III
   High water (over 600 cfs): *very difficult and dangerous*
   Medium water (300–500 cfs): *recommended*
   Low water (100–150 cfs): *skinny but runnable*
   Dam-controlled: *good flow spring and early fall*
   Wild
        USGS: Telos Lake 15, Traveler Mountain 15

Portages:	2 mi	R	**Telos Dam** 25 yds
	14½ mi	R	**Grand Pitch** ½ mi
Campsites:	0 mi		**Telos Landing** AWW $ car
	4½ mi	R	**Webster Stream lean-to**
	8 mi	R	**Little East Branch Grand Lake** (5 sites)
	24¾ mi	L	**Grand Lake Road** (below dam) private $ car

From the end of the Allagash Wilderness Waterway access road at Telos Landing, it is 2 miles to Telos Dam. Below the dam, a 1-mile canal leads to Webster Lake. The flow is controlled at the dam, and it is often possible to arrange for water to be let through for canoeing. It is a fast run in medium water. From the end of the canal it is 3 miles across the lake to the outlet (6 mi).

The first 6½ miles from Webster Lake to Indian Carry (12½ mi) are mostly shallow rapids and fast current. Indian Carry in medium water is a Class III rapid that can be run by experts. However, it requires very difficult maneuvering, and it is recommended that this drop be carried on the right bank.

The next 2 miles to Grand Pitch (14½ mi) contain several very difficult Class III ledge drops, which can be run by experts in medium water. At Grand Pitch, obscure portage trails on each side of the stream require considerable effort to carry this falls. A ½-mile alternative on the right bank follows a trail that leads to a logging road. It bypasses the main falls as well as two more severe ledge drops ½ mile below these falls.

You reach Grand Lake Matagamon (15¾ mi) ½ mile below the last drop, and 8¼ miles down the lake is the dam (24 mi), which you portage on the right.

SEBOEIS RIVER

Seboeis River flows from Grand Lake Seboeis south to the East Branch of the Penobscot, joining the latter 21 miles below the Grand Lake Matagamon Dam. It offers a good alternative to the upper section of the East Branch, and it is particularly suitable for inexperienced canoeists since there are no difficult rapids and only one short carry around a pretty, though impassable, falls. It has a continuous, moderate current to its junction with the East Branch, and it flows through an extremely attractive, unspoiled valley that is rugged and wooded.

The usual starting point is the MFS campground on the Grand Lake Matagamon Road from Patten. Above there, the river has very steep and difficult rapids with poor access, and it is not recommended for canoeing. The first place to take out on the East Branch is at the MFS campsite at Lunksoos Deadwater, 2½ miles below the mouth of Seboeis River.

The flow drops fast after the spring run-off, and the trip should not be attempted after the second week in June. Good campsites can be found along most of the river, although with good water the river can be run easily in one day.

Grand Lake Road—East Branch   17¼ miles

Class I, II
  High water: *May*
  Wild
       USGS: Shin Pond 15, Stacyville 15
  Portage: 1¼ mi   L   **Grand Pitch**   100 yds
  Campsite: 0 mi   L   **Grand Lake Road**   MFS
                          car

There are 1¼ miles of Class II rapids to Grand Pitch, an unrunnable drop with a 100-yard portage on the left. The approach to the falls is marked by a very large, high ledge on the left bank of the river. The remaining 16 miles to the East Branch (17¼ mi) contain fairly continuous Class I rapids.

MATTAWAMKEAG RIVER

The Mattawamkeag River is a large tributary of the Penobscot that flows through a big area southwest of Houlton. The West Branch drains two large lakes in addition to extensive swamps, so in the late spring or early summer its water level is more dependable than that of the East Branch. Below Island Falls, the river is apt to be canoeable after other rivers in northern Maine have become too low.

The Mattawamkeag flows through several small towns, a factor that calls into question the drinkability of the water. Some people can drink it with no ill effects, but it is safe to say that the quality of the water diminishes somewhat as each town is passed and as the level of the river drops after spring run-off.

The longest trip on the Mattawamkeag described in this book—some 90 miles—begins in Patten on Fish Stream. Unfortunately, there are few established campsites.

Haynesville—Kingman   34¼ miles

Flatwater, Quickwater, Class I, II
   Passable at most water levels
   Forested, Rural, Towns
       USGS: Amity 15, Danforth 15, Wytopitlock 15
   Campsite: 28¼ mi L **Meadow Brook** permit,
                                permission

There are two large deadwaters, one below Haynesville and the other beginning at Wytopitlock, and they total 19 miles in length. The balance is a mixture of smooth and quickwater with some rapids.

In two places local highways more or less parallel the river for a total of 15½ miles. Although not a wild river in these sections, it is attractive. Below the ME-171 bridge in Wytopitlock, the river flows slowly for 9¾ miles through a large hardwood swamp with almost no evidence of man.

Rock cribs in the river at Wytopitlock are all that remain from the days of the log drives, which ended about 1950.

Below the US-2A bridge in Haynesville there are 7½ miles of deadwater. It ends a mile below the Ferry Bridge, where the current picks up to Ledge Falls (9½ mi). The latter is wide and about 100 yards long; shallow, but passable, in medium water. It is, as its name implies, all ledge. A short distance beyond is a short, easy rapid.

There is a good current most of the way from Ledge Falls to Wytopitlock. Occasionally there are sections that are Class I. Below the falls 4¾ miles Baskahegan Stream enters left (14¼ mi), and 4¼ miles farther is the Bancroft railroad bridge (18½ mi).

The easy traveling ends 1 mile above Wytopitlock, and after 2 miles of deadwater the river flows under the ME-171 bridge (23¼ mi). The Wytopitlock Deadwater continues for another 9¾ miles and ends at a series of Class I and II rapids that last for 1¼ miles and end at the ME-170 bridge in Kingman (34¼ mi).

Kingman—Mattawamkeag   12½ miles

Flatwater, Quickwater, Class I, II, III
  Passable at most water levels
  Wild, Forested
      USGS: Wytopitlock 15, *Wynn 15,*
           Mattawamkeag 15

Portages:	7¼ mi	L	**Heater** 300 yds
	8¼ mi	L	**Upper Gordon Falls** 50 yds
Campsites:	4 mi	R	**First Pitch** (above) permit, permission
	4¾ mi	L	**Third Pitch** $ car

The best whitewater on the river is to be found in this section. There are also two very dangerous drops to watch for: the Heater and Upper Gordon Falls, which probably rate Class V.

Mattawamkeag Wilderness Park (Box 104, Mattawamkeag, ME 04459) abuts the south bank of the river for a mile beside and downstream of the "third pitch" described below. It is located on the town's Educational and Ministerial Lot, and includes hiking trails and a large automobile campground. Below the Heater and beside both Gordon Falls, the underbrush has been removed in deference to picnickers and tourists traveling on the park's access road.

Below the ME-170 bridge, there are 1¾ miles of quickwater, followed by 2¼ miles of slackwater. Then there are three Class I–III pitches before the rapids that lead into the Heater.

The first pitch (4 mi) is in a small gorge where there are a few heavy waves. Shortly beyond is the second pitch, at a wide right bend. After ¾ mile of slackwater is the third pitch (5¾ mi)—short but with heavy waves.

The third pitch is easily identified because the Mattawamkeag Wilderness Park camping area is on the left bank, but it might not be recognized until after the rapids have been run. Below there is quickwater, which soon becomes easy rapids—Class I. As the river bends to the left, it becomes more difficult—Class II. **Caution!** Stay to the outside of the turn as the river sweeps to the right and stop to scout the Heater. It begins as a passable gorge, very inviting and scenic, with some heavy waves that can be run in medium water in a large canoe. If you choose to run the first part of the Heater, pull out left in the calmer water of the gorge below, for shortly beyond is the main drop, a succession of ledges and holes that would tempt only an expert in a closed boat. A yellow-blazed trail follows the river on the left bank, and it can be used as a portage, although it is not maintained as such.

Below the Heater ¾ mile is Upper Gordon Falls (8¼ mi). Portage on the left bank. Upper Gordon Falls is a Class V run that demands respect of the very best covered boaters. It is a classic horseshoe-shaped drop about 11 feet, with a good rescue pool below. Scout on the left.

Around the corner to the left is Lower Gordon Falls, a classic chute, Class II, with a clear channel and heavy waves, some of which, at least in medium water, will enter an unloaded, open canoe.

Easy rapids continue off and on for 3 miles, but gradually they taper to quickwater about 1 mile before reaching the US-2 bridge in Mattawamkeag (12½ mi). Only a short distance beyond, the Mattawamkeag River empties into the Penobscot (13 mi).

MATTAWAMKEAG RIVER, West Branch

Below Mattawamkeag Lake, the West Branch, already a large river, is mostly rapids and quickwater for 12½ miles. It is a pleasant and easy paddle in medium or high water, and it is similar to the lower Allagash. Like the latter, there are places that are scratchy in low water, requiring you to walk your canoe down. It is wild, although there are about a dozen cabins along the river.

The West Branch above Island Falls is passable in high water, except in a few places, from ME-11 in the township of Moro, but no information is given here.

Island Falls—Haynesville   24½ mi

Lakes, Flatwater, Quickwater, Class I–II
  High and medium water: *mid-May to July*
  Wild
        USGS: Island Falls 15, *Sherman 15,*
                 Mattawamkeag Lake 15, Amity 15
    Portage: 0 mi   R
    Campsite: 11¼ mi   L   **Mattawamkeag Lake**
                            (small)   MFS

Anyone approaching the US-2 bridge in Island Falls should land above or under it, right bank, and lift around the ledges at the old broken dam. Below, right of the island, there is a short pitch followed by 6½ miles of flatwater to Upper Mattawamkeag Lake. Upon entering the latter, turn right and southeast through a thoroughfare for 1½ miles.

It is 3½ miles southeast across Mattawamkeag Lake to the outlet (11½ mi), after which there are ½ mile of Class II and 1½ miles of Class I rapids. The remaining 10½ miles are mostly quickwater, with some easy rapids in the last ½ mile before the confluence with the East Branch (24 mi).

Beyond, in ½ mile is the US-2A bridge in Haynesville (24½ mi).

FISH STREAM

Fish Stream flows eastward to the West Branch of the Mattawamkeag River at Island Falls. It is an easy paddle through wild country where there is also good fishing.

Patten—Island Falls   16½ **miles**

Flatwater, Quickwater
    High water: *May*
    Medium water: *June*
    Wild
        USGS: Sherman 15, Island Falls 15

A side road reaches Fish Stream from ME-159 about 1 mile east of Patten and downstream from a lumber mill. The upper part is all flat, with a few fallen trees blocking the way. After 6¾ miles there is a ledge, passable in high water, ¼ mile before the stream swings around the south end of an esker, a prominent ridge of glacial material that extends north for several miles. The rest of the way to the ME-159 bridge (13½ mi) is mostly flat, but there are a few riffles that are scratchy in low water. In the remaining 2¼ miles to the West Branch (15¾ mi), there is quick and flatwater.

Below the confluence ¾ mile, and past the new ME-159 bridge, is the older US-2 bridge (16½ mi). Take out on the right at or above it, for beyond it at the old dam site there are some ledges that are not passable.

MATTAWAMKEAG RIVER, East Branch

USGS: Smyrna Mills 15, Mattawamkeag Lake
        15, Amity 15

The East Branch is seldom run in comparison to the West Branch. The rapids in the upper part have to be run in high water, and there is no convenient access at the end of the rapids to run the quickwater of the lower end.

Smyrna Mills—Red Bridge   7 miles

This section is small and runnable only at high water. Both the beginning and end can be reached from US-2. The river is mixed rapid and smooth and offers an interesting run early in the season.

Red Bridge—Haynesville   20 miles

Below Red Bridge there are intermittent Class II rapids to the outlet from Pleasant Lake. Below here, around the foot of Outlet Mountain the going becomes very rough. The paddling becomes easier after that. The old dam is now gone. The remaining distance is open going with a slow current. Local people commonly motor up to Nickerson Brook when fishing.

BASKAHEGAN STREAM

Baskahegan Stream, a tributary of the Mattawamkeag River, drains a flat region in eastern Maine. It consists almost entirely of flatwater and large lakes. The shorelines are predominantly lined with hardwood forests, and, except near Danforth, there are few cabins or houses. The water is very dark.

Route 6—Mattawamkeag River   39½ miles

Lakes, **Flatwater,** Class I, II
  High or medium water: *first 5¾ mi*
  Passable at most water levels below first 5¾ mi
  Wild, Town
       USGS: Scraggly Lake 15, Danforth 15
  Portages: 30½ mi   R   **dam at Danforth**   50 yds
              39 mi   R   **ledges in South**
                           Bancroft   150 yds
  Campsite: 17¾ mi   R   **Baskahegan Lake Dam**
                           (poor)   permit

Begin on ME-6 at Lindsey Brook. There are beaver dams in the 1¼ miles before the latter enters Tolman Deadwater on Baskahegan Stream. At the end of this deadwater there is 1 mile of easy Class I and II rapids that end with a short, narrow Class II drop. There is a bridge at the beginning of Middle Deadwater (3¼ mi).

Middle Deadwater is 1¾ miles long, and at its end (5 mi) there is ¾ mile of rapids that begin as Class I and II. **Caution!** About ½ mile after leaving Middle Deadwater, the river widens somewhat where there is quickwater. Then there is a blind right turn before a narrow sluice where there is a series of sharp drops between sloping ledges. A short distance beyond, a dirt road on the right provides a better starting point in low water.

Below the dirt road (5¾ mi), the river meanders for 7¾ miles to Baskahegan Lake (13½ mi). It is passable at low water, but some wading may be necessary.

The washed-out dam on Baskahegan Lake (17¾ mi) is runnable. The next 9¼ miles to Crooked Brook Flowage are flatwater, with the current being stronger in the last 4 miles. There is a 3½-mile paddle on Crooked Brook Flowage northwards to the dam in Danforth.

Below Danforth (30½ mi), Baskahegan Stream has flatwater for 8½ miles. Past a bridge near South Danforth, land on the right and portage along the edge of a field past a series of ledges. Easy rapids continue to the Mattawamkeag River (39½ mi). There is a highway bridge over the latter just above the mouth of Baskahegan Stream.

WYTOPITLOCK STREAM

Wytopitlock Stream rises in Wytopitlock Lake in Glenwood and flows south to the Mattawamkeag River at Wytopitlock. It is a relatively small stream but canoeable in high water from the lake down. It is mixed rapid and smooth, but most of the rapids are runnable. Wytopitlock Lake can be reached from US-2A at Glenwood.

Wytopitlock Lake—US-2A   9¼ miles

Flatwater, Quickwater Class I, II
  Medium water: *late spring*
  Wild
      USGS: Mattawamkeag Lake 15, Wytopitlock
          15

The stream leaves Wytopitlock Lake just to the east of the launching ramp. There are rapids past the bridge, a short deadwater rapids, another deadwater above the third bridge, and then ½ mile of rapids to Thompson Deadwater, where the river is wide and deep through an open marsh, with much wildlife visible.

The deadwater ends at an old dam site (6¼ mi) and rapids continue the next 3 miles to the US-2A bridge.

US-2A—Mattawamkeag River   8½ miles

The remaining distance to the junction with the Matta-wamkeag River is very similar.

MOLUNKUS STREAM

USGS: Sherman 15, Mattawamkeag 15,
        Wytopitlock 15

Molunkus Stream rises in Thousand Acre Bog in Crystal just west of Patten and flows south through Sherman Mills and Macwahoc to the Mattawamkeag River just below Kingman. It is canoeable from Sherman Mills, or with good water from Sherman Station. The upper part is best run with high to medium water, but much of the stream can be run at any time. It is entirely through woods and there are no public campgrounds.

Sherman Station—Sherman Mills   3 miles

One can put in at the crossing of the West Branch just below Sherman Station and run 1 mile down to the main stream and then 2 miles down that stream to Sherman Mills. This is largely through swamp with a good current but no rapids.

Sherman Mills—Macwahoc   20 miles

Just below the put-in spot there is a short rapid down to a deadwater and then another rapid below the deadwater, 1 mile in all. The next 6 miles to the road crossing 1 mile south of Monarda are mostly smoothwater. This spot may be a better place to put in if the water is low up above. Below here there are 2 miles of mixed rapid and smooth-water and then mostly smoothwater with a fast current for the next 10 miles to Macwahoc. For much of this latter part of the run the river is paralleled by US-2 a short distance away. At Macwahoc US-2 crosses the river.

Macwahoc—Mattawamkeag River   **10 miles**

Flatwater, Quickwater
  Medium water
  Wild
        USGS: Wytopitlock 15

Just 100 yards below the US-2 bridge Macwahoc Stream
enters on the left. There is a short rapid for ½ mile below the
start, and then the river meanders through a swamp for the
rest of the way to the Mattawamkeag River, which it enters
2 miles below Kingman, where the only convenient take-out
spot is located.

Alternatively, one can paddle downstream through the
rapids on the Mattawamkeag to Mattawamkeag Wilderness
Park.

MACWAHOC STREAM

USGS: Sherman 15, Mattawamkeag Lake 15,
Wytopitlock 15, Mattawamkeag 15

Macwahoc Stream starts in Macwahoc Lake in Sherman
and flows first southeast, then south and slightly west to
join the Molunkus Stream at Macwahoc. It can be canoed
from its headwaters at Macwahoc Lake all the way to the
mouth, but high to medium stage water would be best for
the upper portions. Macwahoc Lake can be reached easily
from US-2 in Sherman, and if the water is low, Lower Macwahoc Lake, which would provide a better starting place,
can also be reached from this road in Silver Ridge.

Macwahoc Lake—Lower Macwahoc Lake   6 miles

There are several possibilities for the start of this trip. If
the water is high one can put in from a road 2 miles above
Woodbridge Corner on the inlet stream to Macwahoc Lake
and run down the stream ½ mile to the lake, 1½ miles south
down the lake to its outlet, and then ½ mile down the outlet,
Macwahoc Stream, to the bridge where a road that comes in

from Woodbridge Corner crosses. In somewhat lower water this would be a better put-in spot. The next 4 miles to Lower Macwahoc Lake are largely rapids with small ponds or backwaters between them. The inlet to Macwahoc Lake enters at the center of the north shore, and from here it is ½ mile east to the landing on the east shore.

Lower Macwahoc Lake—Macwahoc   20 miles

One can put in at the landing on the east shore of Lower Macwahoc Lake reached by a dirt road from the southeast. After about 1 mile down the lake one enters Macwahoc Stream, which descends with a good current for the next 3 miles, when steep rapids begin for 1 mile to a swampy area. After about ½ mile of easy going, rapids start again and continue for 1 mile to a long swampy area, Reed Deadwater, which continues for nearly 8 miles to the mouth of Reed Stream, where fastwater recommences and continues for the next 5½ miles to the junction with Molunkus Stream at Macwahoc.

PISCATAQUIS RIVER

The Piscataquis River is one of the major tributaries of the Penobscot. Both of its two branches, the East Branch and the West Branch, rise south of Moosehead Lake and join at Blanchard to form the main stream, which then flows eastward to the Penobscot River at Howland. The West Branch has some miles of good canoeing below the crossing of the Shirley Mills-Lake Moxie road, but this is followed by a deep and impassable gorge north of Breakneck Ridge with no way to leave the river. The East Branch has some easy canoeing above Shirley Mills, but with no good way to reach it. Below it is too steep and rapid for some distance, and then it is good but inaccessible canoeing. In effect, then, the river is canoeable only below the junction of the two branches, or from Blanchard on down. From here it is mixed rapid and smooth, with some sections practically all smoothwater. Above Dover-Foxcroft it is usually too low for summer travel, although useable until late in the spring.

Blanchard—Upper Abbot   8 miles

Class II, III
  High water: *spring run-off only*
  Forested
        USGS: Greenville 15, Kingsbury 15, Guilford
                15
  Portage: 3 mi   R   **Barrows Falls**   200 yds

A hundred feet above the bridge in Blanchard is a technical drop over a 2-foot ledge (Class II, III in high water). Another technical Class II rapid starts just under the bridge and extends for 100 yards; it can be heavy if the river is very high. As the paddler leaves the village, he or she will encounter Class I-II rips and quickwater that gradually diminishes until one sights the bridge just above Barrows Falls. This is a small gorge entered via a tight, fast "S"-turn. It is Class III at most water levels, but can be Class IV in high water; scout or carry on the right.

About 2 miles below Barrows Falls there is 1 mile of strong but relatively unobstructed rapids (Class II-III). This entire section of the river is similar in character to that described in the previous paragraph, but somewhat steeper and carrying a larger volume of water. There is a Class II-III chute under the old bridge at Upper Abbott.

Upper Abbott—Dover-Foxcroft   13 miles

Quickwater, Class I
  Spring or unusually wet summer
  Rural
        USGS: Guilford 15, Dover-Foxcroft 15
  Portages: 5 mi   R   **Guilford**   1¼ mi
                (13 mi   R   **Dover Foxcroft**   2
                        dams   ¾ mi)

There is a shallow riffle from the old to the new bridge at Upper Abbott. The riffles and current diminish and disappear as one draws nearer to the dam in Guilford. As there is no convenient take-out at the dam in town, it is recommended that paddlers take out at the senior citizens' housing where the river nears ME-6/15 less than a mile upstream on the left.

From the town athletic field below the mills on the left bank there is quickwater and occasional Class I rips for about 3¾ miles to Lowe's covered bridge. This bridge marks the beginning of Class I-II rapids that are rocky in low water and consist of wide expanses of low, choppy waves in high water. The first two rapids are easier than the rest. Fifty- to 100-yard long rapids alternate with longer, smooth stretches until one reaches an all-but-washed-out dam marked by the remains of a masonry millhouse on the left. This drop is usually run on the left, but varying water levels may allow other routes. Those who found the rips above difficult can carry on the right. The current is almost gone below the railroad trestle, and from there it is one mile of flatwater to the handy take-out and parking spot at "the cove." There are two dams in Dover-Foxcroft, each about 20 feet high. Portage by car ¾ mile from "the cove" to Brown's Mill (also called the Tannery).

Dover-Foxcroft—Derby   18½ miles

Flatwater, Quickwater, Class I, II
    Generally good levels except very dry summer
    Rural
        USGS: Dover-Foxcroft 15, Boyd Lake 15,
            Schoodic 15

Below Brown's Mill there are two ledges, each 1 to 1½ feet, followed by a rocky rapid around a long left turn. Both the ledges and rapid are Class II at moderately high water. There is a good current and easy rapids for 3 miles to the bridge at East Dover, below which there is a 100-yard long rapid, which is a fast, wavy, Class I on the left and a mild Class II on the right at most water levels. Seven more miles of smooth river bring one to the bridge at South Sebec, and 8½ miles farther is the confluence of the Sebec River and the bridge near Derby.

Just above the confluence with the Sebec is a railroad bridge, under which there is a rather steep and rocky rapid 100 yards long, Class II at low runnable level and potentially heavy when the river is high. A quarter-mile downstream is the ME-11 bridge, which has a shorter and easier rapid under it.

Derby—Howland   24¼ miles

Flatwater, Quickwater, Class I, II, III
   Medium water
   Forested, Towns
      USGS: Schoodic 15, Lincoln 15,
            Passadumkeag 15
   Portage: (24¼ mi   L   **dam**)

The beginning and end of this section is smooth, broken in the middle by 5 miles of rapids, which can be portaged by car. This is a large river, and the rapids generate heavy waves even in medium water.

Downstream from the ME-6/11/16 bridge 4 miles, the Pleasant River enters on the left. It flows over several easy rapids, and then drops over a steep Class II rapid. Occasional easy rapids continue to the high former railroad bridge (9 mi). Persons not wishing to run the heavier rapids below should take out at a dirt road just above, on the left. This is the last reasonable access, as the banks become steep and high.

Easy rapids start immediately and run to Schoodic Point (10¾ mi) where the Schoodic River enters left in an impressive rapid. The Piscataquis River turns sharply right and begins dropping more steeply, creating large waves, Class III in medium water. The rapids decrease in difficulty for the next couple of miles. Persons portaging the rapids can start again 3½ miles from Schoodic Point where the river comes close to the road near the Medford-Maxfield town line.

Seboeis Stream enters left ½ mile above the I-95 bridge (21¾ mi). The river gradually slows to flatwater. Take out at a launching ramp on the left above the dam at Howland. The confluence with the Penobscot is just below.

PLEASANT RIVER

The Pleasant River rises east of Greenville and Moosehead Lake. The West Branch flows out of Gulf Hagas to Katahdin Iron Works to Brownville Junction where it joins the East Branch, which flows out of lower Ebeemee Lake, northwest of Seboeis Lake. The combined river then flows south to Brownville, where it turns southeast to meet the Piscataquis east of Derby. The upper part is steep and should be run in moderately high water. The lower river is broad and shallow but can usually be run in the summer. The stream is clear and the banks wooded and attractive.

Brownville Junction—Brownville   5½ miles

This section would primarily be paddled at the end of a trip on the East or West Branch. There is a "water level" put-in on the left bank of the East Branch a mile above the confluence with the West Branch.

From the confluence it is 1½ miles of easy paddling to Brownville Junction and another 4 miles to the dam in Brownville.

Brownville—Piscataquis River   11 miles

Quickwater, Class I
  Medium water
  Forested
      USGS: Sebec 15, Schoodic 15, Boyd Lake 15

There is a ledge just below the dam in Brownville. The remainder of the distance is very pleasant with easy rapids and quickwater for 5 miles to the ME-16 bridge north of Milo and then another 6 miles to the Piscataquis River, which is reached about 5 miles below the bridge at Derby. There is no road near the river at this point, but 1 mile downstream at the Upper Ferry one can take out on either side of the river.

PLEASANT RIVER, West Branch

Long Pond Road—Katahdin Iron Works   4 miles

Quickwater, Class I
  Medium water, mid-May to mid-June
  Wild
      USGS: Sebec 15

Put in near where Long Pond Road first comes near the river after crossing the log bridge. This is near "X609" on the topo map. The river is narrow with good current. It is generally shallow with gravel riffles, downed trees, and forest debris forming Class I obstacles. The stream becomes broader, deeper, and slower in the last mile above Silver Lake. One can take out at the log bridge on Long Pond Road or continue ¾ mile down Silver Lake to Katahdin Iron Works. The old dam at "K.I." is completely gone, leaving a swift, shallow, and rocky rapid down past the bridge at "K.I."

Katahdin Iron Works— Brownville Junction   9¾ miles

This part can be reached by a private road from ME-11. The upper part is particularly steep and passable only in moderately high water. These rapids decline in severity until the stream becomes generally smooth by the time it is joined by the East Branch above Brownville Junction.

PLEASANT RIVER, East Branch

Lower Ebeemee Lake— West Branch   3½ miles

Class I, II
    Medium water, May
    Forested
        USGS: Sebec 15
        Portage: near start   R   **100 ft**

Put in at the log bridge at the foot of Lower Ebeemee Lake. The two-foot drop just above this bridge would be runnable (Class II–III) in medium or high water if it were not blocked by a partially detached bridge timber. Drift down 50 yards to where a jumble of small boulders marks the site of an old dam. In high water the extreme left might be runnable in decked boats (Class III–IV). Most paddlers will carry 100 feet on the right. A 50-yard-long pool leads into a Class II rapid that quickly splits into two channels;

75% of the flow goes left. The first 50 feet of this channel are tight and fast, possibly Class III at some levels; the remaining 100 feet are technical Class II at medium water. One now comes to a series of mild (Class I–II) rapids alternating with short stretches of quickwater.

One and one-half miles below the put-in the river suddenly kinks to the right. At the apex of the kink a one-foot ledge divides the stream into two chutes. The left chute has most of the flow and forms an irregular sousehole of significant dimensions. The right chute is shallow and entails two 90° turns. Between the two chutes is dry ledge at medium or lower water. Just below this drop, which is the last one that should take your mind off the scenery, the river divides into multiple channels, with most of the water going to the left again. The extreme right channel comes quite close to a gravel pit just north of "the prairie," which makes an acceptable put-in for those wishing to avoid the rapids above. The remaining two miles to the high ME-11 bridge are very scenic and the rapids are less frequent and diminish from easy Class II to Class I and then disappear.

The smaller Middle Branch enters a short distance below the bridge. A short side road comes near the left bank, making an easier take-out than the steep climb up to ME-11. The river is smooth the remaining mile to the West Branch.

SEBEC RIVER

The Sebec River drains Sebec Lake, located in Willimantic and Bowerbank, and flows east and south to the Piscataquis River at Derby. Together with the lake it provides an easy 20-mile canoe trip on smoothwater available during most seasons of the year.

Earley's Landing—Derby   22¾ miles

Lake, Flatwater
  Generally all summer
  Forested, Rural
     USGS: Sebec Lake 15, Sebec 15
    Portages: 12½ mi   **Sebec Lake Dam**
               20½ mi   **Milo Dam**

One can put in at Earley's Landing or ¾ mile further at Packard's Landing on Sebec Lake. From Packard's Landing it is 4 miles to the Narrows, where the lake narrows to less than ¼ mile. For the next 7½ miles to Sebec the lake is generally less than one mile wide. At Sebec there is a dam with a short rapids below. Approximately 4 miles farther along there are about 100 yards of rocky Class II rips.

The dam in Milo is right in the middle of town, and the river splits into 2 channels just below it. The left channel has a small powerhouse put on line in 1982. Choice of channel and portage route will vary with day of week and amount of water in the river. The rapids for the next ½ mile will be bony Class I–II if one gate is open, heavy with more water. The confluence with the Piscataquis is ¼ mile above the ME-11 bridge, which has an easy Class II rip under it.

BIG WILSON STREAM

Big Wilson Stream rises in Wilson Pond near the Kennebec/Piscataquis divide south of Moosehead Lake. It is a major inlet to Sebec Lake.

Bodfish Crossing—Willimantic   5 miles

Quickwater, Class I, II, III
 High water
 Wild, Forested
  USGS: Sebec Lake 15
 Portages: 1¾ mi   L   **2 falls**

There is a formidable series of cascades just below the bridge near Bodfish Crossing. Put in from either side in the pool below. About 1½ miles of quickwater and Class I riffles bring the canoeist to a Class III rapid (medium to high water) caused by three ledges. The first ledge is abrupt on the left, blocked in midstream by a barely visible flat rock below it, and sloping on the right. The second is impassable at medium water on the far right, has a sizable sousehole right of center and a chute with waves left of center. The third ledge has obvious routes on the left and center if you've gotten past the other two.

In about ¼ mile there is a Class II rapid around an island,

easily run on either side. The next two miles are smooth
with occasional riffles. Several boulders on the left, into
which the river seems to disappear, mark the beginning of
the strenuous last mile and a half. The main flow turns
abruptly left into a twisting Class III series of sloping drops,
waves, and avoidable souseholes. In roughly 75 yards there
is a 4- or 5-foot drop over a ledge; the easy route is on the
far left where the drop is a series of small steps. A 150-yard
stretch of flatwater brings the now apprehensive paddler to
a 10-foot all-but-vertical falls, to be carried on the left.

Below this falls the river makes a meander to the right,
which includes a Class III rapid with good-sized waves.
While carrying around the first falls you will see the lip of
the second; boaters with reliable eddy turns can drift down
and take out on the left 10 yards above the lip. The second
falls is a damlike sloping ledge of about 12 vertical feet or
15 on the slant. The roller at its bottom looks like a keeper
at any water level. Put in amongst the rocks just below it.

The next landmark is an "S"-turn with a cabin on the
right bank. Opposite the cabin and below it are two 2-foot
ledges with fairly obvious slots right of center and left of
center, respectively. The second ledge is followed by a 1/4-
mile-long, Class II rock garden down the right side of a
large island. There is a house high on the right bank where
the river turns left into a short Class II rapid culminating in
another 2-foot ledge best run on the far left. Look up and
you will see the bridge at Willimantic, which is also known
as Norton's Corner.

Willimantic—Sebec Lake   4 miles

Class I
    Generally all summer
    Forested, Wild
        USGS: Sebec Lake 15
    Portage: (4 mi   **Falls at Earley's
                              Landing)**

Below the Willimantic bridge the river is Class I with fast,
shallow riffles in mid-June. This section is canoeable almost
anytime. From the bridge in Willimantic, it is 4 miles to

Earley's Landing on Sebec Lake. Portage around two waterfalls at Earley's.

SHIP POND STREAM

Ship Pond Stream is the outlet of Onawa Lake, and flows
to Sebec Lake at Bucks Cove, from where it is 2 miles of
lake paddling to a road access.

During early spring the road access to the start is impassable, and the lake may also be frozen.

Cow Yard Falls—Sebec Lake   3 miles

Flatwater, Quickwater, Class I
   Medium water: *May–June; after heavy rains*
   Wild
      USGS: Sebec Lake 15
      Portage: 2¾ mi   e   **waterfall 50 yd**

Cow Yard Falls can be reached by a private road that
leaves ME-150 at Earley's Landing at Willimantic. The road
runs right through Twin Falls Camps, and it is about 2½
miles to Cowyard Falls, an 8-foot ledge.

Put in below the falls or below the Class II ledges, if you
prefer. After a few Class I rips the stream flows quickly
over a gravel bed for ½ mile. After a mile of meandering
river it spreads out over a shallow stretch, which may have
to be waded for ¼ mile at low water at summer levels. A
short piece of deep flatwater leads to the falls at Bucks
Cove.

The falls is about 5 feet in several quick steps followed by
a rocky pool and a 2-foot ledge drop at the apex of a bend
to the right, whose rocky out-run leads into Bucks Cove, an
isolated arm of Sebec Lake, which contains three wooded
islands and many glacial boulders.

It is a mile southeast to the mouth of the cove and
another mile west to Packard's Landing. A further ½ mile
will bring you to the lower of the two falls at Earley's on
Big Wilson Stream.

It is not unduly strenuous to do this trip in the upstream
direction as the finish of a trip on Big Wilson Stream or
Sebec Lake.

PASSADUMKEAG RIVER

The Passadumkeag River rises in Lee, flows south for
some miles, then southwest, and finally west to the Penobscot River at Passadumkeag. It has many miles of good
canoeing on it, but the upper part is best done at moderately
high water.

Weir Pond—Pistol Green   18 miles

Flatwater, Quickwater, Marsh
  Anytime
  Wild
      USGS: Springfield 15, Nicatous Lake 15,
            Saponac 15
  Campsites: 9 mi   R   **Brown Brook**
                12¾ mi   L   **Cold Spring**
                 18 mi   L   **Pistol Green**

The stream is fairly small. The described put-in is at the
bridge below Weir Pond.

One can put in at Weir Pond or at a road crossing just
below the pond, both reachable by the same road off ME-6
west of Springfield. If one puts in at Weir Pond there are
½ mile of pond and ½ mile of swampy stream to the lower
put-in spot. The next 17 miles are all smoothwater with the
river meandering through swampy going all the way to the
mouth of Nicatous Stream at Pistol Green.

An alternative start, which may miss some fallen trees, is
via the West Branch starting at Number 3 Pond. In this case
there are 2 miles of lake and a mile of river to the Passadumkeag reached 1¼ miles below the bridge.

Rand Brook (3¾ mi) marks the start of the old portage
across to Upper Sysladobsis and the St. Croix drainage.

Pistol Green—Passadumkeag   **32¼ miles**

Pond, Flatwater, **Quickwater,** Marsh, Class I, II
  Anytime
  Wild, Forested, Rural
      USGS: Saponac 15, Passadumkeag 15
  Portages: 4½ mi L **Grand Falls** ¾ mi
              18½ mi R then L **Lowell Dam**
             (32 mi L **dam at**
                            Passadumkeag)
  Campsites: 5 mi L **Grand Falls**
              13 mi L **Saponac Pond**

The river is smooth for the first 4 miles. Grand Falls is a wild rapid in which the river drops 100 feet in a mile, and should be carried. There is a good carry road.

The river winds through flat bottomlands to Saponac Pond (12¼ mi). In high water the river is hard to find in the maple swamp before the pond. A campsite is on the south shore; it is somewhat buggy. There is a mile of river beyond the pond to Pond Rips and White Horse Rips, which some may wish to line or carry.

The river is smooth again for 3 miles to the dam at Lowell (18½ mi), now broken. Portage right through a field, cross the river on the bridge, and take the trail along the left bank. The ledges make fearsome waves in high water. Except for Rocky Rips (25½ mi), the river is smooth all the way to Passadumkeag.

The usual take-out is at an iron bridge 2 miles upstream of Passadumkeag. Persons continuing on to the Penobscot should watch for an eel weir above the US-2 bridge. There is a bad portage left through driftwood and poison ivy.

NICATOUS STREAM

Nicatous Stream drains Nicatous Lake and flows northwest to the Passadumkeag River at Pistol Green. It is part of a major Indian canoe route.

"Nicatous" means "Little Fork" and applies to the junction of this stream and the Passadumkeag. At that point a person ascending the Passadumkeag had a choice of routes to follow. Nicatous Stream led to "Kiasobeak," now

called Nicatous Lake, from which one can easily reach the
headwaters of four major river systems.

Nicatous Lake—Pistol Green   7¾ miles

Flatwater, **Quickwater,** Marsh, Class I, II, III
  Medium water
  Wild
        USGS: Nicatous Lake, Saponac 15
  Portage: ¼ mi   **dam**

From the public landing on the north shore of Nicatous
Lake it is a short paddle to the small dam at the outlet. The
river flows for 2 miles through boggy areas separated by
short, bouldery sections. Class I rapids commence after a
long boggy stretch and increase without letup to Idiot Dog
Falls, which is Class III if there is enough water, flowing
over 50 yards of granite ledges (3 mi). Right at the bottom a
crumbling log bridge has posed some hazards in the past.
The bridge is a good lunch spot; just upstream on the left at
bank level is a cold spring of cedar water.
  Below the bridge is another short, sharp pitch, then rapids diminish quickly. The final 3 miles flows through a
swamp with gravel bars and pools. Good moose country.
There is a bridge half a mile above the Passadumkeag.

GASSABIAS STREAM

This stream is part of a major east-west Indian canoe
route, and also used to be the traditional approach to the
Machias river in preroad days. One can easily pole or paddle up and down Gassabias Stream with only a minimum of
dragging in low water.

Gassabias Lake—Nicatous Lake   3 miles

The low bridge at the outlet of Gassabias Lake may have
to be carried if the water is high. After a mile of deep water
swamp comes a mile of mossy boulders, but no rapids,
where you must be alert for problems in the low water. This
ends at the CCC road bridge, where marsh begins again and
continues to Great Falls. At Great Falls the stream narrows

and plunges 5 feet vertically in the next 200 yards. Nicatous Lake is soon reached, just south of the "Snakka," a long, undulating stone ridge that almost cuts the lake in two.

The 2-mile portage to Fourth Machias Lake starts on the east shore of Gassabias Lake just to the left of a large stand of red pines. The portage trail begins as a 12-foot groove cut into the peat bog from heavy use. The trail is still passable, but difficult.

Campsites: Red pine grove by the portage
Outlet of Gassabias Lake
North side of "Snakka," good sand beach

KENDUSKEAG STREAM

Garland—French Stream   7½ miles

Quickwater, Class I, II
High water: *spring run-off or pond drawdown*
Forested
USGS: Dover-Foxcroft 15, Stetson 15
Portages: 2.8 mi   L   **dam at Twin Brook**   lift over
2.9 mi   L   **ledge**   lift over

Just below the dam at Garland, a side road from ME-94 crosses the stream. Put in here at relatively high water levels only. Note that the quadrangle does not reflect recent road construction: ME-94 does not cross the stream twice in this area. The first mile is mostly quickwater, with sharp turns and minor alder tangles. After the first mile a rock-strewn channel requires quick maneuvering in spots, generally with stretches of quickwater below each rapids. This continues for about ½ mile to a road crossing and another ½ mile to the back-up of a small, washed-out milldam at Twin Brook. Burnham Brook enters on the left in this area but may be missed in the meanders.

Another 0.8 mile brings the paddler to the old dam at Twin Brook. It may be lifted over on the left, or might be

run after scouting if water level is advantageous. Within
0.1 mile of the dam is another road crossing. Beneath this
bridge is a ledge drop of 2–3 feet over which the current
takes a sharp "S"-turn. After scouting from above the
bridge, and with careful execution, the stream may be run
to the left bank above the ledge, and the canoe lifted over.
It is slightly over a mile below the ledge to the next road
crossing. Between the ledge and the crossing are more rapids
interspersed with quickwater, much like the section above
the pond. The remainder of the run to the ME-11/43 bridge
is comprised of occasional rapids with numerous beaver
dams, blowdowns, and tangles. The crossing of ME-11/43
is just (30 yards) upstream of the confluence with French
Stream, which at this point is approximately the same size
as the Kenduskeag. Take out here on the right under the
bridge.

French Stream—Kenduskeag   13½ miles

Flatwater, **Quickwater,** Class I, II, III
  Medium to high water: *April, May*
  Forested, Rural
    USGS: Stetson 15, Bangor 15
  Portages: 11½ mi   **ledge**   lift over
              13½ mi   **ledge**   lift over

Below the ME-11/43 bridge the river is doubled in size by
French Stream entering right. The bridge at McGregor Mill
is 1¼ miles, and it is another 1¼ miles to the second bridge.
The current is fast, with some rapids up to Class II, then
the river pools up for a couple of miles, with little current
and deeper to a rapid above a covered bridge at Robyville
(7 mi). The bridge cannot be seen from the beginning of the
rapid, but the change in terrain is obvious, as the river
makes an "S"-turn over a ledgy drop, Class III.
  The rapids for the next ¾ mile are slightly harder. Just
above the fourth bridge is a 3½-foot drop over a ledge,
which may need to be lined or carried. The next ledge
before the bridge in Kenduskeag is even more difficult.

Kenduskeag—Bangor   16 miles

Quickwater, Class I, II
  High water
  Forested
    USGS: Bangor 15
  Portages: 15 mi   L   **Flour Mill Dam**
                15¼ mi   R   **Maxfield Dam**

The bridge in Kenduskeag is the start of the Kenduskeag to Bangor race, the largest in the state. The first 10 miles are meandering quickwater with a few riffles to Six Mile Falls, immediately above the ME-15 bridge. Six Mile Falls is a 200-yard Class III rapid at most runnable levels, which is easier scouted and run on the left. The next 5 miles vary from quickwater to Class II. Flour Mill Dam, just above the interstate bridge, is generally not run, and is the usual end of a day trip on the Kenduskeag.

It is ¼ mile to the bridge near Maxfield Dam. Both of these are short, powerful ledge drops. Scout the rapids at the end of the portage.

The remaining ¾ mile to the Penobscot River is quickwater unless the tide is coming in.

SOUADABSCOOK STREAM

Souadabscook Stream (alternate spelling: Sawadapskook) rises in Etna Pond and flows east to join the Penobscot River south of Bangor. It was one of the major Indian waterways, connecting the Penobscot and Kennebec watersheds; a portage connected to the Sebasticook River.

Black Stream—Vatiades Landing   3½ miles

Pond, Quickwater, Class I
  High or medium water: *mid-April to early June*
  Rural, Settled
    USGS: Bangor 15

Put in from US-2 at a culvert 3¾ miles west of Hermon. This culvert connects Black Stream, a tributary of the Kenduskeag River, to Souadabscook Stream in high water. Parking is poor.

The 1¾ miles to Newburgh Road and the Maine Central Railroad crossings is all flatwater except for a Class II chute over what appears to be a sunken stone wall at the halfway point. Newburgh Road offers good parking, and this section can be paddled upstream.

The pond is another ¼ mile, and the outlet of the pond is 1½ miles to the southeast. Vatiades Landing on Bogg Road is an additional ½ mile.

Black Stream, while a tributary of the Kenduskeag, is more likely to be paddled as an extension of this trip. It can be ascended from the culvert at the start of this trip ½ mile to a washed-out culvert, or descended 1 mile to Black Stream Road (an alternate start).

Vatiades Landing—Hampden   9 miles

Lake, Flatwater, **Quickwater,** Class I, II, III
  High water: *April to mid-May*
  Forested, Rural, Settled
      USGS: Bangor 15, *Bucksport 15*
  Portages: 6¼ mi   **Crawford drop (Class IV ledge)**
               7 mi   e   **Grand Falls ¼–½ mi**
               (9 mi   **Waterworks)**

Put in at Vatiades Landing on a side road just north of I-95. The stream is smooth at the start, as it goes south under I-95, then soon flows into Hammond Pond, which is often still frozen when the stream is at its best. The outlet is ½ mile east across the pond on the northeast corner.

The current gradually quickens, flowing through a deep-water swamp, heading first northeast under I-95, then turning southeast back under it for the third time. Some warm-up around scattered rocks gets you ready for the first ledge just above Manning Mill Road, a drop of 2–3 feet at a right turn, nearly vertical at the inside (right) and sloping on the outside. After a short pool the stream narrows to pass under the road bridge. In another ½ mile near Camp Preutis is a steep 3-foot ledge. After another ¼ mile, at Emerson Mill

Road, is another ledge similar to the first. Next is a quick chute into a pool, which sets you up for Crawfords a few hundred yards further along.

Crawfords is a collection of low, offset, broken ledges offering a variety of routes, all of which require adroit maneuvering. Shortly there is a narrow chute under Hopkins Bridge on Papermill Road where most people start the portage of Grand Falls.

The falls are an impressive drop over ledges and through boulders, but the stream no sooner emerges from the falls than it is held up by a 4-foot dam. Put in below the dam. The 1-foot weir can be run.

Near the cement plant the stream zig-zags around a series of ledges. These obstructions are not as abrupt as those above, but the souseholes below them are more powerful. The stream winds down with ½ mile of shallow, rocky rips leading to ½ mile of flatwater ending at the waterworks under US-1A. If the tide is not too low, you can carry down a long, steep bank and run the last ¼ mile of the Soudab (as it is commonly called) to join the Penobscot River.

These rapids are mostly steep ledges over sharp shale and can really chew up boats.

MARSH STREAM

Marsh Stream flows eastward from Monroe to tidewater on the Penobscot.

Monroe Center—West Winterport   9½ miles

Flatwater, Quickwater, Class I, II
  High water: *spring*
  Forested
    USGS: Brooks 15, *Bucksport 15*
    Portage: 9¼ mi e **dam in West
                            Winterport**

There is a good trail on the left to the put-in at the base of the falls. A mile of Class I rips slows down through bottom farmland. The ME-141 bridge is passed at 3 miles. Just before the Marsh Stream Road bridge (5¾ mi) is Crooked Rip, a right-left-right ledge drop, Class II in low to moderate water. The junction with the North Branch is another ¼ mile.

The deadwater starts above the dam in West Winterport.

West Winterport—Frankfort   6½ miles

Quickwater, Class I, II, III
  High water: *spring; after heavy rain*
  Forested
    USGS: Bucksport 15
  Portages: 5 mi   L   **Flatrock Falls**   100 yd
              (6½ mi   e   **dam)**

This is a nice day trip with a variety of whitewater. Put in from Loggin Road in West Winterport just off ME-139. It starts with a couple of miles of quickwater, which is followed by three Class I rapids.

Just above a snowmobile bridge (3¼ mi) is a double ledge, running at 45° to flow (Class II). In another ¾ mile is a rock garden (Class I–II).

Beyond the railroad bridge (possible access) are Railroad Rip with complicated currents and Pine Island Rip (Class II). Run on left of island; to the right is disaster. Portage or line from island if necessary. Scout before running.

Around another corner is Flatrock Falls (5 mi), Class IV–V. The run-out is poor, as the river immediately becomes wider, shallow, and full of boulders and logs. One Class II drop comes before the final 1½ miles mostly on flowage above the dam at Frankfort.

The last mile on the North Branch of the Marsh River is tidal on the Penobscot River.

CHAPTER 5

Allagash
Wilderness
Waterway

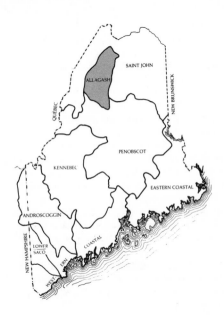

ALLAGASH RIVER

The Allagash is "the River of Maine" because the shore-line is owned by the state. Since it attracts canoeists from all over the East, it is also the best-known river in Maine. Those who travel down it do so under varying circumstances; for some it symbolizes an achievement, the culmination of a series of canoe trips, with the Allagash providing the finishing touch. For others, it is the beginning, maybe the first experience in a canoe, with other rivers to follow depending upon the individual's affinity for, or ability to cope with, back-woods and black flies, rain and rapids, winds and waves, and all the things that are a part of an extended canoe trip.

After ice-out and into June, the most common use of the Allagash River and its headwaters is for fishing. As the season progresses, those seeking primarily fish are replaced by those attracted by the wilderness setting, although the latter group frequently includes part-time anglers. August is the month that brings the heaviest use, with July close behind. In the summer, solitude may be hard to find, but a survey of visitor use in 1973 indicated that campsite utilization on Allagash Lake and Allagash Stream was significantly below that of the rest of the river.

There is no need to purchase USGS maps unless you are canoeing into the Allagash Wilderness Waterway via one of the access routes described below, including Johnson Pond. Any Waterway Ranger or the Allagash Wilderness Water-way (Bureau of Parks and Recreation, Station 22, Augusta, ME 04333) can supply you with a good map, free. It shows the location of the seventy-odd campsites, about which no mention is made in this book.

In 1973 the Waterway started charging fees. By 1986 the rate will be $3.00 or more per day. If you canoe from Telos Landing to the Saint John River, the distance is 96¾ miles. That will take about six days, so bring enough money to pay for campsites for the duration of your trip. Camping fees are collected at North Maine Woods gates on private roads leading to the Waterway. There are Waterway Ranger Stations at the Chamberlain Thoroughfare Bridge, on the northeastern arm of Allagash Lake, at Lock Dam on the northern bay of Eagle Lake, at Churchill Dam, on Umsaskis Lake near the Thoroughfare, and at Michaud Farm.

Establishment of the Allagash Wilderness Waterway

A hydroelectric dam on the Saint John River was first suggested in the 1920s in order to supplement the proposed Passamaquoddy Tidal Power Project. The site chosen was Rankin Rapids, 9 miles downstream from Allagash Village. A dam at that location would have wiped out the lower portions of both the Allagash and the Saint John rivers. In the late 1950s, there was renewed interest in damming up the Saint John, but plans to harness the tides were dropped. Public pressure ultimately prevented the construction of a high dam downstream from the mouth of the Allagash River.

In August 1962, the Natural Resources Council of Maine recommended land acquisition and management of the Allagash by the state or federal government. The following year, the Bureau of Outdoor Recreation in Washington recommended federal protection for the river. Pressure from the federal government for protection of the river through land acquisition led to the state's establishment of the Allagash Wilderness Waterway on December 28, 1966. The act setting up the Waterway authorized a bond issue of $1,500,000 that was matched by federal funds. The state has acquired a corridor averaging 500 feet wide along the shore of the river and all the lakes it flows through from Telos Dam north to West Twin Brook, including also Allagash Lake and Allagash Stream. The act also placed restrictions on land use within one mile of the shorelines of the Waterway.

One of the first projects undertaken by the state was the reconstruction of Churchill Dam so that the flow through Chase Rapids could be regulated and maintained throughout the canoeing season. Some private camps have been removed, while the rest have been taken over for use by the Waterway itself.

The protection afforded the Allagash River applies to commercial development, dam construction, and uncontrolled logging, but there may have to be protection from overuse by the people that the Waterway was set up to serve. In the eight years from 1967 through 1973, the number of people visiting the Allagash doubled. Use since 1973 has leveled off to approximately 45,000 to 50,000 visitor nights between ice-out and the end of September. If one wishes to encounter fewer people on the Waterway, visit it in September.

Early Logging Along the Allagash

Over a hundred years ago, logging began to have an impact on the Allagash region. As was the case all over the state, the early loggers built dams at the outlets of the lakes in order to be able to store and release water into the rivers below so that they could drive their logs to a mill. Today, only a trace remains of the dam that raised the level of Allagash Lake, and the one on Mud Pond is only slightly better preserved. Much of Long Lake Dam, built in 1908, still remains, although it no longer controls the level of the lakes behind it. Today, the shoreline exposed when that dam "went out" supports only an alder thicket, that layer of bushes seen along the waterline of many of Maine's lakes whose water level has dropped. When Churchill Dam was rebuilt in 1968, it reflooded areas where alders had established themselves along the shoreline exposed when, in July 1954, the previous dam was washed out.

Dams are of particular interest on the Allagash because of the diversion of much of its headwaters into the East Branch of the Penobscot. A dam at the site of Lock Dam on Chamberlain Lake raised the level of that lake and Telos Lake as well so that the water would flow east, rather than north. Telos Dam was built to control the flow into the East Branch. A dam at the site of the present Churchill Dam raised the level of the water in Eagle, Churchill, and Heron lakes, therefore making it possible to boom logs on these lakes to another dam at the south end of Eagle Lake that functioned as a lock, where the logs were raised up to Chamberlain Lake, down which they were boomed to Telos Dam.

There are two other examples of stream diversion that can be seen today. The first is a sluiceway on Allagash Stream above Little Round Pond, where the river was channeled. The remains of this can be seen easily at low water. The other is at Allagash Falls, where a dike still keeps most of the river out of the far right-hand channel.

Unique to the Allagash were the Eagle Lake Tramway, used for six years from about 1902, and the two railroads, the Eagle Lake Railroad and the Chesuncook and Chamberlain Lake Railroad, that operated over a 13-mile roadbed between Eagle and Chesuncook lakes from 1927 to 1933. The remains of the tramway can still be seen close to the old locomotives near Eagle Lake; the roadbed itself, with the rails still in place at the northern end, can be traced to Chesuncook Lake.

The history of the river is told in *The Allagash,* by Lew Dietz (Holt, Rinehart and Winston, 1968). The reading of this book will add meaning to many of the places of interest along the river, and it will give you a picture of life in the Maine woods during the past several centuries.

Access to the Allagash Wilderness Waterway

In the Introduction you will find information on the region to the north controlled by North Maine Woods.

By car: The most popular access points at the southern end of the waterway are Telos Landing and the Chamberlain Thoroughfare Bridge. Both are reached from Greenville or Millinocket via private logging roads that are open to the public. From Ashland, you can use the American Realty Road to reach Long and Umsaskis lakes, and Churchill Dam.

By Canoe: To Allagash and Chamberlain Lakes

A trip on the Allagash Wilderness Waterway, with Allagash Lake on the itinerary, takes 8 or 9 days, somewhat less if you fly into Johnson Pond. If it is desirable to plan a longer trip, this can be done by beginning at Chesuncook Lake on the West Branch of the Penobscot. It takes an additional 3 or 4 days from Chesuncook Dam to the Allagash via Mud Pond or Caucomgomoc Lake.

The easiest comparison of the two routes involves portages: a total of 4½ miles via Caucomgomoc Lake versus the 1¾-mile Mud Pond Carry. However, the longer portages lead to Allagash Lake, while to reach the same point via Mud Pond requires that you pull up Allagash Stream, a day's work unless the water is high, in which case it would be extremely difficult.

Another comparison deals with esthetics. The end of the Caucomgomoc Portage is along a logging road, and shortly thereafter you paddle up a stream lined with dead trees still standing in the water that killed them. And, if you plan to camp on Round Pond before the Allagash Portage, or between trips across it, you will do so close to a major logging

road. You will not be spared dry-ki or roads if you go via
Mud Pond, but there is considerably less of each. Mud
Pond and the lake before it are attractive bodies of water
that give a feeling of remoteness that is not always easy to
find on a trip down the Allagash.

Early trips on the Allagash usually began at Greenville
and followed a route that went up Moosehead Lake, across
North East Carry to the West Branch of the Penobscot,
down the latter to Chesuncook Lake, and then via either
Mud Pond or Caucomgomoc Lake. The routes detailed below use Chesuncook Dam as the starting point, but it is possible to drive to the West Branch below Seboomook Lake,
canoe downstream to Chesuncook Lake, and choose either
one. You can also drive to Caucomgomoc Lake.

Chesuncook "Dam" is located on a peninsula that separates Chesuncook and Ripogenus lakes. The construction
downstream of Ripogenus Dam in 1916 replaced an earlier
structure, and, with a 75-foot head of water, it flooded out
Chesuncook Dam. Today, the place known as Chesuncook
Dam is a convenient launching area, with parking space
available.

Chesuncook Dam—Allagash Lake   35¼ miles

Lakes, Class I–II (if traveled in reverse)
  Wild

USGS:	Harrington Lake 15, Ragged Lake 15, Chesuncook 15, Caucomgomoc Lake 15, Allagash Lake 15	
Portages:	26 mi L	**Caucomgomoc Stream** 1½ mi
	32¼ mi	**Allagash Carry** 3 mi
Campsites:	5 sites	**on Chesuncook Lake** MFS
	19¾ mi L	**Black Pond** (S end) permit
	26 mi L	**Caucomgomoc Portage** NMW $
	32¼ mi	**Round Pond** (N shore) NMW $ car
	35¼ mi	**Allagash Portage** (N end) AWW $

From the "dam" there are 26 miles of paddling up Chesuncook Lake and across Black Pond to the 1½-mile Caucomgomoc Portage. The trail begins on the left at the campsite and leads to a logging road, which you follow to the right. A second road comes in on the left not far from the Caucomgomoc Dam (27½ mi).

The rapids in Caucomgomoc Stream are easy enough that you can pull up the stream if there is enough water. The only difficulty, going up or downstream, is a ledge approximately two-thirds of the way from the bottom, about opposite where the trail joins the logging road.

The next leg of the trip is a 4¾-mile paddle up Ciss Stream and across Round Pond to the campsite (32¼ mi).

The 3-mile Allagash Carry begins on the logging road that goes around the north end of Round Pond. You have to walk along the road to reach it, either north from the bridge over the stream from Poland Pond or west from the campsite. The trail is well-used, but there may be no marker where it meets the road. As you near the end of the portage, an old trail at a fork leads left to the forest service camp at the base of the trail to Allagash Mountain.

The outlet of Allagash Lake (40 mi) lies 4¾ miles northeast of the end of the portage.

Johnson Pond—Allagash Lake   3 miles

Flatwater
  Wild
        USGS: Allagash Lake 15

In high water you can paddle a canoe most of the way down the stream from Johnson Pond to Allagash Stream. But it was reported in 1975 that one of the natives, by name *Castor canadensis,* had stopped maintaining his dam at the outlet, with the result that travel became impossible in low water.

If it becomes necessary to portage, a trail follows along logging roads close to the right bank. It continues straight when the logging road turns left to cross the stream. The trail ends where the stream from Johnson Pond joins Allagash Stream.

It is 1¼ miles from the island in Johnson Pond to Alla-gash Stream, followed by a 1¾-mile paddle down the latter to Allagash Lake (3 mi). To the east 3¼ miles, is the outlet (6¼ mi).

Allagash Lake Outlet—Lock Dam   9½ miles

Lakes, Quickwater, Class I-II
  High water: *best*
  Medium water: *passable*
  Low water: *wading and dragging required*
  Allagash Mountain Firetower: The ¾-mile trail begins at
              the forest service camp at the south end of
              Allagash Lake.
  Deer: Notice the "browse line" along the edge of Little
              Round Pond. In the winter, the deer stand
              on the ice and eat all the cedar needles and
              twigs they can reach.
  Point of interest: Trestle of the Eagle Lake and West
              Branch RR (1927–33)
      USGS: Allagash Lake 15, Churchill Lake 15
  Portages: 3¼ mi   L   **Little Allagash Falls**
                          150 yds
              9½ mi   **Lock Dam**   10 yds
  Campsites: See map issued by Allagash
              Wilderness Waterway.

The remains of the old dam are barely visible. Below the lake, Allagash Stream flows for 2¾ miles to Little Round Pond. There are many rapids, up to Class I, in the first part, but the last mile consists of quickwater.

The portage around Little Allagash Falls (3¼ mi), at the outlet of Little Round Pond, is on the left. The stream below, 2¼ miles long, has Class I rapids, except for three places. The first is a ledge about ¼ mile below the falls that can be avoided by staying along the right shore and going to the right of a small island. A second ledge farther on must be lifted over on the right. Finally, be on the lookout for a logging bridge, because underneath it there is a short rapid that should be scouted.

The gradient gradually lessens as you approach Chamberlain Lake (5½ mi). It is a 4-mile paddle down the lake, past the railroad trestle (6½ mi), to Lock Dam (9½ mi).

If you are enroute from Allagash Lake to Churchill Dam, you may avoid 7½ miles of paddling, an important consideration if there is a strong headwind, by portaging along the abandoned tramway from the northern tip of Chamberlain Lake to Eagle Lake. Included in the bargain is a ½-mile carry, as well as a visit to the trains.

Chesuncook Dam—
Lock Dam via Mud Pond   31¼ miles

Lakes, Class I
   Wild
       USGS: Harrington Lake 15, Ragged Lake 15,
             Chesuncook 15

Portages:	21½ mi	R	**Umbazooksus Lake Dam** 10 yds
	22¼ mi	R	**Mud Pond Carry** 1¾ mi
	31¼ mi		**Lock Dam** 10 yds
Campsites:	4 sites		**on Chesuncook Lake** MFS
	22½ mi		**Mud Pond Carry** (S end) NMW $

It is a 20¼-mile paddle from the "dam" to the head of the lake at Umbazooksus Stream, where a low bridge must be portaged. After the bridge, you paddle past dry-ki for ¾ mile, after which you work your way up what remains of the free-flowing Umbazooksus Stream. There is a short carry around the dam on Umbazooksus Lake (21½ mi).

The Mud Pond Carry begins on the northeast shore of the lake, ¾ mile from the dam. The trail crosses the old roadbed of the Chesuncook and Chamberlain Lake Railroad (1927–1933), passes through the campsite, crosses a logging road, and then continues through attractive woods to Mud Pond (24 mi).

Across Mud Pond, 1¼ miles, is the outlet (25¼ mi). The brook below can be run in high water, but part of it must be waded down in medium water. In ¼ mile it reaches

Mud Pond Inlet, a part of Chamberlain Lake. Lock Dam
(31¼ mi) lies 5¾ miles to the north.

Telos Landing—Lock Dam   15 miles

Lakes
    USGS: Churchill Lake 15, Umsaskis Lake 15
    Portage: 15 mi   **Lock Dam**   10 yds
Campsites: See map issued by Allagash
                    Wilderness Waterway.

Many people begin the trip at the bridge across the Chamberlain Thoroughfare (4½ mi), where there is a Waterway
Ranger and ample parking space.

By Canoe: To Eagle and Churchill Lakes

Haymock Lake—Eagle Lake   8 miles

Smith Brook is mostly a small, easy stream, with a fall to
lift over not far above Eagle Lake.

Indian Stream Access

Follow the Indian Pond road as far as the gate. Continue
down Indian Stream to Eagle Lake.

Cliff Lake—Churchill Lake   4 miles

Cliff Lake can be reached by private road from Ashland. It
is used mainly by those coming from the north and wishing to
make the Allagash run. The road reaches the lake near the
south end of the east shore. There is a campsite here and one
farther north on the east shore. It is 2 miles across the lake
and through Twin Lake to the dam at South Twin Brook. If
the water is high enough to run, this brook provides 2 miles
of easy rapids to Churchill Lake. If the water is too low,
wade with the canoe. It is then 4½ miles across Churchill Lake
and through Heron Lake to Churchill Dam.

Lock Dam—Long Lake Dam   37½ miles

Lakes, Quickwater, Class I–II
   Dam-controlled: *Chase Rapids only*
   Portage service available around Chase Rapids—see
         ranger.
   Points of interest: Tramway and trains—southwest end
         of Eagle Lake.
   Moose: Moose feed on underwater plants. They
         apparently find plenty of them in the
         marshes along the river as you approach
         Umsaskis Lake, and you stand a good
         chance of seeing the big beasts in the
         evening and in the early morning.
   Priestly Mountain Firetower: 4-mile trail begins at MFS
         camp on west shore of Umsaskis Lake.
      USGS: Churchill 15, Umsaskis Lake 15
   Portage: 18¾ mi   L   **Churchill Dam**   15 yds
   Campsites: See map issued by Allagash
         Wilderness Waterway.

At the right end of Lock Dam, there is a short lift-over into the stream below. In ½ mile you reach Martin Cove at the south end of Eagle Lake. If you are using the Churchill Lake quadrangle, you should realize that the map was made prior to the rebuilding of Churchill Dam, so that you are likely to find the unshaded areas bordering Eagle and Churchill lakes covered with water. The water level normally drops during the summer months, and on October 1st it is supposed to be at its lowest point, in deference to the lake trout, who need shallow water and a relatively stable level in the lake for spawning.

No trip down the Allagash is complete without a visit to the tramway and the trains. About 100 yards east of the remains of an old pier on the southwest shore of Eagle Lake is where the trail begins (6 mi). It leads past the locomotives to Chamberlain Lake, just to the east of the old tramway.

There is a bridge (12¼ mi) across the thoroughfare between Round Pond and Churchill Lake, and 6½ miles beyond is Churchill Dam (18¾ mi).

Enough gates at Churchill Dam are usually kept open in the daytime to provide a medium water level for Chase

Rapids. Usually this means two gates open when the lake is high, more when it is low. The rapids at the beginning are easy. After about a mile, you come upon the most difficult drop, still only Class II, at a point where the river takes a turn to the right. It is a good idea to scout these rapids, because you cannot see them well as you approach the turn. Shortly beyond, the river widens out and gets shallow. This is a section for which medium water is not quite enough. After that, easy rapids and quickwater continue for most of the remaining distance to Umsaskis Lake (27¼ mi).

The next 9¾ miles up Umsaskis and Long lakes and beyond are flat. At the north end of Harvey Pond, there are some minor rapids as you approach Long Lake Dam. They become flooded out in high water. Just beyond is Long Lake Dam (37½ mi), which is washed out. It can be run in high water, but in medium water you may hit old spikes. **Caution:** Not only have canoes been ripped open, but canoeists have also been injured.

Long Lake Dam—Saint John River   44¼ miles

Lake, Quickwater, Class I–II
  High and medium water: *mid-May through July*
  Low water: *wading and dragging in places*
  Points of interest: Recent scars on the trees along the
        riverbank above Allagash Falls, the result of
        the severe ice-out, May 1974. The falls
        apparently broke up the large blocks of ice.
        Round Pond Firetower: 2-mile trail begins at
        site of forest service camp, ½ mile north of
        Jalbert's Camp on Round Pond.
  USGS: Umsaskis Lake 15, Round Pond 15,
        Allagash Falls 15, Allagash 15
  Portage: 30 mi   R   **Allagash Falls**   150 yds
  Campsites: See map issued by Allagash
        Wilderness Waterway.

In a dry season, you should not have any illusions that the water level of the Lower Allagash will be similar to that in Chase Rapids. The flow from Churchill Dam, where all but the fish ladder may be closed at night, is, by itself, not sufficient to provide good canoeing farther downstream, where the riverbed is much wider. The depth of the water below Long Lake depends a great deal on the contributions of all the small streams along the way. If they are low, you will have to pick your channels carefully, and occasionally you will have to walk your canoe down.

Below Long Lake Dam, intermittent riffles continue for 9¾ miles to Round Pond. After the outlet of Round Pond (11¼ mi), there is more of the same, with riffles and quick-water alternating for 18¾ miles to Allagash Falls (30 mi). The only long stretch of flatwater is Musquacook Dead-water, which begins a little before the mouth of Musqua-cook Stream (15¾ mi) and extends for about 2 miles north of it. There is a Waterway Ranger Station in the field at Michaud Farm (26¾ mi), beside a wide bend in the river to the right.

Allagash Falls (30 mi) is 3¼ miles below Michaud Farm. **Caution!** You should stop at the portage on the right bank above the rapids that precede the falls.

Below the falls, the river continues much as it does above for the remaining 14 miles to Allagash Village. The only rough water to speak of begins 7½ miles below the falls at Twin Brook Rapids (37½ mi). These are Class II, ½ mile long.

In Allagash Village you can take out on the left just above the ME-161 bridge (44 mi), or a little way below on the right where the Allagash meets the Saint John (44¼ mi).

CHEMQUASABAMTICOOK STREAM

This stream flows north from the lake of the same name, known also as Ross Lake. The latter has a large surface area, a factor that contributes to a relatively steady flow in Chemquasabamticook (pronounced 'se-bém-sicook') Stream, particularly above Clayton Lake. Nonetheless, this river requires the high water of May and early June, because above Clayton Lake there is a section of over a mile in length with a gradient of 40 feet per mile that requires a good flow. The drop in this section is a steady one, and there are no large rocks in the riverbed, so the rapids are Class II.

Seventeen miles of the river, over half of it, are in rapids, all relatively easy, with the most difficult being below Clay-ton Lake. It is a very scenic, semi-wilderness trip that can be done in a little over half a day in high water.

Chemquasabamticook Stream joins the Allagash Wilderness Waterway at Long Lake 4½ miles north of the American Realty Road, from which Ross Lake can be reached. For those continuing down the Allagash, it is 47¼ miles to the Saint John River, in which case the most practical access to Ross Lake may be via floatplane.

Ross Lake—Long Lake   27 miles

Lakes, Flatwater, Class I-II
  High water only: *mid-May to early June*
  Wild
         USGS: Clayton Lake 15, Umsaskis Lake 15
  Campsites: Ross Lake (NE shore)   NMW $ car

The first 3½ miles below Ross Lake are easy rapids, which begin to slacken at a bridge. Then, for 1½ miles, there is a deadwater, in which there are two dry-ki dams; the first must be lifted over, but the second may be paddled around on the left. The flatwater ends (5 mi), the current picks up, and the river drops steadily for 4 miles to an old logging camp left (9 mi) where the current slackens. After 4 miles of meandering, the stream opens into Clayton Lake (13 mi). It is about 1 mile across the lake to the outlet (14 mi).

Below Clayton Lake the stream drops steadily for 9½ miles, providing good Class II whitewater. The river gradually becames shallower and wider until it reaches slackwater (23½ mi). After 3½ miles of flatwater, it ends at Long Lake (27 mi). To the north, 3 miles, is Long Lake Dam (30 mi).

MUSQUACOOK STREAM

Musquacook Stream flows north from a series of lakes east of the Allagash River, joining the latter 4½ miles below Round Pond (T13 R12). In the spring when the water is high, it offers many miles of enjoyable whitewater up to Class III. The trip from Fifth Musquacook Lake to Allagash village, a total of 53½ miles, can be done in 3 days.

The stream begins at Clear Lake, an appropriately named body of water that has no tributaries to bring in the organic matter that colors most of Maine's canoeable waters. It is hard to get to since the logging roads to it are not generally open to the public. Thus, a floatplane is the only practical access. The mile from Clear Lake to Fifth Musquacook Lake is a hard one, requiring portaging (including bushwhacking) into and out of a deadwater between the two lakes.

The remainder of the stream from Fifth Musquacook Lake makes an excellent trip of lakes and rapids for 25¼ miles to the Allagash River. Fifth is not accessible by road, but Second can be reached at the campground on the American Realty Road.

Fifth—Second Musquacook Lake   7 miles

Lakes, Quickwater, Class I–II
> High water: *mid-May to early June*
> Wild
>> USGS: Musquacook Lakes 15
> Portages: 4 mi   L   **Fourth Musquacook Lake Outlet**
>   5¼ mi L   **Musquacook Dam**   ¾ mi

Fifth Musquacook Lake is a horseshoe-shaped lake 2¼ miles long, whose only access is via floatplane. The ½-mile long stream from the outlet is wide and deep when the water is high, but narrow and difficult when low. There is a 3½-mile paddle on Fourth Musquacook Lake to its outlet, which is clogged with dry-ki, requiring a short carry left. The 1-mile run to Third Lake (5 mi) is a fast run of easy Class II rapids.

It is ½ mile across Third Lake to the outlet, where the dam is washed out and easily run in high water. The 1½ miles of stream to Second Musquacook Lake (7 mi) is Class I and II. Just before Second Lake, the American Realty Road crosses the stream.

Second Musquacook Lake—
Allagash River   18¼ miles

Lakes, Flatwater, Class I–III
  Wild
        USGS: Musquacook Lakes 15, Allagash Falls
              15
1 long portage
  Campsites: (0) mi   R   **Squirrel Pocket**   NMW $
                             car
              5¼ mi   L   **Musquacook Dam**
                             NMW $

The washed-out dam at the end of first Musquacook
Lake (5¼ mi) is followed by Horse Race Rapids, which are
extremely rough. A portage leads through the campsite left
to an old tote road that follows the stream for ¾ mile to
where you can put in. There may still be a deadfall across
the river a short distance farther down, in which case you
should let down to it, and then portage or lift over it.

Below the portage the gradient lessens, and there follow
about 2½ miles of flatwater to Lower Horse Race Rapids (9¼
mi), which are Class III and can be heard as you approach
them. A loaded canoe may have to be lined in a few places.
The remaining 8½ miles to the Allagash River at Musquacook Deadwater are all rapid, Class I and II.

CHAPTER 6

Saint John Watershed

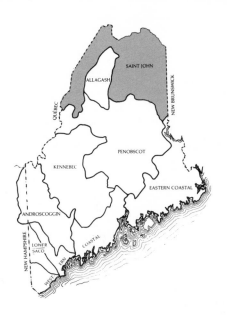

SAINT JOHN WATERSHED

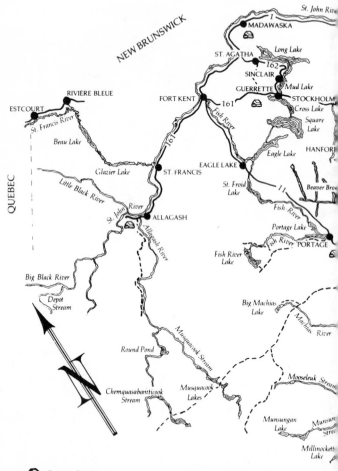

Ranger Stations

SCALE IN MILES
0 1 2 3 4 5 6 7 8 9

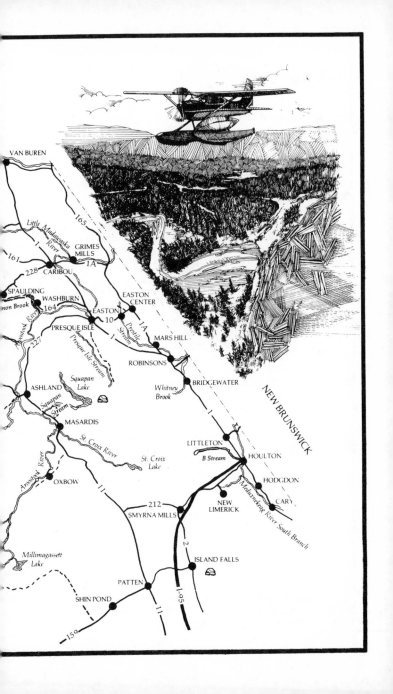

SAINT JOHN RIVER

The Saint John River flows from a series of ponds just north of the headwaters of the Penobscot River in northwestern Maine and runs parallel to the Quebec boundary for many miles until it turns east and, at Saint Francis, forms the northern boundary of Maine as far east as Hamlin. The river was named by Pierre de Guast and Samuel de Champlain, who sailed into the mouth on June 24, 1604, the feast day of Saint John the Baptist.

From Fourth Saint John Pond to the ME-161 bridge in Dickey, the Saint John River flows for 128½ miles through an extensive semi-wilderness area that has no equal east of the Mississippi. It is a commercial forest owned by many landowners who manage the area for the production of lumber and pulpwood and for recreational use. There are no public roads, although most of the privately owned and maintained logging roads are open to the public. Some may be closed to recreational traffic during active harvesting operations.

Below Baker Lake, the Upper Saint John has an unusually even gradient, and there are no portages for almost 200 miles. The portion above Dickey is wild, with remarkably few twentieth century infringements, and for many miles below it flows through an attractive rural valley.

The best section for running rapids is between Fourth Saint John Pond and Baker Lake, but it must be run early, for the water level drops rapidly as summer approaches. Below Baker Lake the river is passable through June, but only when the rainfall is above normal is it canoeable after the first week in July. Since there are few lakes and ponds in its headwaters, the level of the river is remarkably responsive to rainfall, or the lack of it, and a stick driven into the bank at the water line will frequently show an appreciable change in the water level overnight.

In the high water of mid-May, you could conceivably canoe from Fourth Saint John Pond to Allagash, 131¾ miles, in five days. By late June, the reduced flow would probably make it necessary to take six days to cover the 105¼ miles from Baker Lake to Allagash, since the current is not as strong and the shallow sections above Big Black River require more careful selection of channels.

Above Baker Lake, the paddler must be capable and alert to unexpected blowdowns and other low-lying obstructions. For 12 miles below the Fifth Saint John Dam, the current is fast, with many continuous, though easy, rapids. After Baker Lake, the river is wider and the gradient is less. The only dangerous drops are at Big Black Rapids and at Big Rapids. A good Class II paddler should be able to run the river with competence and style, provided he or she can accurately measure his or her ability when it comes time to decide whether or not to run the two difficult rapids.

You can drive to Baker Lake from Saint Aurelie, Quebec, and farther downstream the river can be reached from Ashland or Daaquam, Quebec over the American Realty Road. The only practical way to reach Fourth Saint John Pond is via floatplane. Parties also frequently fly into Baker Lake. Planes can land on the river itself at Priestly Deadwater and just above the village of Saint Francis. Contact North Maine Woods (see Introduction) for current information on access to and use of the privately owned woodlands of the area.

Many years ago the Saint John was reached by traveling up the North Branch of the Penobscot past Big Bog to a canal that led up to Fifth Saint John Pond. Today, the canal has very little water in it, and it is so overgrown that it is completely impassable.

The river itself is now less a center of activity than it used to be when logs were driven down in the spring and farms along the way helped supply food and fodder for the loggers and their animals. Today, the abandoned fields at Seven Islands, Simmons Farm, and Castonia Farm are in a state of transition from field to forest, and as such they provide excellent habitats for the wildlife of the region. The old implements rusting in the field at Seven Island become hidden in the tall grass by late June, leaving scant reminder that here was a large community at the place where the old California Road forded the Saint John.

Across Nine Mile Brook from the ranger station are a few remains of a logging camp. Helen Hamlin's book, *Nine Mile Bridge* (W. W. Norton, 1945, out of print) gives a picture of life here and elsewhere in the Maine woods in about the late 1930s.

Springs

Since the water in the Saint John River tends to be muddy in high water, and warm and off-color in lower water, canoeists may wish to carry extra containers for drinking water to fill at springs.

Baker Lake: East on the access road from St. Aurelie 1½ miles on the left.

Knowles Brook: On the same side of the river 100 yards upstream, best reached by canoe as it spills directly into the river.

American Realty Road: A 5-minute walk east on the road.

Big Black River: Upstream on Big Black River on the point ¼ mile above confluence.

Where springs are not available, the very small side streams may be used as a water source.

American Realty Road—Allagash   71¾ miles

Quickwater, Class I–III
  High water: *fast and easy except for 2 rapids, mid-May to early June*
  Medium water: *shallow rapids, some are scratchy, mid-June to early July*
  Wild
  Points of interest: Abandoned logging camp at Nine Mile Brook; abandoned farms at Seven Islands, Simmons Farm
      USGS: Beaver Pond 15, Clayton Lake 15, Seven Islands 15, Round Pond 15, Rocky Mountain 15, Allagash 15

Campsites:				
1½ mi	R	**Red Pine Grove**		
		(poor) NMW $ car		
11½ mi	L	**Nine Mile Brook**		
		(poor) NMW $ car		
20½ mi	L	**Seven Island** NMW $		
25 mi	L	**Priestly Bridge** (poor)		
		NMW $ car		
30¾ mi	L	**Simmons Farm** NMW $		
40¾ mi	L	**Big Black River** NMW $		
55½ mi	L	**Ouellette Stream** NMW		
		$ car		
57½ mi	L	**Fox Brook** NMW $		
72 mi	R	**Mouth of Allegash**		
		(north end)		

For the next 25 miles, from the American Realty Road to Priestly Bridge, the river has good current with occasional, easy rapids. In medium water the river is shallow in many places, requiring that you choose your route carefully. Occasionally it will be necessary to walk your canoe down. In high water, travel is almost effortless. Nine Mile Bridge (11¼ mi), closed for many years, finally succumbed to ice-out in May 1970. The western section was dragged downstream for 3 miles before it became lodged in the riverbed. The remains of both spans have since been removed.

One mile below Priestly Bridge is Priestly Deadwater (26 mi), where floatplanes sometimes land. The river continues for another 12¾ miles to Big Black Rapids, with good current most of the way. Priestly Rapids, shown on the Seven Island quadrangle, will very likely be passed unnoticed in high water. In medium water, it is Class I. Simmons Farm (30¾ mi) is shown on the Round Pond quadrangle as BM 835. Below the farm there is a shallow section for several miles, and there are two small rapids (34¾ mi, 37¼ mi) located at the two right-hand turns that precede Big Black Rapids.

Caution! Big Black Rapids are 1 mile long and Class III. They begin (38¾ mi) where the river bends sharply to the left and since you cannot see them as you approach the turn, it is advisable to stop on the left shore and look them over. They are the most difficult rapids between Baker Lake and Big Rapids farther on, and because of their remoteness, they deserve a great deal of respect. Below them, the Big Black River (40¾ mi) enters on the left after 1 mile of mostly smoothwater.

The Saint John, swelled by the flow from the Big Black, continues for the next 24 miles with a good steady current, broken several times by short drops that are Class I in high water and somewhat more difficult when the river is lower. Then you reach the beginning of the Big Rapids (64¾ mi), located below a sweeping left turn in the river with a field on the left, where there is also a road if you wish to portage. **Caution!** Big Rapids is 2 miles long, Class III, and dangerous in high water. It should be scouted from the left bank. Most of the rapids on the Saint John get easier as the water rises because they are flooded out, but this one does not because it has many large boulders, which produce heavy waves.

Below Big Rapids the river flattens out, passes under the ME-161 bridge (68¼ mi) in Dickey, and 3½ miles farther on the Allagash River enters on the right (71¾ mi).

Allagash—Fort Kent   28 miles

Quickwater, Class I–II
High or medium water: *mid-May to mid-July*
Rural
    USGS: Allagash 15, Saint Francis 15, Eagle
        Lake 15, *Fort Kent 15*

Campsites:				
	5 mi	R	**Cross Rock**	private $ car
	8½ mi	R	**Rankin Rapids**	(not easily recognized, dirt road leads up from river) public, car
	11 mi	R	**Pelletier** private $ car	

**numerous islands below
Saint Francis**

For the first 11½ miles, the north bank of the Saint John
is wild and the south bank has a few houses and fields along
the highway, which follows the river closely some of the
way. Below Saint Francis, it flows between Maine and New
Brunswick in a rural setting all the way to Fort Kent. This
section can be run easily in less than a day except when the
water is low.

The drinkability of the water below Allagash is question-
able, but above Saint Francis there are several small streams
that empty into the river along the north bank.

The current is strong for 11½ miles to the Saint Francis
River, which enters on the left. There are three short rapids,
Cross Rock (4¼ mi), Golden (5½ mi), and Rankin (8¾ mi).
They rate up to Class II in medium water, but they are
largely flooded out when the river is high. If you are going
to be picked up by floatplane in Saint Francis, stop at least
a mile above the town so as to avoid having to paddle back
upstream to the plane.

Below the Saint Francis River (11½ mi), the Saint John is
broader and flatter, but with good current, for the rest of
the way to Fort Kent, where the Fish River enters on the
right (28 mi).

Fort Kent—Madawaska-Edmunston   19 miles

Quickwater, Class I
  Anytime
  Rural
      USGS: Fort Kent 15, Grand Isle 15

At normal water levels this stretch is all good current with one easy rapid, the Fish River Rapid, 2 miles below Fort Kent. In low water there are numerous gravel bars through which one must pick one's way, choosing the deeper channels. The low water also causes many rips and short easy rapids. The water is clear and the trip a pleasant one. Probably the best and easiest place to take out is at one of the docks on the left, Canadian, bank about 2 miles above Edmundston.

Madawaska-Edmundston—Hamlin   35 miles

      USGS: Grand Isle 15, Stockholm 15, Van
            Buren 15

In the past this section of the river has suffered from excessive industrial pollution in addition to technical difficulties in the first few miles.

The New Brunswick Bureau of Tourism has been attempting to start inn-to-inn canoeing on the lower Saint John below Frederickton, which is mostly flatwater through mostly rural countryside.

NORTHWEST BRANCH via DAAQUAM RIVER

The Northwest Branch rises in Beaver Pond near Lac Frontière and flows south to Powers Gore (T11 R17), where it is joined by the Daaquam River, a stream running north, parallel to the Southwest Branch, until it turns east and crosses the boundary to join up with the Northwest Branch. The American Realty Road, which comes in from Daaquam, Quebec, follows the Daaquam River and the Northwest Branch, and then crosses the main Saint John River several miles below. The customs stations on this road are not open nights or Sundays. If the water is high enough one can canoe down the Daaquam River and Northwest Branch practically from the border.

Daaquam—Southwest Branch 8½ miles

Quickwater, Class I
 High water
 Wild
     USGS: Beaver Pond 15

Put in on the Daaquam River at Daaquam Forest Service Headquarters. It is nearly 2½ miles down the Daaquam River to the junction with the Northwest Branch, where it becomes a broader stream, and then 6 miles to the junction with the main stream. In this distance the river is mostly smooth. Below the confluence with the Southwest Branch, there is a large boulder patch followed by riffles and good current for the remaining 4½ miles to the American Realty Road.

SOUTHWEST BRANCH via BAKER BRANCH

This is a common approach to the Saint John River early in the season, giving the longest continuous run.

Fourth Saint John Pond—Baker Lake Outlet
Baker Branch   26½ miles

Lakes, Flatwater, Class I-II
High water only above Fifth Saint John Pond: *mid- to late May*
High water below Fifth Saint John Pond: *mid-May to early June*
Wild

USGS: Saint John Pond 15, Baker Lake 15

Campsites:	0 mi		**Fourth Saint John Pond Outlet** (small) permit
	(6) mi	L	**Fifth Saint John Pond** (northwest end, by canal) NMW $
	7 mi	R	**Fifth Saint John dam,** poor permit NMW $
	24 mi	R	**Baker Lake** (southeast end, right shore) NMW $
	26½ mi		**Baker Lake Outlet** NMW $ car

Here the Baker Branch is still small enough to be crowded in places by alders and blocked by dry-ki dams. Viewed from the air, the sides of the river below Fifth Saint John Pond seem heavily logged, but you are not aware of this as you canoe down the river, for the forests lining the banks appear thick and deep.

The old dam (0 mi) in Fourth Saint John Pond is washed-out and runnable. Below, the river consists mostly of fast, shallow rips with no big rocks. About halfway down there is a dry-ki dam in an alder swamp. In 3½ miles it empties into Fifth Saint John Pond.

It is 3½ miles down Fifth Saint John Pond to the dam (7 mi), which is presently washing out.

Below the Fifth Saint John Dam, the first 4 miles are the most difficult. The river runs fast with sharp turns that require quick maneuvers to avoid being swept against the outside of the turns. The rapids are not difficult, but they are more or less continuous. In this section there are two old logging bridges, which may block the river, depending on the water level, and two dry-ki dams that require short portages, first on the left and then on the right. Other than a possible log or fallen tree, there are no other obstacles.

For the next 8 miles the current remains strong, with rapids most of the way to a large deadwater (19 mi). After 4½ miles of flatwater, the river empties into Baker Lake (23½ mi). It is a 3-mile paddle down the lake to the MFS camp at the outlet (26½ mi).

Baker Lake—American Realty Road
Baker and Southwest Branches   33¾ miles

Flatwater, **Class I–II**
  High water: *fast and easy, mid-May to early June*
  Medium water: *shallow rapids; likely to be scratchy, mid- to late June*
  Wild
    USGS: Baker Lake 15, Beaver Pond 15
  Campsites: 9¼ mi   R   **Baker Branch**   NMW $
               24¼ mi   R   **Knowles Brook**   NMW $
               31¾ mi   L   **below Northwest Branch** (small)   NMW $

In this section the Saint John grows to become a large river. Below Baker Lake, the Baker Branch is still small enough so that the forest grows right to the water's edge. As you approach the confluence with the Southwest Branch, you can begin to see the effect of the tremendous force behind the ice as it breaks up in the spring. Where there are sharp bends and a strong current, the ice has scraped and sometimes broken off the trees on the outside of the turns. Continuing downstream, the size of the river increases, and the scouring of the riverbank is such a regular occurrence during ice-out that no trees at all grow near the water except alders, which are relatively unaffected as the ice rides over them.

There are numerous easy rapids for 5¼ miles to Turner Brook, which enters on the right. For the next 8 miles the river is mostly flat, and partway along you pass the Baker

Branch Campsite (9¼ mi) located on the right bank a little south of the forest service camp marked on the Baker Lake quadrangle. Approximately 14 miles north of Baker Lake the current picks up, and in the remaining 4 miles the rapids increase to Class II as you approach the southwest Branch.

Below the confluence with the Southwest Branch (18¾ mi), there are 10½ miles of smooth and quickwater all the way to the Northwest Branch. Halfway down on the right is the Knowles Brook Campsite (24¼ mi). There are a few riffles as you approach the Northwest Branch.

After the confluence with the Northwest Branch (29¼ mi) there is a large boulder patch followed by riffles and good current to the American Realty Road (33¾ mi).

BIG BLACK RIVER

In many respects the Big Black River resembles the Saint John. It is a large river with alternating sections of slow and fast-moving current. The rapids are generally shallow, and they tend to get easier as the water gets higher, although a few may generate large waves at times of heavy run-off. The water level is very responsive to rainfall, and the river is likely to show daily fluctuations that can be easily measured.

Below the mouth of Depot Stream and above the bridge near the top of Connors Sluice there are a few cabins, but the remainder of the river is very wild. Many of the banks are heavily forested, but Ninemile Deadwater, which used to be flooded, is bordered by extensive and open low-lying areas. At the end of Connors Sluice there is a large meadow that is similar to the one at Seven Islands on the Saint John River.

The Big Black River can be reached by road most easily from Quebec. At Saint Pamphile, a North Maine Woods road crosses the border and soon divides. The road to the left crosses Shields Branch, which provides a flatwater access to Ninemile Deadwater that is used by fishermen in motorboats. Straight ahead leads to the bridge near the top of Connors Sluice. The one to the right crosses the river close to the border. The river from that point to Depot Stream is mostly flat.

An alternative means of access is to fly into Depot

Lake, provided the water is high enough to negotiate Depot Stream.

Depot Stream—Saint John River   22½ miles

Flatwater, Quickwater, Class I, II
   High water: *fast and easy, mid-May to early June*
   Medium water: *shallow rapids likely to be scratchy by mid-June*
   Wild
   Points of interest: Abandoned log structures along north shore of Ninemile Deadwater in T14 R14 at two sharp bends where the river swings to the right
         USGS: Seven Islands 15, Round Pond 15
   Campsites: 5 mi   R   **Connors Sluice**
                                   (meadow at end)   NMW
                                   $
                     10¼ mi   L   **Ninemile Deadwater**
                                   (1st right turn in T14
                                   R14)   NMW $
                     13¾ mi   L   **Big Black Dam**   NMW $
                     17½ mi   L   **Fivemile Brook**   NMW $
                     20½ mi   L   **Twomile Brook**   NMW $

Below the mouth of Depot Stream there are 2½ miles of flatwater to the beginning of Connors Sluice, a fast and easy 2½ mile Class II run that ends at the beginning of Ninemile Deadwater (5 mi). In 2¾ miles Shields Branch enters on the left.

Ninemile Deadwater extends all the way to Big Black Dam (13¾ mi). The washed-out dam is runnable. The remaining 8¾ miles to the Saint John River are a mixture of intermittent Class I and II rapids and quickwater, with the most difficult sections being just above and below Fivemile Brook (17½ mi).

DEPOT STREAM

Depot Stream is a tributary of the Big Black River. Depot Lake, below which the stream is runnable, is located close to the Quebec border; it is a very remote body of water. A trip from the lake to Allagash is 72½ miles. There are no portages, and the hardest rapids, other than Big Rapids on the Saint John, are Class II.

Depot Lake cannot be reached by road, but it is possible to drive from Quebec to at least 3 places along the upper half of the stream.

Depot Lake—Big Black River   19 miles

Flatwater, Quickwater, Class I, II
  High water: *mid-May to early June*
  Wild
    USGS: Depot Lake 15, Seven Islands 15
  Campsite: 8 mi   L   **Old MFS camp**   (grassy
                                bluff)   NMW $

From the outlet at the north end of Depot Lake there are 3 miles of flatwater to a logging bridge, followed by ¾ mile of easy Class II rapids that lead to another flatwater section 4 miles long. Much of this way is through alder swamps and extensive low-lying areas where there are occasional views of Depot Mountain up ahead.

As it passes around the north side of the mountain, the stream enters a narrow and densely wooded valley and Class II rapids begin (7¾ mi). In ½ mile there is a bridge where the road to the firetower crosses. (To reach tower follow the road to the south (right). Keep left at the fork. Distance is 1 mile.)

Rapids and quickwater continue for the next 7 miles to the bridge on the logging road from Saint Pamphile to Allagash (15¼ mi). There is quickwater for most of the remaining distance to the Big Black River (19 mi).

SHIELDS BRANCH

Shields Branch rises in Quebec and flows across the international boundary into Maine in T15 R15. Although the upper part is canoeable, it has no access. The road from Saint Pamphile mentioned in the description of the Big Black River crosses Shields Branch about 3 miles above the junction of that stream with the Big Black and provides an opportunity to reach the latter below Connors Sluice. The 3 miles of meandering river provide an easy and pleasant paddle through wild country.

LITTLE BLACK RIVER

The Little Black River rises in Quebec and flows in a southeasterly direction to the Saint John River, which it reaches at Dickey. It is canoeable from the international boundary all the way to the Saint John. The river is most easily reached by a private road of the Seven Islands Land Company, which runs south from Estcourt in Quebec. This road reaches the river about 2 miles from the international boundary. There is a public campground here, and this makes a good point to start the trip. The trip is fastwater most of the way, with two rapids, both usually runnable.

T19 R12 bridge—Saint John River   27 miles

Quickwater
  High water: *spring or after heavy rain*
  Wild
        USGS: Rocky Brook 15, Rocky Mountain 15,
                Allagash 15

One can put in at the campground on the private road at the bridge over the river in T19 R12. From here there is a good current to the forks where the West Branch comes in. There is a very fast rapid here, about ⅝ mile long. Below this rapid the river has a good current for the 9 miles to Boat Landing Camp at the end of a spur of the same private road from Estcourt. There is a public campground here on the north bank of the river. Below Boat Landing Camp, the river meanders for 10 miles through a boggy section, although it does have well-defined banks. About 1 mile more below this section, Johnson Brook enters on the right and there is a public campground here near the road that comes upstream from the mouth. From Johnson Brook there are 5 more miles of fastwater to the mouth, with a falls about halfway down. This is usually runnable but should be looked over first. In high water a carry will be necessary. The carry trail is on the left. From here to the Saint John

River it is all easy but with a good current. Almost directly across the Saint John is the town of Dickey, where a paddler may take out on ME-161 if he or she does not wish to run down that stream.

SAINT FRANCIS RIVER

The Saint Francis River rises near Whitworth, Quebec, and flows southeast into Pohenegamook Lake. Upon its exit from this lake it becomes the international boundary for the rest of its course to its confluence with the Saint John River. It flows eastward on a very meandering course to Blue River, Quebec, where it turns almost due south for a number of miles, until finally just above Glazier Lake it flows southeast toward the Saint John. The water holds up well because of the many lakes, so that from Blue River down, at least, it may be run at any time. The best approach is from the Maine side of the river.

Estcourt—Blue River   24 miles

Quickwater, Class I
  Medium or high water: *spring and early summer*
  Wild
      USGS: Beau Lake 15

This section is very winding. Although the water holds up well, it may become quite scratchy in a dry summer, so the best time for running is probably spring and early summer. There are no serious rapids and few obstructions, but some of the former dams, which have been largely washed out, may require a lift over or lining down. At Blue River the Riviere Blue enters from the north, adding considerably to the volume.

Blue River—Beau Lake   10 miles

Quickwater
  Anytime
  Wild, Rural
      USGS: Allagash 15, Beau Lake 15

This portion of river carries somewhat more water and can usually be run at any time. It has many meanders but no rapids of any consequence. It provides a pleasant easy paddle with forested banks on the Maine shore; most of the time, there are fields on the Canadian side.

Beau Lake—Saint John River   22 miles

Lakes, Quickwater, Class I, III
  Anytime
  Wild
      USGS: Saint Francis

This is probably the most interesting stretch of the whole river, as it comprises lake, rapid and fastwater paddling. Like the Allagash, which it resembles to some extent, it can be run at any time. The road running south from Blue River ends at Beau Lake, but it gives the canoeist a chance to select this section without the necessity of running the 10 miles down from Blue River if he or she wishes. One can put in at the upper end of Beau Lake and paddle down the 6 miles to the narrows at the south end, after which there is 1 mile more of wide, lake-like stream. Halfway down one passes the Quebec-New Brunswick boundary on the left, before the river becomes narrow for another 1 mile, with a small pond partway down. The river then enters Cross Lake, down which one paddles less than ¼ mile to the outlet on the east shore, or all the way down the lake, ½ mile to the south end, where there is a ½-mile carry to the upper MacPherson Pond. If the canoeist selects to run the ¾ mile of river through the Cross Lake Rapid (Class III) to the upper MacPherson Pond, he or she should look over the rapid, about ⅜ mile long, before running. The water is heavy and in high water can be dangerous or impossible for a loaded canoe. The ½-mile carry from the south end of Cross Lake to Upper MacPherson Pond should be used in such a case and would be preferable for less experienced canoeists. Upper MacPherson Pond is ¾ mile long. At its southeast corner the river turns southeastward and in 300 yards flows into Lower MacPherson Pond, down which one paddles 1 mile to the short stretch of river leading into Glazier Lake.

This lake is 4 miles long to the Narrows, then ½ mile more to the outlet. From the outlet of Glazier Lake there are 2 miles of fastwater to Falls Brook. Here, where the brook enters on the right at a sharp left turn, is the ⅜ mile-long Falls Brook Rapid. This can be a difficult spot and should be looked over, especially at high water. In another mile, after the river has made a sharp right turn, one comes to the Horseback Rapids. These are composed of two short but sharp drops and will well repay being looked over before running. There are a number of twists and turns in the next 2 miles to the MacDonald Rock Rapid. This is marked by a large boulder standing in midstream. It is about ⅜ mile long and has high waves in high water. In low water there are many rocks and fast canoe handling is necessary. From here it is about 1 mile to the Saint John River, which is reached opposite the town of Saint Francis, Maine.

FISH RIVER

The Fish River rises from the confluence of a number of brooks in Township 13 Range 8, 2 miles south of Fish River Lake, but for all practical purposes the lake may be considered as its source. From here it flows eastward to Portage Lake, on which the town of Portage is located. It then takes a northerly route to flow into the Saint John River at Fort Kent. The upper headwaters are in wild country, and must be canoed early in the season when the water is fairly high. Except for wet seasons summer travel may be impractical. From Portage Lake down, the stream is larger and much of it is composed of lakes, so that travel at most seasons is practical. Many canoeists combine it with the lakes of the East Branch, which joins it at Eagle Lake, to make a long trip.

Fish River Source—Portage   24 miles

Lake, Flatwater, Quickwater
  High water
  Wild
        USGS: Fish River Lake 15, Winterville 15,
               Portage 15
    Portage: 8½ mi   **Fish River Falls**

A private road from Portage crosses the Fish River practically at its source above Fish River Lake. A branch of this road, which swings north and down the Red River to Eagle Lake, has a side road, which reaches Fish River Lake at the outlet. One can also fly in to the lake, where there are two sporting camps. If one puts in at the road crossing above the lake, there are 2 miles of easy travel with a good current north to the lake. There is a sporting camp ¼ mile away from the inlet on the west shore and another halfway down the lake on the east shore. It is 3 miles down the lake to the game warden's camp at the outlet at the northeast corner.

From the lake, there is ½ mile of river to Round Pond, where there is a public landing and campsite; then it is ½ mile across the pond. Just below the pond, the Fish River Falls are located, and a short portage is necessary. Fish River Falls may be run, but it is a heavy Class III + section. The next 2½ miles are quickwater, with minor rips. The river then becomes smoothwater through marshland fringed by forest, good moose country, for most of the 10 miles to Portage Lake. It is then 3 miles down the lake to the village of Portage at its southeast corner.

Portage Lake—Eagle Lake   24 miles

Lakes, Flatwater
  Anytime
  Forested, Cottages
    USGS: Portage 15, Eagle Lake 15

This section is all smoothwater or lakes. It is often canoed in the reverse direction by those starting at the head of the East Branch chain of lakes. From Portage it is 4 miles down the lake to the outlet at the north end. For the next 10 miles to Saint Froid Lake the Fish River offers smooth paddling through boggy woodlands. There is an excellent beach as you enter Saint Froid Lake.

Saint Froid Lake is 7 miles long and less than 1 mile wide. About 4 miles down the Red River enters on the left. In another 3 miles the foot of the lake is reached, and here the 3-mile long Nadeau Thoroughfare leads to Eagle Lake, where this route meets that coming down the East Branch.

There is a good campsite across Eagle Lake from the inlet, at Cozy Point on the northeast shore just east of Oak Point.

Eagle Lake—Saint John River   20½ miles

Lakes, Flatwater, Quickwater, Class I, II
   Medium water
   Forested, Rural
      USGS: Eagle Lake 15, Fort Kent 15
   Portage: 16 mi R **Fish River Falls**   20 yds

From the inlet of Eagle Lake to Eagle Lake village is less than 2 miles. Eagle Lake is a very beautiful, narrow lake. It is some 6 miles from Eagle Lake village to the outlet near Wallagrass. Below there are 4 miles of smooth river to Soldier Pond, where there is a bridge (10 mi). Here the quickwater begins.

A mile below Soldier there is a 4-foot drop, which may be run on the right (Class II) or lifted over on the left. There is quickwater for the next 5 miles to the second Fish River Falls, a Class V drop. **Caution!** Stop well above the falls on the right and line the canoe down to the carry trail, starting from an eddy at the lip of the falls on the right. If the falls is run, it must be run on the right over the drop, because the easy-looking left chute has many very sharp rocks and cross-currents.

Below the falls it is 2½ miles to a railroad bridge; then comes Martins Rapid, a Class II drop 200 feet long, which must be run on the right. In another ½ mile, below the road bridge, the river splits. To the right is easy Class I, but to the left is a Class II + drop, which may be re-run because of the nice pool at the bottom. The remainder of the way is Class I to the Fort Kent Blockhouse, an excellent take-out just above the confluence with the Saint John.

FISH RIVER, East Branch

The East Branch of the Fish River is little more than a chain of lakes, on which there are many cottages and year-round homes. The trip comprises the major part of what is commonly called the Fish River Lake Trip. The northern end of Long Lake, the highest in the chain, is in the towns of Saint Agatha and Madawaska, only a few miles from the Saint John River. Most of the lakes run in a northwest-southeast direction, with the short bits of connecting river cutting at right angles to this trend, so that you travel in a zigzag route, which finally brings you to Eagle Lake considerably to the south. Here you meet the main stream of the Fish River and can either go up that stream to its headwaters or down it to the Saint John River at Fort Kent, only a few miles from where you started. This trip is one of the best known in northern Maine and can be done by novice canoeists, if they are careful.

Saint Agatha—Eagle Lake   28 miles

Lakes
   Anytime
   Forested, Cottages
      USGS: Frenchville 15, Square Lake 15,
            Stockholm 15, Eagle Lake 15

The usual starting point is Saint Agatha at the northwest end of Long Lake. Although this lake is 10 miles long, the canoeist wishing to make a fast trip will turn into the east arm in 6 miles and follow this 3 miles to the town of Sinclair at the west end. There are three state campsites on the lake: one at Berube Point on the east shore opposite the west arm, one on the southeast shore at the mouth of Mud Brook, and one on the south shore of the west arm 2½ miles from Sinclair. At Sinclair there is a short ½-mile passage through the thoroughfare to Mud Lake, sometimes called Salmon Lake. There is a 2-mile paddle the length of this lake. A lunch site is located on the south shore about 1½ miles down. At the southwest corner the outlet leaves. It is 1½ miles down this thoroughfare to Cross Lake, which is reached on the east shore about halfway down. The northern end of the lake has a number of cottages on both shores. The only campsite on this lake is 1 mile diagonally northwest across the lake from the inlet, at Matrimony Point. From this campground or from the inlet it is 3 miles to the outlet at the southwest corner, where a short thoroughfare 1 mile in length leads into Square Lake, which is a large lake some 7 miles long and 2 miles wide with an extensive shoal in the middle. Because of this shoal and the fact that the wind is funneled between mountains, this lake can be dangerous in the wind, which may come up very suddenly; therefore, stay close to the shore.

It is about 3 miles northwesterly across the lake to the outlet far up on the northwest shore. This is a wilder lake than Cross Lake, and many canoeists will want to spend some time on it using some of the four campsites available: one at Salmon Point on the southeast shore, one at Goddard Cove on the south shore at the mouth of Little Goddard Brook, another on the west shore at the big hill $3\frac{1}{2}$ miles south of the outlet, and another on the west shore $1\frac{1}{2}$ miles south of the outlet at Limestone Point. The thoroughfare from Square Lake to Eagle Lake is 3 miles long, with a good campsite halfway down on the north bank at the mouth of Halfway Brook. Eagle Lake is formed in the shape of an "L." The thoroughfare from Square Lake reaches the lake at the halfway point of the east-west leg on the north shore. From here it is 4 miles west to the inlet of the main stream of the Fish River 1 mile east of Eagle Lake village on the south shore. From this point one can ascend the main stream or descend to the Saint John River. There is a nice campsite on the north shore just east of Oak Point, on Cozy Point. Many canoeists may wish to spend some time on the east bay of the lake east of the inlet, and there are 3 campsites here: one on the south shore in Three Brooks Cove at the mouth of Middle Brook, one on the southeast shore 3 miles east of the thoroughfare, and another 4 miles from the thoroughfare. One can take out at Eagle Lake village or continue the trip as desired.

AROOSTOOK RIVER

The Aroostook River is formed by the union of Munsungan Stream and Millinocket Stream in the unincorporated townships north of Baxter State Park, and follows a winding course northeast to the Saint John River in New Brunswick. The first part of the river is forested and wild; the lower portion is through farmland; and the last few miles are difficult whitewater.

Pending settlement of the boundary between the United States and England, the Aroostook valley became the prey of lawless trespassers who removed large amounts of timber. The Maine legislature authorized a company of volunteers to suppress this illegal traffic. On February 8, 1839, 200 men under Captain Rines reached Masardis Stream and fell unexpectedly upon the trespassers, who offered but slight resistance. Flushed with success the company advanced to the Little Madawaska River, where they met a reverse. Captain Rines was captured and carried off to Fredericton. These events precipitated the Aroostook War, a general call to arms in which there was no loss of life, and which was finally settled by the Webster-Ashburton Treaty of 1842.

Around 1900 the Aroostook River was used to gain access to the Upper East Branch of the Penobscot River from Moose Brook, which flows into Millinocket Lake. The Aroostook was also used, as it is still by a few, to gain access to the Seboeis River and Grand Lake Seboeis, with a ¾ mile carry from the West Branch of Carry Brook. This brook flows into La Pomkeag Stream and then into the Aroostook River about 10 miles west of Oxbow.

Libby Camp—Oxbow Landing   17 miles

Quickwater, Class I
  High water: *spring recommended*
  Wild
      USGS: Millinocket Lake 15, Grand Lake
            Seboeis 15

Libby Camp is at the confluence of Millinocket Stream and Munsungan Stream, and can be reached by either. The first 7 miles to Mooseleuk Stream have a fast current with occasional riffles, then 1 mile of deadwater to La Pomkeag Stream. Then after 7½ miles of current to Baste Rips (Class II), it is 1½ miles to Oxbow Landing, where motorboats can be launched.

Oxbow Landing—Washburn   **44 miles**

Flatwater, Quickwater, Class I
  High water: *spring, fast current*
  Medium water: *summer and fall, some shallow spots*
  Forested, Towns
    USGS: Grand Lake Seboeis 15, Oxbow 15,
          Ashland 15, Presque Isle 15, Caribou
          15

After 3 miles of deadwater, the river swings north, and
the barely noticeable entrance to the Oxbow is passed on the
right. A side trip of 1 mile can be made to this overgrown
marsh. The deadwater continues 3 miles to Shepard Rips
(Class I), where there is a camp on a bluff on the left. The
river runs slowly east/north, where there is an excellent
campsite at the turn, and then east again for 8 miles to the
mouth of the Saint Croix Stream (and a good take-out just
upstream at ME-11 bridge) in Masardis (14 mi). Several
small ledges are found here. The 5 miles of slow water to
Squa Pan Brook is largely through farmland, which cannot
be seen from the river. In 5 more miles you pass the site of
an old logging bridge, and shortly after that the Machias
River (24 mi). The next mile contains some Class I rapids to
the Ashland bridge. It is another mile to the Little Machias,
and 1 mile more to Sheridan, with a railroad bridge and the
remains of an old logging dam, which can be run, lined, or
carried on the right. Six miles below is Pudding Rock, a
large rock face on the right with some ledges on the left;
there's good access to the river here. At the island before
Beaver Brook, 3 miles further, the left channel leads to a
campsite on a high bank on the left. The river winds
through islands for 2 miles to Gardiner Brook Rapids (easy
Class I). This is the end of the wilderness run, as many
camps are along the shore for the 6 miles of quickwater to
Washburn. At the railroad trestle are the remains of an old
logging dam, and then a landing and a good parking place
just above the Washburn Bridge (44 mi).

Washburn—Fort Fairfield   37 miles

Flatwater, Quickwater
  Canoeable whenever ice-free
  Rural, Towns
        USGS: Caribou 15, Presque Isle 15, Mars Hill
             15, Fort Fairfield 15
    Portage: 14 mi   e   **Caribou Dam**   ½ mi

Much of this run is through potato fields, although the
banks are often wooded. The river is swift, with many small
rips through islands to Crossville, where there is a white
church steeple on the left. The river passes under a railroad
bridge a mile below Crossville and enters Rum Rapids,
Class II in low water, but tending to wash out in higher
water. The next 7 miles to the US-1 bridge in Presque Isle
(11 mi), where Presque Isle Stream enters, has good current
and passes many islands. The 14 miles to the dam at Caribou are smooth. The carry on the right is shorter but difficult, the left is half a mile on a good road behind the power
plant. It is 5 miles to the Little Madawaska River at Grimes
Mill, and 7 miles to the ME-165 bridge at Fort Fairfield
(37 mi).

Fort Fairfield—Saint John River   11 miles

Flatwater, Class II–V
  Above 15,000 cfs—*dangerous*
  2800-5000 cfs—*best play level for all boats*
  Wild
        USGS: Fort Fairfield 15
    Portages: 4 mi   R   **Dam**
                 5 mi   **Dam**

Persons wishing to paddle this section should report to
customs, located 3 miles east of town on ME-167, and also
check the dam release for the day.
  Flatwater continues to the dam, 4 miles from Fort Fairfield, and 1 mile beyond the Canadian border. Portage
right.
  The next mile is through a canyon, Class IV–V, where the

river drops 75 feet. The canyon should be run only after complete scouting because it contains very few eddies and a 180° turn in the middle of the gorge. The last drop is the worst, where the river makes a right-angle turn against a rock wall.

Below the second dam, you enter immediately into Class II rapids for 1½ miles, to a Class III ledge with the chute on the left, and then into more Class II rapids to the Limestone River on the left. The last major rapid starts under the Trans-Canada Bridge; the size of this rapid is deceiving because of the height of the bridge, and it can easily swamp a canoe. The last 2 miles to the Saint John are flatwater.

MUNSUNGAN STREAM

In the past, the headwaters of Munsungan Stream have best been reached by floatplane, but now both the upper end of Chase Lake and the outlet of Munsungan Lake can be reached by good gravel roads.

Chase Lake—Libby Camp   16 miles

Lakes, Flatwater, Class I, II
  High water: *spring*
  Wild
        USGS: Spider Lake 15, Millinocket Lake 15

Chase Lake is 1½ miles long. The outlet is a ½-mile long shallow stream with Class I rapids. It is then 5 miles down Munsungan Lake to a broken logging dam, which can be run. There are 1½ miles of Class I rapids and ledge drops to Munsungan Falls, a heavy Class III rapid, which should be scouted from the right bank. The worst drop is around a corner and cannot be seen from the start. Just below is a new steel logging bridge.

There follows 6 miles of quickwater to a collapsing bridge, which must be carried due to low clearance, and then 3 miles of Class I rapids to Libby Camp, where Millinocket Stream joins to form the Aroostook River.

MILLINOCKET STREAM

This Millinocket Stream is the outlet of the Millinocket Lake north of Baxter State Park, and a tributary of the Aroostook River, and should not be confused with another Millinocket Stream, which is the outlet of another Millinocket Lake and a tributary of the West Branch of the Penobscot. Millinocket Lake can be reached by a short portage from a branch road from the Grand Lake Road. Inquire locally for directions.

Millinocket Lake—Libby Camp   6 miles

Lakes, Flatwater, Class I, II
  Dam-controlled: *runnable anytime*
  Wild
        USGS: Millinocket Lake 15

Portage the dam at Millinocket Lake. It is a short distance to Round Pond, with an old logging dam at the outlet. Just below is Millinocket Falls, a short Class II–III rapid, which should be scouted from the left bank. This is followed by 1½ miles of Class II rapids to Millimagassett Stream. It is possible to ascend ½ mile of stream and ½ mile of log sluice to Millimagasset Lake, which features beautiful islands and a view of Baxter Park mountains.

Below is 1½ miles of deadwater and ½ mile of Class I water to the bridge at Moosehorn Crossing, which is followed by 1 mile of quickwater to Devils Elbow, a ½ mile series of Class II ledge drops. It is then ½ mile to Libby Camp, where Munsungan Stream joins up to form the Aroostook River.

MOOSELEUK STREAM

The Mooseleuk Stream, which rises in Mooseleuk Lake just off the American Realty Road in T10 R9, is one of the major tributaries of the upper Aroostook River. The trip can make an excellent weekend in the wild. The stream is swift, and the major problem is being swept into the bushes in the many bends.

Mooseleuk Lake—old Fire Warden's camp
18 miles

Lake, Quickwater, Class I
High water: *spring*
Wild
    USGS: Mooseleuk Lake 15, Millinocket Lake
        15, Grand Lake Seboeis 15

It is a very pretty 2-mile paddle down Mooseleuk Lake to the outlet and the remains of an old logging dam. At once you enter a swift stream (Class I) with many sharp bends. At 10 miles the large, heavily used bridge from Ashland crosses just above Chandler Stream. In 2 more miles there is a sharp right bend in the stream to Boars Head Falls, where the river narrows into Class II rapids. Boars Head Falls is an excellent camping spot. It is only 3 more miles to the Aroostook River in a large deadwater just below the old fire warden's camp, which is now privately owned.

SAINT CROIX STREAM

The Saint Croix Stream rises in Saint Croix Lake in T8 R4 and flows north to the Aroostook River at Masardis. Although the Bangor and Aroostook Railroad parallels the stream, it is a very wild area, which is full of history of past logging days. The stream is a large one and drains a large swamp above the Saint Croix River, so it makes good canoeing in all but the lowest water season. The stream varies from smooth to very rough water in the middle section.

Howe Brook—Aroostook River   18 miles

Flatwater, Quickwater, Class II
High water: *difficult*
Medium water: *excellent*
Low water: *scratchy in spots*
Wild
Point of interest: Griswold, an old logging city
    USGS: Howe Brook 15, Oxbow 15

There is about 1 mile of lakelike river below the lake before you enter Saint Croix Stream. From here it is 5 miles of slow swampy going to a bridge where the water quickens, with several sets of Class II rapids and a falls, which is a Class III + stretch of water with ledges. This can be run, lined, or carried on the right side. In ½ mile Pride is reached; then there are 4 miles of Class II whitewater from Pride to Griswold (9½ mi). In Griswold are the remains of an old mill site with a very nice chute (Class II +). Below Griswold are 7 miles of flat swampy stream, until the Blackwater River enters on the right (16½ mi). Below there is a section filled with rocks, which can be hard going in low water. In another 1½ miles Masardis is reached, and the US-11 bridge, below which is the confluence with the Aroostook River.

SQUA PAN STREAM

Squa Pan Lake, south of Castle Hill, is a dogleg-shaped lake about 15 miles long and 1 mile wide, for the most part wild and unspoiled. The lake is used to hold water by the Maine Public Service Company. The outlet stream is short but swift, and flows into the Aroostook River above Ashland.

Squa Pan Lake—Aroostook River   3 miles

Flatwater, **Quickwater**, Class I, II
  Anytime dam is open; call MPS (768-5811 for
  information)
  Wild, Settled
          USGS: Ashland 15, Presque Isle 15

When the water is low, you can see the remains of the original dam a few miles up the lake.

The dam and bridge at the outlet must be carried about 100 yards on either side. Below the bridge are continuous Class II rapids for 2½ miles. In this distance the river drops 63 feet through wild, wooded country. Then you go under several railroad bridges and finally the ME-11 bridge into a deadwater for the last ½ mile to the Aroostook River.

MACHIAS STREAM

The Machias Stream flows south and then west from
Machias Lake in T12 R8 to the Aroostook River near Ashland. The river is about 39 miles long and drops 420 feet,
making it an excellent whitewater trip for a weekend.
In the early spring the river can be run in a day with water
up to Class IV. The Machias runs through mountainous
and heavily forested country, with many signs of the old
logging days. Because of heavy logging in the last few years,
the river must be run early because there is a very fast run-
off. It also can be run after heavy rains.

Pratt Lake—Big Machias Lake Outlet   8 miles

Lake, Quickwater
  High water: *spring*
  Wild
     USGS: Mooseleuk Lake 15
  Campsites: 7 mi   **on north shore at
                               Twentymile Brook**
                8 mi   **Big Machias Lake
                               outlet** car

The outlet of Pratt Lake is at the northernmost point,
where you enter a small but swift stream. This flows
through some ponds for about 2 miles. After 3 miles you
enter Big Machias Lake. The outlet is 3 miles down the lake
at the east end.

Big Machias Lake—Aroostook River   32 miles

Flatwater, Quickwater, Class I, II, III
  High water: *very fast—Class III*
  Medium water: *can be scratchy*
  Wild
     USGS: Mooseleuk Lake 15, Greenlaw 15,
           Ashland 15
  Campsite: 15 mi L **Rand Crossing** car
             many other undeveloped
             campsites

Scout the old logging dam at the outlet, which can be run but contains many rocks. Below the dam is good current for a mile, and then 2 miles of Class II rapids to Russell Crossing, where there was once a bridge on the American Realty Road. The heavy rapids continue about a mile, then 3 miles of Class II rapids to McKeen's Crossing and Rowe Brook (6 mi). After 9 miles of good current you go under the Rand Crossing Bridge from Ashland, where there is a large public campsite on the left side. Below here the river has good current 8 miles to the deadwater behind a logging dam. In the middle of the swamp just before the South Branch enters is a set of Class I rapids where a clay deposit was mined from the river. Six miles below Rand Crossing is a deadwater 3 miles long formed by an old logging dam, now almost gone, which can easily be run in the log chute on the right side. Below are Class II + rapids for 4 miles, then good current for 4 miles. Suddenly, around a bend is Ashland. Just below the town is a Class III + set of ledges, which should be run left to right in medium and low water, but on the far right in high water. Then go under a bridge and in ½ mile enter the Aroostook River in a forested setting.

LITTLE MACHIAS RIVER

The Little Machias River rises to the southwest of Portage, flowing southeast to Little Machias Lake. From there it flows southeasterly through wild but swampy land to the Aroostook River below Ashland.

Little Machias Lake—Aroostook River   6 miles

Flatwater, Quickwater, Class I
  High water best
  Wild
        USGS: Greenlaw 15, Ashland 15

The first 3 miles are wild, swampy country; the lower 3 miles are swift current with occasional rips. The confluence is halfway between Ashland and Sheridan.

BEAVER BROOK

Beaver Brook drains an extensive forest area to the east of Portage Lake. The brook is smooth with good current and about 10 good permit campsites along the way. The country is wild and untouched by camps, roads, or signs of logging; it is a good place to see moose and waterfowl. The nicest campsite on the Aroostook River is at the mouth of Beaver Brook.

West Branch Beaver Brook—
East Branch   5 miles

This section can be run down from the ME-11 bridge in Winterville in high water only, and is rapid, with many blowdowns.

Confluence—Aroostook River   8 miles

Quickwater, Class I
  High or medium water
  Wild
        USGS: Ashland 15, Portage 15

From the bridge on a dirt road just below the confluence, the brook is mostly smooth, with a few rips and chutes for the first 3 miles to liven the trip. It then winds through the alders in a swamp, but the last 3 miles to the Aroostook are again rips and quickwater. When the brook takes a sharp bend to the left, the Aroostook River is beyond the high bank directly ahead.

SALMON BROOK

Salmon Brook is a rapid stream, which rises in Salmon Brook Lake and flows southeast to the Aroostook River at Washburn.

New Dunn Town Road—Aroostook River   4 miles

Class II
  High water only: *spring*
  Wild
        USGS: Caribou 15

Put in from the Story Brook Fire Tower road. The stream drops 40 feet to the Aroostook River, all in an even gradient, providing easy Class II rapids for the entire distance. It makes a good stream to warm up on in the spring. Take out at the town landing in Washburn.

LITTLE MADAWASKA RIVER

The Little Madawaska River rises in Bog Pond about 6 miles west of Perham in T14 R5, and flows northeast to Stockholm, and then southeast to the Aroostook River at Grimes Mill. The beginning and end of the river are very swift, but the middle section is swampy and slow going. Above Blackstone, access is poor and there are many blowdowns.

Blackstone Siding—Stockholm   13 miles

Quickwater
  High or medium water
  Forested, Town
        USGS: Portage 15, Caribou 15, Stockholm 15
   Portage: (13 mi   L   **dam in Stockholm**   400
                              yds)

The first 5 miles to Madawaska Lake Outlet are quickwater and easy rapids through softwood swamps. An alternate starting point is Madawaska Lake, running the 1 mile down the outlet, which increases the size of the river considerably. The next 4 miles to the ME-161 bridge and the following 1 mile are swift, and then 2 miles of deadwater and swamp bring one to the dam in Stockholm.

Stockholm—Aroostook River   22 miles

Flatwater, Quickwater
  High water: *dangerous below ME-89*
  Medium water: *recommended*
  Low water: *except very dry spells*
  Forested, Rural, Towns
        USGS: Stockholm 15, Caribou 15, Fort
              Fairfield 15

There is 1 mile of quickwater below the dam, then 7 miles of meandering swampland to the US-1 bridge at Acadia. There follows 3 miles of quickwater, and after another 5 miles there is a dam, then 2 miles of meanders through open farmland to another bridge on the Loring Access Highway, where the river quickens for the next mile to the ME-89 bridge, which should be approached on the extreme left.

The last 3 miles to the Aroostook are very swift and meandering. Almost every bend has overhanging or fallen trees, so the boater should stay near the inside of these bends and be prepared to land should the river be blocked.

PRESQUE ISLE STREAM

Presque Isle Stream rises in the unorganized townships southeast of Ashland and flows northerly to the Aroostook River at Presque Isle. Starting at Presque Isle Lake, the stream is steep and blowdowns are frequent, so the recommended starting point is Grindstone.

Grindstone—Aroostook River   15 miles

Flatwater, Quickwater
  High water: *spring*
  Wild, Town
        USGS: Presque Isle 15

The first 8 miles are swift, with the Presque Isle Rapids (Class I) at the foot of Hobart Hill. The next 5 miles are the backwater from the rock dam at Presque Isle, located directly below a bridge. This can be run on the right center

(Class III +) in high water, or roped on the right at low water. The last 2 miles to the Aroostook River are quickwater with a few rips.

PRESTILE STREAM

Prestile Stream is formed by the junction of a number of brooks in Fort Fairfield. It flows south through Easton, Mars Hill, and Blaine to Bridgewater, where it turns east, crosses the international boundary, and flows into the Saint John River a few miles south of Florenceville, New Brunswick.

Westfield—Canadian border   14½ miles

Flatwater, Quickwater, Class I	[23½ km]
High water: *upper sections*	
Medium or low water: *lower section*	
Wild	
USGS: Mars Hill 15, Bridgewater 15	
Portage: 6 mi R **Robinson Dam**	

From Westfield to Mars Hill the river runs southeasterly with fine views of the long ridge of Mars Hill. The going is hard, with many low trees and blowdowns, to the backwater of the washed-out Mars Hill Dam (4½ mi).

Below the old dam there are easy rapids for about a mile, then 3½ miles of good current to the backwater of the Robinson Dam (10½ mi), which is best carried on the right.

Below Robinson Dam the stream is much larger, and canoeable at most seasons. About 1 mile below the dam at Robinsons the river crosses the town line into Bridgewater and turns east. About 3½ miles down, Whitney Brook enters on the right and in less than ½ mile the international boundary is reached. The customs station is on the road on the left bank. For those not wishing to continue on into Canada, a take-out here is possible, or one can take out at the bridge just above the entrance of Whitney Brook.

WHITNEY BROOK

Whitney Brook is formed in Bridgewater by the junction of the north and south branches. About 1 mile below this

junction the brook is crossed by Rumford Road and US-1.
Below here it is navigable, although best done with relatively high water. The brook flows on a northeasterly course
to meet the Prestile Stream less than ½ mile west of the
Canadian border.

Bridgewater—Prestile Stream   4 miles

Quickwater, Class I
  High water
  Forested
      USGS: Bridgewater 15

From the pond at Bridgewater, there are 4 miles of easy
rapids and fast current to the junction with Prestile Stream,
passing a very low bridge 2 miles down. Take out in the
large field in front of customs.

MEDUXNEKEAG RIVER

The Meduxnekeag River rises in Ludlow, flows southeast
to New Limerick, then east to Houlton, where it turns north
and slightly east to the Canadian border. Here it turns definitely east to join the Saint John River near Woodstock,
New Brunswick.

New Limerick—Houlton   11 miles

Flatwater, Quickwater
  High or medium water: *spring and early summer*
  Forested
      USGS: Smyrna Mills 15, Amity 15
  Portage: (11 mi   **dam in Houlton)**

Below the dam at New Limerick the river has a good current partly through swamps for the 2 miles to Green Pond,
where the outlet is only 200 yards away along the south
shore to the east. From here the river is larger, and in 3
miles of a somewhat meandering course, the outlet of Nickerson Lake on the right is reached. This lake, a favorite spot
for summer cottages, is only 1 mile up the outlet. In 3 miles

more Carys Mills is reached and the entrance of the South Branch just below on the right. With the added water the stream is now quite large for the 3 miles to the dam at Houlton.

Houlton—Canadian Border   9 miles

Flatwater, Quickwater
    Anytime
    Forested, Rural
        USGS: Houlton 15, Amity 15

The stream is now large and flows northward for some 8 miles with no obstructions, then turns east and in 1 mile more crosses the border between Monuments 27A and 27. The nearest customs station is 1 mile south at the road crossing, so most canoeists will probably take out at the road bridge some 2½ miles upstream from the international boundary.

Since at present trying to cross the Canadian border in a canoe in this area is a hassle, and furthermore since the rivers drop precipitously off the plateau to the Saint John River in only a short distance, the description of the Saint John tributaries ends on the American side of the border.

MEDUXNEKEAG RIVER, South Branch

The South Branch of the Meduxnekeag River is formed by the junction of a number of brooks in Cary. From there it flows north through Hodgdon to Houlton, where it joins the main river at Carys Mills.

Cary—Meduxnekeag River   9 miles

Flatwater, Quickwater, Class I
    High or medium water
    Forested, Rural, Towns
        USGS: Houlton 15
        Portages: 5 mi   L   **dam at Hodgdon**   10 yds
                    (9 mi   L   **waterfall at Carys Mills**)

Just above the Oliver Road Bridge at Cary the South
Branch is joined by Davis Brook and becomes quite large.
There are 4 miles of meandering stream to the big pond at
Hodgdon, then 1 mile down the pond to the town. There is
a dam just above the bridge; portage 10 yards on the left via
a small public landing. There are Class I and II rips for 100
yards below the dam, then 1 mile of good current to a broken log dam. This dam may be runnable, but is apt to be
blocked by debris. Two more miles of quickwater and riffles
bring the canoeist to a bridge on the dirt back road from
Hodgdon to Carys Mills. Within ½ mile one comes to an
area of meanders and alders that continues for ¾ mile. Once
out of the bushes, the current quickens again and occasional
Class I rapids appear.

These become more frequent and interesting after a nearly right angle turn to the right. A slight turn to the left signals the beginning of a series of low ledges above the first of
two bridges at Carys Mills. There is a falls dropping in several sections just below the bridge. Below the fall there are
100 yards of Class I water to the main river.

B STREAM

B Stream rises in Hammond and flows southeast to the
Meduxnekeag River in Houlton. It is fed by a number of
brooks with swampy areas on their courses, so it should
hold water well. From B School in southeastern Hammond
the river drops 120 feet in 8 miles to Houlton.

Hammond (Sixth Bridge)—Houlton   4¼ miles

Quickwater, Class I, II
  Medium water
  Forested
      USGS: Houlton

Starting at the sixth bridge above the confluence with the
Meduxnekeag, this stream can be paddled in mid-June if it
has not been too dry. There is quickwater and Class I riffles, occasionally obstructed by trees, to the high bridge
near BM 373 (1½ mi). Below this bridge the stream is some-

what larger and deeper and one is not so hampered by trees. The third bridge marks the beginning of a mile-long section where ledges cross the stream at varying angles, creating intermittent Class II rapids, one or two of which could be tricky at high water. This section ends at a bridge on the back road to Ludlow, which is the last convenient take-out; beyond, access from the Interstate is impractical and the area around the US-2 bridge is urbanized, with a low dam just above it.

CHAPTER 7

Western Coastal Watersheds

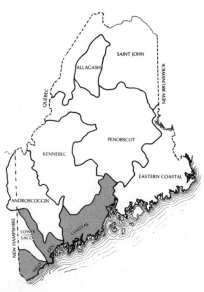

WESTERN COASTAL
WATERSHEDS

SCALE IN MILES

LITTLE RIVER

The canoe season is short but exciting on the Little River. Canoe early in the morning or on an overcast day, because it heads into the afternoon sun for most of its length.

Lebanon—Salmon Falls River   11¼ miles

Flatwater, Quickwater, Class I, II
  High water: *late March to early May*
  Forested
      USGS: Berwick 15

The usual put-in is below the broken dam beside an old mill in Lebanon. In high water the river can be run above the mill, either from Fall Road (a mile upriver) or from ME 11/US 202 (3 mi above the mill). Determined explorers occasionally start even higher up. The river above the mill is quite narrow with Class I and II rapids and numerous obstructions.

From the mill there are two rapids—one at a broken dam—in the first mile. In the next 1 mile, from the Lord Road bridge to the bridge on Little River Road, the river is smooth and winding. The next 4¼ miles to Stackpole Bridge pass through an area known as "the Marshes," where the river maintains a good current around numerous tight twists and turns. Occasional breakthroughs create some confusion, but careful observation of the current will guide you through easily.

Whitewater enthusiasts frequently begin at Stackpole Bridge (6¼ mi), under which there is a small drop over a ledge. The next 2 miles are smooth and slow until the river reaches a small Class I rapid, followed soon after by ¼ mile of Class I rapids up to Messenger Bridge, where Pine Hill Road and Little River Road meet.

Below Messenger Bridge (8½ mi) there is another Class I rapid, then an easy Class II rapid, and finally a ¾-mile-long, hard Class II rapid. The river is narrow enough that you must pick either the left or right side—there is no room for a middle route—and the only clear passage involves switching occasionally from a course down one side to a course down the other. Stop and scout frequently unless you like piling up onto ledges and into impassable rock gardens. One particularly interesting spot has a car-sized boulder perched on top of a ledge left of center; the usually runnable channels lead you within an arm's length of it.

The long rapid ends with a small ledge in a sharp right turn. The last ½ mile of this rapid, down to a back-road bridge (9½ mi), is very scratchy when the rapids above are marginally canoeable. Flatwater follows. One-half mile above the Hubbard Road bridge (11¼ mi), there is a broken dam at the end of a sharp "S"-turn that can be run with extreme caution or lined from the right bank.

The Little River empties into the Salmon Falls River (11¼ mi) just below the Hubbard Road bridge. Somersworth is 5 miles downstream (16¼ mi).

GREAT WORKS RIVER

This unassuming little river claims the distinction of having turned the first water-powered mill in the United States, in the section of South Berwick called Great Works. Mills continued there without a break for over three hundred years, until the 1940s, when the remaining few fell into disuse.

North Berwick—South Berwick   11½ miles

Flatwater, Quickwater, Class I
  High water: *late March to mid-May*
  Passable at most water levels for last 3½ miles
  Forested
     USGS: Kennebunk 15, York 15, Dover 15
  Portage: 11½ mi   **Rocky Gorge** 1 mi

The first 5 miles to Emerys Bridge on Hooper Sands Road are narrow and winding, and the river shallows out early in the season. The next 3 miles to Junction Bridge, at the west end of Emerys Bridge Road, hold water a little longer. Both sections are prone to blowdowns.

The final 3½-mile section from Junction Bridge to the village of Great Works is canoeable except in very dry summers, and it is entirely flatwater. Take out at the Brattle Street bridge (11½ mi) ¼ mile below the ME 236 bridge.

Caution! Below the Brattle Street bridge there is a series of falls and rapids called Rocky Gorge. Stay well above it. Continuing to the Salmon Falls River, into which the Great Works River flows, is not feasible because this obstruction requires a 1-mile portage.

There is a dam on the Great Works River at the confluence with the Salmon Falls river.

MOUSAM RIVER

The Mousam River flows into the sea at Kennebunk. There is usually not enough water in the upper section for good canoeing except in the spring and just after Labor Day, when Mousam Lake is drawn to permit lakeshore work to be done.

Mousam Lake—Estes Lake   14 miles

Lakes, Quickwater, Class I, II
  High water: *early spring and early September*
  Dam-controlled: *annual drawdown of Mousam Lake*
  Forested, Rural, Settled
    USGS: Berwick 15, Kennebunk 15
  Portages: 3½ mi   L   **1st and 2nd dams in Springvale**
                  4 mi   R   **small dam in Springvale**
                4½ mi   e   **1st dam in Sanford**
                  6 mi   L   **2nd dam in Sanford (cross over 1st bridge)**
                (14 mi   R   **Estes Lake Dam)**

The river below the dam on Mousam Lake can be reached by turning off ME-11/109 at the Emery Mills Post Office. If there is a boiling flow at the base of the dam, there is sufficient water for this trip.

In the 3 miles to the first millpond in Springvale, there are three sharp drops to watch out for. The first is under a powerline, the second is a short distance below the ME-11/109 bridge (1¼ mi), and the third one is about a mile farther on.

At Holdsworth Park in Springvale, there is good access to the pond above the first dam. If continuing downstream, take out left of the dam (3½ mi), portage along Water Street, and put in below the second dam. There is a third dam (4 mi) just upstream of an abandoned stone railroad bridge.

The first dam in Sanford (4½ mi) is followed by quickwater to the millpond above the second dam (6 mi). Take out on the left, cross the river via Washington Street, follow Pioneer Avenue downstream, and put in by the Emery Street bridge. Then there is quickwater with some debris for 3 miles to the ME-4 bridge.

Below ME-4 (9 mi) it is ½ mile to the ruins of Jagger Mill Dam, which can be run. Quickwater continues for most of the way to Mousam Lane (13 mi), which is near the head of Estes Lake. When the lake opens up, turn right to reach the dam (14 mi).

Estes Lake—Kennebunk   12 miles

USGS: Kennebunk 15

Below the powerhouse there is a short rapid, followed in ½ mile by a gauging station on the right, the Whichers Mills Road bridge, and a dam. This dam should be carried on the right and the put-in made below a sharp fall and rapid, at the head of Old Falls Pond. There are then 1½ miles of paddling down the pond to the high power dam at the end. This should be portaged on the left, down a steep hill 150 yards. Below the start about 200 yards, just around the bend, is a sharp rapid, which should be scouted before running if the river is in flood. Once through the rapid, the river becomes quiet with a fair current and good hemlock woods on the right bank. The valley soon widens out, and in 4½ miles the bridge at West Kennebunk is reached. The old dam just below the bridge has a short rapid just below it. In ½ mile more the railroad culvert is reached, and then in another 200 yards a dam at a mill, where there is a short, steep carry on the right bank to the rapids. These ¼-mile-long rapids are easily run to the slackwater, which continues for 1 mile to the Maine Turnpike bridge. The next 2 miles of meandering river to the Route 1 bridge in Kennebunk pass through farmlands on both sides. In Kennebunk, it is best to take out above the bridge: the rapids below drop to tidewater.

TIDAL RIVERS SOUTH OF PORTLAND

Canoeing in tidal marshes does not involve either the risks or the specialized equipment of "sea kayaking" along exposed shorelines. Typical open canoes and basic quickwater paddling skills are generally sufficient. Birders and amateur naturalists will find salt marsh exploration particularly enjoyable.

Scarborough, Nonesuch, Libby, and Spurwink Rivers

Tidal
    Anytime: *check tide chart*
    Rural, Settled, Salt marshes
        USGS: Portland 15

SCARBOROUGH RIVER

The Scarborough River is formed by the joining of Cascade Brook and Dunstan River near West Scarborough, which is also called Dunstan Corner. It is the largest of several streams emptying into the estuary that separates Pine Point from Prouts Neck. For a 4¾-mile trip put in at the Scarborough Marsh Nature Center (which provides canoe rentals and guided trips) near the time of high tide.

For the first ½ mile or so you will actually be on the Dunstan River. Cascade Brook enters through a culvert on the right. About 3 miles further on, the river passes under a railroad trestle. The current at the strength of the ebb can be quite strong, and it passes through the trestle at a 45° angle. Paddlers without whitewater experience, or who are not alert, can get into difficulty here. Another mile through the widening estuary brings you to the Pine Point town landing.

NONESUCH RIVER

The Nonesuch River has a long course through the upland parts of Scarborough, but paddlers attempting portions of it in the 1960s and 1970s found it to be so frequently obstructed by alders and fallen trees that it can be recommended only to dedicated bushwhackers.

For the recommended trip put in at ME-207 just west of Black Point village. The river can be ascended at least 1½ miles from here or paddled 4 miles down with the tide.

Downstream of this point one encounters a railroad trestle. Alternatively, you can put in at the state boat ramp on Clay Pits Road and skip it. Other than that, there are no impediments to take-outs at either Pine Point or Ferry Beach on Prouts Neck.

LIBBY RIVER

The Libby River is substantially smaller than either the Scarborough or the Nonesuch, and the first ¼ mile can only be paddled within 1 hour of high water. Put in from ME-207 just west of ME-77. Take out at Ferry Beach, which has a parking fee in the summer.

SPURWINK RIVER

The Spurwink River is not connected to the others, and is of a somewhat different character. Those wishing to tour the narrow passages of the marsh can put in from Spurwink Avenue for the East Branch or from Fickett Road for the West Branch. From either point it is ½ mile to ME-77, where a side road on the right comes right down to the river. This is a better start for the lower Spurwink.

The side road ends at what appears to have been an old ford, and its remnants form a Class I riffle and eddies on the ebb. There is also a lot of current under the ME-77 bridge. From ME-77 to Higgins Beach is about a mile past scenery that is more varied than the typical marsh. There is no good take-out or any free parking at Higgins Beach, which is a popular bathing beach. There is often an impressive surf that closes out the mouth of the river at half tide or lower. Plan to return to ME-77, about a 5-mile round trip. If you start at high water and set a leisurely pace down and back, you may end up dragging your canoe over sandbars the last ¼ mile up to ME-77.

PRESUMPSCOT RIVER

The Presumpscot River is the outlet of Sebago Lake and flows to tidewater at Casco Bay. It "has a dam every 5 miles," so most of the river is short stretches of rapids and quickwater and much deadwater behind dams. It suffers also from pollution.

There is a short, pleasant section of quickwater downstream of the covered bridge replica and another section from Blackstrap Road to US-302 that have been reported as fairly enjoyable.

CROOKED RIVER

The Crooked River flows from Songo Pond near Bethel south to the Songo River and Sebago Lake. For the most part it is clean and attractive, and for 53 miles it has scenery that includes forests typical of northern Maine, alder swamps, and stands of red maples. There are many sections that have a remoteness that road and topographic maps do not suggest. From the river, North Waterford is not very pretty, but the settlements of Bolsters Mills and Scribners Mill farther downstream are slices from New England's past.

In the spring the river offers a pleasant combination of rapids and smoothwater. Below the ME-118 bridge in East Waterford, there are ten sets of rapids, which are mostly Class II with a few Class III drops. In high water there are several sections with heavy waves. Because of the river's relatively small drainage area, the water level changes from hazardously high to undesirably low in a matter of weeks.

Albany—North Waterford   9 miles

Flatwater, Class I–II
  High water: *April*
  Forested
        USGS: East Stoneham, North Waterford

The Crooked River here is small. In a few places fallen trees block the stream, and in the middle section alders crowd the channel. The current is fastest at the beginning where it flows through forests, portions of which have been selectively cut. Where the gradient lessens, the river meanders through alder thickets.

A convenient starting point within sight of the highway is from a bridge on a logging road that leaves ME-5/35 just over 5 miles north of Lynchville. For ¾ mile there is a mixture of rapids and flatwater. Stop above an old bridge by an abandoned farm (1½ mi) to scout the rapids below. One-half mile below the second highway bridge, the stream enters an alder swamp through which it meanders for 2½ miles to the ME-35 bridge in Lynchville (7½ mi). For the next 1½ miles to the ME-35 bridge in North Waterford (9 mi), the river is flat and wider.

North Waterford—East Waterford   12 miles

Flatwater, Quickwater, Class II–III
  High water: *April*
  Medium water: *shallow rapids, May*
  Forested, Towns
      USGS: North Waterford, Norway 15

The banks of the river in North Waterford are not very attractive, but beginning at the broken dam below town, there are a couple of miles of good rapids mixed with quickwater. The last 6 miles are very crooked, with leaning swamp maples crowding the stream.

Below the ME-35 bridge less than ½ mile, there is a broken dam that should be scouted. Then there are easy rapids as the river flows past a lumber yard. About 100 yards beyond the point where the stream approaches the highway again, stop just above a cabin on the right (1 mi) to scout the steep Class III rapids beside the roadside rest area. Near the top, large boulders produce heavy waves in high water with no obvious channel. The lower section is ¾ mile long, and it contains two easier Class II drops, which can be scouted from ME-118.

Below the last drop (2 mi) the river leaves the highway and runs deep and slow. A jam of fallen trees by a gravel pit on the left must be lifted over on the left. Two and a half miles below the rapids, the outlet from Papoose Pond enters on the right, and in another ¼ mile there is a bridge (4¾ mi). After 1 mile the river passes below the cliffs of Pulpit Rock (5¾ mi). The second bridge below the rock is ME-118 in East Waterford (12 mi), and it is reached after 6¼ very crooked miles.

East Waterford—Scribners Mill   17 miles

Flatwater, Class II–III
  High water: *April*
  Medium water: *scratchy rapids, May*
  Forested, Towns
    USGS: Norway

Portages:	14 mi	L	**dam at Bolsters Mills** 30 yds
	(17 mi	L	**dam at Scribners Mill** 20 yds)
Campsite:	4¾ mi	L	**bottom of 1st rapids**

This stretch makes a pleasant one-day trip with a mixture of rapids and smoothwater. There are some cabins along the river below East Waterford and Twin Bridges, and also beside McDaniel's Rips near Sodom, but other than that the river is secluded all the way to Bolsters Mills. The section between Sodom (a name that originated in the enmities aroused by a nineteenth century land feud) and Twin Bridges is especially scenic.

The rapids between East Waterford and Sodom provide nice whitewater runs for people with skill and good judgment. Not all who try to run them possess these qualities, and many canoes have been wrecked in McDaniel's Rips.

Below the ME-118 bridge there are 4½ miles of winding river that lead to a ¼ mile-long set of rapids that begin innocently enough, but soon lead to a very sharp Class III drop followed by easier rapids that have heavy waves in high water. It should be scouted from the left bank. Below it there are two pools separated by some riffles, and then you reach McDaniel's Rips (5 mi). Stop on the right bank and scout them, because they begin with a drop over a ledge at the site of an early paper mill.

After the ledges associated with the mill site, there is a narrow and surprisingly steep pitch ending with a boulder smack in midstream. Because this rock is often covered by water and hard to spot, many paddlers have been too slow to choose a path around it and have broached on it.

Beyond, about 100 yards, the drops continue as Class II or III rapids (depending on the water level), which are ½ mile long and taper to smoothwater at the Sodom bridge.

Below Sodom (5½ mi) there is slackwater for 3 miles to a powerline (8½ mi). Shortly after that there is a nice, 100-yard Class II rapid with clear channels and large waves in high water, followed almost immediately by another shorter pitch, also with heavy waves in high water. In about ½ mile there are more Class II rapids at Twin Bridges.

For ¼ mile below ME-117 at Twin Bridges (9½ mi), the rapids continue; then there is smoothwater for 4¼ miles to the dam at Bolsters Mills (14 mi). Portage on the left. Past the dam there is ½ mile of Class II rapids. The latter are followed by 2½ miles of slackwater that is broken by one short, easy pitch about halfway to Scribners Mill (17 mi). If you are continuing downstream, portage on the left.

Scribners Mill—Route 302   15 miles

Flatwater, Class I–II
   Passable at all water levels
   Forested, Rural
      USGS: Norway 15, Sebago Lake 15
    Portage: 10 mi L **Edes Falls** 10 yds

This section is passable all summer, although there are a few short rapids that may have to be walked down. Between Scribners Mill and Edes Falls, the river meanders for many miles through a high-banked flood plain where some sandy beaches are exposed in low water.

The portion of the river from US-302 to the Songo River is not recommended. The banks are lined with a veritable Hooverville of small cabins, and there are other encroachments of civilization, such as powerboats, that the sections upstream generally lack.

To reach Scribners Mill, head south from ME-35 from the junction with ME-117 in Harrison. In 2.7 miles, continue straight onto a side road when ME-35 bears right. Go straight past a crossroads in 1 mile, and turn right when the road ends in another mile. Take the first left and follow that road for 1.2 miles to the Crooked River.

Put in below the dam on the left. After ½ mile of rapids, the river is flat and winding for 9¼ miles. Near the end of the flatwater, there are a few camps on the left, then some Class I rapids, and finally a portage on the left around the old dam at Edes Falls. Sometimes it is possible to pass the breached dam by running over a sloping ledge on the far right (Class III).

Below Edes Falls (10 mi) there is ¼ mile of Class I rapids, which end just below the bridge. The last 5 miles are mostly flatwater. There is a good access on the left bank at the ME-11 bridge (12¾ mi) and fair access at the US-302 bridge (15 mi).

The last 4¼ miles to the Songo River (19¼ mi) are flat, crooked, and unattractive. From the mouth of the river, continue straight ahead through the locks to the Bay of Naples (20 mi), or turn left to Sebago Lake (21¾ mi).

PLEASANT RIVER

This Pleasant River is a tributary of the Presumpscot River, which drains Sebago Lake. The Pleasant River rises east of Little Sebago Lake and flows southwest to its confluence with the Presumpscot.

US-302—River Road   4 miles

Flatwater, **Quickwater**, Class I, II, III
  High or medium water: *April or May after heavy rain*
  Forested, Rural
    USGS: Yarmouth

Put in from US-302 where the river is near the road 0.2 miles west of the junction with US-202. The rapids are easy for the first half of the distance to a 6-foot drop in two stages (Class III). Scout or portage on the right. Quickwater continues below for another ¼ mile to another double ledge combination (Class II+)—a good surfing spot. The remainder of the distance is mostly quickwater. Take out on River Road at Lovet Bridge.

ROYAL RIVER

The Royal River rises in Sabbathday Pond in New Gloucester and flows east, north, and then south in that town and continues southward through North Yarmouth to reach the sea at Yarmouth. Except for one or two short bits, it is mostly smooth; the parts that can be most easily canoed are wholly smooth. As a consequence, the river can be run almost any time of year. The upper river can probably be run in high water, but the steep drop at Upper Gloucester must be carried.

Mill Rd.—ME-231   1¾ miles

An old-fashioned brickyard is still in operation at the put-in. After a Class I chute below the bridge it is quickwater to the next bridge.

ME-231—Yarmouth Waterworks   7½ miles

Flatwater, Quickwater (in spring)
  High water: *April, early May; passable most summers*
  Forested, Rural
    USGS: Freeport 15

One can put in at the ME-231 bridge about ¾ mile north of BM 167 on the Freeport topo map, but parking space is limited. There is a Class I rip directly under the bridge. In the spring this part of the Royal has a strong but smooth current, occasionally interrupted by fallen trees and beaver dams, which may effectively block the small river. Thick undergrowth may make portage difficult.

In 1½ miles the Chandler River enters from the left. At the confluence the Chandler is wider but the current is slower. One can easily ascend the Chandler ¼ mile to North Road, where there is a short, rocky rapid (Class II in medium water) under the road bridge. A short carry on either bank gives access to flatwater, which continues upstream for about one mile before the increasing frequency of fallen trees becomes a nuisance.

ME-9 is a little over ¼ mile below the confluence of the two streams, at Dunns Crossing, which offers a good off-road put-in. In summer, unless there have been heavy rains, there is no perceptible current below Dunns, and above it the current is not enough to impede upstream travel. The next 5¾ miles are smooth and meandering with no obstructions. Only a few houses and one lovely farm will be seen. The second of two railroad bridges signals the end of this section, with Yarmouth Waterworks on the right. The Waterworks is on East Elm Street, which joins North Road and leads back to Dunns, making for an easy car shuttle.

The Royal River now loses its placid demeanor as it plunges over the dam below East Elm Street and continues to fall until it reaches tidewater at ME-88.

Yarmouth Waterworks—Town Landing   1 mile

Quickwater, Class II–IV
  High water: *April, early May*
  Settled, Urban
    USGS: Yarmouth
    Portages: R **Below East Elm St.** 100 yds
                       R **First old mill site** 150 yds
                     L/R **Sparhawk Mill** 200 yds
                       L **Second old mill site** 100 yds

The first half of this section runs through a partially developed municipal park. Because of the four portages (total ⅓ of a mile), it is hard work for the amount of paddling actually done. Water levels are critical for safe and enjoyable canoeing on those rapids that can be run.

Just below the East Elm Street Bridge is a dam built on either side of a sloping outcropping of ledge. At an ideal water level an expert kayaker might be able to slide down this ledge (Class IV) and run the short rocky Class III rapid just below it. There is also an old ten-foot wide mill canal that exits the pond above this dam very near the waterworks parking lot and runs under the street. It looks runnable but isn't, as it contains two 90° turns, a four-foot drop, and a lot of debris. Carry around the dam on either side of the canal.

Less than 50 yards below the confluence of the canal and the main river, the banks become vertical and the river turns into a Class II rapid that is the lead-in to a 12-foot drop over a nearly perpendicular ledge. This was the site of a mill complex, the ruins of which make up the right bank. This fall could be run at some levels in a decked boat, but would be at least Class IV, as the run would require maneuvering both above and below the steep part. Carry via the paved path on the right; by the time one comes to a suitable launching spot the stream has subsided to Class I. In 200 yards the river passes under US-1 and into the 100-yard-long pond formed by the dam above the Sparhawk Mill.

In high water one can put in just below the fishway and run a strong Class II–III rapid down past the mill parking lot. Most of this rapid is too rocky to run at medium or lower levels, so one must take out on the right, carry across the bridge down into the mill parking lot, and put in from the left bank. Below the Sparhawk Mill rapid are 200 yards of quickwater and easy Class I rips. Now the river swings right and then slides into a series of broken and offset ledges at another old mill site. The lower half of this rapid is under the ME-88 bridge and is flooded out by high tide. With medium water and high tide, one has a choice of highly technical routes through the ledges down to flatwater just above the bridge. At low tide and high run-off one still has several options on the upper part, but all routes lead to two successive heavy drops under the bridge. This rapid can vary from bony Class III to thundering Class IV depending on the interaction of runoff and the tides. A vacant lot on the right provides a carry to ME-88. Below the rapid is a pool and the high I-95 bridge. The town landing is 200 yards downstream on the left. It is reached via Bayview Street. There are two miles of pleasant tidal paddling to the Cousins River and Casco Bay, for those wishing an opportunity to relax.

CHANDLER RIVER

The Chandler River rises in Pownal and flows southwest to the Royal River.

Runaround Pond—Royal River   10 miles

Flatwater, Quickwater, Class II
  High or medium water: *April or May*
  Some sections passable after heavy rain
  Rural, Settled
     USGS: Freeport 15
  Portages: 2¾ mi   R   **dam**   50 yd
               7½ mi   **ledge** lift over

The dam at the foot of Runaround Pond is on Frickett Road halfway between North Pownal and ME-9, which are 3 miles apart. A paddle up the pond is possible for a warm-up.

Put in on the left. The first mile is choked with alders, but the struggle is rewarded by a subsequent mile of lovely woodland paddling in fair current to Poland Range Road. Just below this bridge is a ¼ mile of millpond. Portage on the right along Lawrence Road to where the stream is again large enough for a canoe. A few yards of riffles bring you to the Lawrence Road bridge. In ½ mile there is a small broken weir that requires a lift-around unless the water is high. In ½ mile Sweetser Road is passed, and ¼ mile below is ¼ mile of rapids that are Class II when runnable. The one possible channel has lots of turns. Beyond the rapids is a mile of quickwater to Elmwood Road. To Chadsey Road is ¾ mile of quickwater; the hardwoods give way to alders, but there is still room to paddle. The last mile is uneventful except for two ledges halfway along. The first is a sloping drop of 1½ feet, the second is a one-foot vertical drop. These might be up to Class II in high water and must be lifted around in low water. People often take out at Milliken Road, but the climb up is steep on either side.

Just below Milliken Road is a jagged ledge drop, which can probably never be run clean. The ledge drop is surrounded by barbed-wire fences. The river meanders 3 miles with some current to North Road and is occasionally obstructed by fallen trees.

Under the North Road bridge is a short rip. It is ¼ mile to the Royal River and another ¼ mile down it to ME-9 at Dunns Corner, where there is good off-road parking.

Paddling upstream from the lower end is also possible for a mile or more.

CATHANCE RIVER

The Cathance River rises north of Bradley Pond and flows south to Topsham where it turns abruptly and flows northeast to tidewater at Bowdoinham. The river is very small, alternating smooth stretches with short rapids and ledges. These may be run, lined, or carried depending on water height, type of canoe, and skill of party. This is a fun river for canoeists with some skill in whitewater and a realistic estimate of their abilities.

US-201—Bowdoinham   6½ miles

Flatwater, **Quickwater**, Class I, II, III, Tidal
   Medium, Medium low water
   Forested, Settled
      USGS: Bath 15
     Portage: up to 5 or 6 mi as desired
          3½ mi   R   **waterfall**   25 ft

Put in where the old road dead ends at the river. At the start the river is 20 feet wide, deep, and with almost no current. For ½ mile it follows under and along I-95. As it curves away the current becomes noticeable. A mile from the start the first rapid is reached, runnable but scratchy—a taste of things to come. There are many short, steep pitches, each with a quiet pool below and easy to scout. Several are narrow, sharp curves with a width of 4-6 feet. Ledges and rocks prevent running some drops, and higher water would increase the size of the waves and the problems.

Below Cathance Road bridge is a 15-foot waterfall, which can be carried on the right. Access is very poor at the bridge. From this point the river is a tidal marsh. The scenery is good with only a few scattered cottages and many birds. The tide is a couple of hours later than Portland. Take out at boat launching ramp at Bowdoinham.

SASANOA RIVER

The Sasanoa is an entirely tidal passage that runs north-west-southeast connecting the tidal parts of the Kennebec and Sheepscot rivers. Midway through its course, at Hockomock Bay, it meets and mixes with the Back River. The Back River also connects the Kennebec to the Sheepscot, but goes northeast-southwest.

The trip can be done in either direction, but timing the tide is critical if one wants to go with the current at the two tidal rapids known as Upper and Lower Hell Gate. High water at Bath is 1 hour later than at Portland; at Upper Hell Gate, 1 hour and 11 minutes later than Portland; Mill Point, 35 minutes later; and Robinhood, 14 minutes later.

Knubble Bay—Bath   7 miles

Tidal, Tide race
  Anytime
  Rural, Settled, Urban
    USGS: NOS chart 13293 preferred to Bath 15
        and Boothbay 15

The AMC Knubble Bay Camp is reached by following gravel Webber Road that turns left off the paved road to Robinhood. From the camp it is about ½ mile to Beal Island (camping by previous registration only). Lower Hell Gate is between Beal and Westport islands. The current swirls through the crooked passageway creating many low waves, irregular eddies, and, occasionally, small whirlpools. It might be considered Class II at maximum strength on the ebb 3 or 4 hours after high water; near slack it is more like Class I. The correct exit from Hockomock Bay is hard to find without a chart or knowledge of buoy markings. The white dome of the Maine Yankee nuclear power plant on the northeast arm of the Back River is the only real landmark.

Upper Hell Gate is one mile west of where the Sasanoa leaves Hockomock Bay; it is nothing more than the constriction of the already narrow channel and will appear trivial to whitewater paddlers. A Class I chute with waves at most times, it can be tricky if powerboats are trying to pass at the same time.

In another ½ mile the Sasanoa opens into Hanson Bay, which is fairly shallow and can be quite choppy in a blow. Follow the current between Preble and Sasanoa points and out into the Kennebec. Take out at the municipal floats just upstream of the US-1 bridge on the west or at the boat ramp near the sewage treatment plant 1 mile further up the Kennebec.

KENNEBEC RIVER

Bath to Lines Island and Return   6 miles

As a continuation of the Sasanoa River trip, or separately, it is not too difficult to continue up the Kennebec River to round Lines Island and return.

If the tide is ebbing, hog the west bank and use the eddies to get upstream, then ferry across and go up Burnt Jacket Channel east of Lines Island and come back down the west channel with the main current.

SHEEPSCOT RIVER

USGS: Liberty, Palermo, Razorville,
Vassalboro 15

The Sheepscot River rises in Montville and flows southwest through Palermo and Somerville to Whitefield, where it is joined by the West Branch. From there it flows southward past Wiscasset to the sea between Georgetown and Southport.

Sheepscot Pond—Coopers Mills   12½ miles

The upper part of the Sheepscot River consists of small sections of river connecting ponds that are artificially raised by dams. It may be best enjoyed as side trips upstream of Sheepscot Pond or upstream or downstream of Long Pond.

From ME-3 it is ¾ mile to Sheepscot Pond. A dam and fish hatchery are at the outlet. Below the next bridge the river is only a canoe-length wide with steep rapids underneath overhanging branches. It can be reached another ¾ mile downstream at a logging ford by a heavy-duty vehicle. The rapids are alleged to moderate below here as it slows down and becomes more winding. It can be paddled up a considerable distance from Long Pond.

Below Long Pond it is wide and flat to the 7-foot dam above the old bridge at Coopers Mills.

Coopers Mills—Whitefield   9½ miles

There is 1 mile of rapids below the dam, the first ½ mile of which is Class III in high water and too rocky at other levels. It is narrow with one sharp drop and overhanging obstacles, which make it quite dangerous. The next mile to the junction with the West Branch (2 mi) is mostly smoothwater.

If one wishes to put in at the junction of the West Branch, it is probably better to use the side road that crosses the West Branch just above the junction rather than attempt to take the canoes down the steep bank from ME-218 on the east shore. The next 2 miles to the ME-126 bridge at North Whitefield (4 mi) are smooth going. There is a gauging station on the east bank above this bridge. The next 5½ miles of winding river to Whitefield are quite smooth, past many fields and some wooded banks to a dam.

Whitefield—Head Tide   6 miles

Quickwater, Class II
   High water: *early to mid-April*
   Medium water: *late April to early May, or after heavy rains*
   Forested, Rural
      USGS: Wiscasset 15
      Portage: (6 mi   **dam**)

This is a very popular open canoe run in early to mid-April, as it is not too difficult and it usually ices-out before most other streams.

Below the deteriorating dam at Whitefield is a 2-foot ledge that makes an interesting sousehole at high water. The put-in is easier from the right, but take care not to block access to the private home just downstream. The pool below the ledge has a fast jet down its middle, which divides around a low island. Most of the river goes left, and beginners often have difficulty crossing the jet to get to a deep channel; the right channel is usually too shoal to run.

Fast current with some waves and occasional rocks continues for about a mile, then winds down to mostly smooth-water that continues to a pair of old bridge abutments. There is a short Class II pitch here, then mixed quickwater and mild rapids. One soon reaches a stretch of nearly 2 miles of continuous Class II rapids through wooded banks. These rapids ultimately diminish to Class I riffles, then the river kinks left and right by a large rock outcrop on the left, 100 yards above the muddy take-out at the dam at Head Tide. If water is going over the crest of this dam, the rapids above will be mostly low waves with few visible rocks. If more than 6 inches of the upstream face of the dam is dry, the rapids will be rocky and technical.

Head Tide—Wiscasset   11½ miles

Although the tidal effect is felt as far up the river as this point, the river is still moderate in size and provides a very pleasant paddle for the 7 miles to the bridge at Sheepscot. This is the second bridge to replace the original bridge, a toll bridge from 1794 to 1894 that provided the earliest crossing of the river. Some canoeists may wish to take out here. Others will want to continue on around the right turn ¼ mile below, where at low tide there is a small rapid, and take out at the gravel pit just below on the east bank, easily reached by a dirt road from Sheepscot. Others will wish to go down the widening estuary 5 miles to Wiscasset, well worth visiting with its charming old houses and interesting museum.

SHEEPSCOT RIVER, West Branch

The West Branch rises in Palermo and flows south through China to join the main river in Whitefield. The first few miles below Branch Pond the river is small as it wanders through a swamp, is obstructed with debris, and has a few rocky rapids that are scarcely runnable. The remainder of the river is a mixture of quickwater and rapids, with the blockage by trees becoming less frequent as the river becomes larger.

Weeks Mills—Sheepscot River   11¼ miles

Quickwater, Class I, II
  Medium high water
  Forested
      USGS: Vassalboro 15, North Whitefield
  Portage: 11 mi L **ledge**   25 ft.–100 yds
                                 depending on water level

This section of river is primarily gentle current flowing between evergreen-lined banks, interspersed by occasional rocky rapids.

The section of river immediately below Weeks Mills may be blocked by fallen trees. Check locally before starting. If the river is blocked, put in at the next bridge.

A mile and a half above the ME-105 bridge is an abutment with a chute through it. Starting shortly above the bridge is a rocky Class II rapid with a small ledge continuing down to the bridge. More smoothwater is followed by ½ mile of scratchy rapids. More easy rapids and some interesting rocks by a pool lie above the ME-11 bridge (9 mi). Anyone who has had difficulty with the rapids above should take out here.

Rapids start half a mile above the next bridge, gradually increasing in difficulty, culminating in an unrunnable drop over a ledge visible from the bridge. Those watching for it can see the bridge from above in time to get to shore before the ledge.

Rapids continue below the bridge to the confluence with the Sheepscot River ¼ mile below. The next take-out is 2 miles down the main river.

DAMARISCOTTA RIVER

The Damariscotta River is a long freshwater lake separated by a high dam from a tidal inlet.

Damariscotta—South Bristol   13 miles

Tidal
  Anytime
  Rural, Settled, Towns
      USGS: Wiscasset 15, Boothbay 15 or NOS
            chart 13293
  Campsite: 10½ mi   **Fort Island**

Put in from the public boat ramp in Damariscotta at or shortly after high water, which occurs 16 minutes later than at Portland. The river is wide and the well-marked channel is deep enough for sizable yachts. In about 5 miles the channel makes a sharp kink to the right around a hidden ledge off the end of Fitch Point. The ledge, which uncovers at half tide, creates a minor tide rip when covered and large eddies when bare. Another 2½ miles on the left is the University of Maine's Darling Center Marine Lab on Wentworth Point. A mile further one passes between Miller and Carlisle islands, which make good lunch stops.

Two miles beyond Carlisle Island is Fort Island, which boasts a campsite and the remains of a very small redoubt. Between Fort Point, the east end of the island, and the left bank is a powerful tidal race. At strength it sometimes tows the navigational buoy completely under. Give it the same respect as a Class II rapid. Even though wide open, the eddy lines are irregular and abrupt.

East Boothbay is 1½ miles beyond Fort Island on the west. One could take out here, but parking near the water is limited and the shuttle route is somewhat circuitous. Better to cross 1½ miles to South Bristol on the east bank and take out near the town float on the south side of the gut near a small grey store.

PEMAQUID RIVER

The Pemaquid River starts at Pemaquid Pond and flows through Biscay Pond, and then southward past Bristol until it reaches tidewater at Pemaquid.

The dam at Bristol has raised the level of the connecting streams above, but the dams further downstream are out, leaving shallow rapids.

Pemaquid Pond—Bristol Dam   6½ miles

Lake, Flatwater
   Passable at all water levels
   Forested
      USGS: Waldoboro West, Louds Island, Bristol
   Portage: (6½ mi R **dam at Bristol)**

This is a trip highly suitable for beginning canoeists, as it is all flatwater, but rather pleasant, best suited as a lake paddle rather than a through trip.

Start at the launching ramp at the north end of Pemaquid Pond. Paddle 6¼ miles south to the outlet or take a side trip up its outlet stream 1¾ miles to Duckpuddle Pond. Two commercial campgrounds allow for a longer stay.

Continuing south it is 2½ miles down Biscay Pond to its outlet, a short, marshy paddle to the ponded Pemaquid River and another 2¼ miles to the dam above Bristol.

Bristol—Pemaquid   5 miles

Pond, **Flatwater**, Quickwater, Class I, II
   Medium, medium low water
   Forested, Rural
      USGS: Bristol
   Portage: 5 mi   **gorge**   200 yd

The middle section of this river is a delightful paddle, but has no good access. It is guarded by awkward rapids at the beginning and end. The rapids, if runnable, may be Class III. It should be enjoyed on a warm day with fairly low water and the canoe waded down the rapids. Portaging is not feasible at either end.

Because of the rapids below the dam and the gabions in the river, it is best to put in below the last bridge in Bristol, ¾ mile below the dam. A short stretch of rapids leads to an open marsh with occasional beaver dams. In another mile the old dam above Bristol Mills Road is reached. The steep drop there should be waded down.

From this bridge (do not trespass on private property) a ½-mile of river with some beaver dams leads into Boyd Pond. Going down the pond, keep right into outlet, where it is 1¾ miles of marsh and riffles to the final ledges, 0.1 mile above the ME-30 bridge at Pemaquid. Below the bridge the river drops steeply for 200 yards through an old mill site and another 200 yards to tidewater.

MEDOMAK RIVER

The Medomak River rises in Liberty and flows south to the ocean at Waldoboro. The river is small and meandering above Medomak Pond. Below the pond much of the distance is flat and probably passable at most water levels, but interspersed are several rapids, which are impressive at high water and impassable at low water. Formerly all these drops were dammed, but all traces of the dams are now gone except for the one below Flanders Corner.

Carroll Road—Medomak Pond   6½ miles

Flatwater, **Quickwater**, Class I, II
  High water
  Forested
          USGS: Liberty, Washington, Union

While it might be possible to put in further up at Lucas Corner, several streams come in above this bridge, making it more passable. The river is small and winding with occasional rapids. Below ME-17 (2½ mi) it is slightly larger as it flows through mature woods to Medomak Pond. This is a sizable pond, but the river leaves it ½ mile down on the west shore and in a few hundred yards passes under ME-220.

Medomak Pond—Waldoboro   12¼ miles

Flatwater, Quickwater, Class I, II
 Flatwater: *most water levels*
 Rapids: *medium to medium high water*
 Forested
       USGS: Jefferson, Waldoboro West

The first mile below the ME-220 bridge is smooth. Just above the next bridge the river drops through the rocky site of an old dam. This section should give a fair representation of water conditions for the rest of the river.

Shortly below the bridge, the Medomak fans out through a boulder field, which necessitates some lifting over for passage at any safe water level. A ¼ mile below the bridge a breach in the old dam can probably be run. After dispersing briefly through another boulder pile below the dam, the river flattens out into the beginning of a long, quiet section. Most of the remaining distance to Winslow Mills is flat, with occasional quickwater and riffles. Three ledges break this placid run. The first and easiest is around a left turn, and ends in a pool. The second is slightly more difficult. The third is at least Class III, and may be unrunnable at some water levels. It should be scouted in any case.

The current picks up as the next bridge (8 mi) is reached. Around the corner below it is a scratchy drop, then easier going to the next bridge (10½ mi) at Winslow Mills, with a drop through the old dam site. The rapid below soon smooths out to slow current to the US-1 bridge at Waldoboro. Take out at the picnic area downstream on the right on ME-32.

Rapids start around the corner leading to a dangerous waterfall at an old dam site behind the Legion hall. In another ¼ mile, immediately below the next bridge, is a dam. Following a short rocky section the river opens up into a wide, flat expanse above town. At the Main Street bridge, another ¼ mile, the river falls over another rocky drop to tidewater.

SAINT GEORGE RIVER

A number of lakes near Liberty form the headwaters of the Saint George River. West of Searsmont it becomes large enough to run in high water, and lower down it is passable at all seasons. It is an easy river, but there are nonetheless half a dozen places where caution must be exercised.

The Saint George is an outstanding choice for someone who wishes to canoe through rural Maine. Although many miles of its banks are forested, the river flows through several small towns and past numerous farms. There are three large ponds where the typical view is one of hillside fields and barns, although there are some cottages along the shores. An occasional pair of stone bridge abutments confine the river momentarily, and two washed-out dams suggest that the river prefers to be left unharnessed.

The upper section of the river offers the most interesting canoeing. Flatwater alternates with rapids and ponds. In high water it is probably possible to put in below the dam on Trues Pond in Montville, but a start above Woodmans Mills is not recommended in medium water. You may also begin on Quantabacook Pond off ME-3 and paddle south to the river at Searsmont.

The lower Saint George River can be canoed at all water levels. It is all lake or flatwater except for a total of ¾ mile of rapids, where it will be necessary to wade or drag in low water.

The 5½ miles from Warren to Thomaston are tidal. The river here, somewhat wider and lined with salt marshes, is attractive.

A road map and the text that follows will supply all the information needed to run this river. Of the USGS maps, the Union quadrangle is the most helpful.

Woodmans Mills—Seven Tree Pond   21½ miles

Lakes, **Flatwater**, Quickwater, Class I, II
  High water: *recommended, early May*
  Medium water: *some wading required, early June*
  Forested, Rural, Towns
     USGS: Washington, Searsmont, Union
  Portages: 5½ mi   L   **ledge drops in**
                               Searsmont
                7¾ mi   R   **dam**   100 yds
               17¾ mi   e   **dam**   50 yds/¼ mi
  Campsite   18 mi   L   **in pine-hemlock grove**

Woodsmans Mills is located on ME-173 about 3 miles
west of Searsmont where a tar road branches left (south)
and almost immediately crosses the river. There is a small
ledge drop and some minor rips just below the bridge. Then
for ½ mile the river is small and occasionally crowded with
alders, but the current is strong.

For the next 4 miles the river is mostly smooth. The
flatwater is occasionally broken by short rips, which in high
water are barely noticeable, but after the first 1½ miles there
is a ¼-mile Class II rapid with a ledge near the beginning
that must be lined in medium water and should be scouted
in high water.

More rapids (4½ mi) begin as you approach ME-173 west
of Searsmont. **Caution!** They begin as Class II, but just
above the ME-173 bridge (4¾ mi) there is an old washed-out
milldam that must be scouted. Class II rapids continue to a
short flatwater section above the bridge in Searsmont.

Caution! In high water stop above the ME-131/173
bridge in Searsmont (5½ mi), because there are two unrunnable ledge drops directly below it. In medium water it is
possible to lift over the left side of each ledge, but you are
likely to get wet doing it. Below, easy rapids taper to flatwater by the time you reach the outlet from Quantabacook
Lake (5¾ mi). The next two miles to the low, wooden dam at
Ghent are mostly flat with some riffles. Lift over the dam
on the right.

Below the bridge at Ghent (7¾ mi) there is about 1 mile of
Class II rapids. After ½ mile of quickwater, there is a short

rapid, impassable in medium water, where the river flows between two old bridge abutments (9½ mi). The next 4 miles to Appleton are mostly flat, but there is a ¼-mile Class II rapid that begins at the ME-105 bridge (10¼ mi). Another one begins ¼ mile above Appleton, where the banks of the river become steep (13 mi). These last rapids continue past Appleton, but under the bridge there is another ledge drop that can be lined in medium water and should be scouted in high water.

Below Appleton (13¼ mi), wide, shallow rapids continue for ½ mile, followed by 1¾ miles of flatwater to Sennebec Pond (15½ mi). There is a boat landing at the south end where ME-105/131 skirts the pond (17½ mi). There is a dam ¼ mile below Sennebec Pond. If you carry on the right and put in below it, there is ¼ mile of Class II rapids with a sharp ledge drop halfway down in the middle of an "S"-turn. You may also portage the dam and rapids by following a dirt road between the river and the canal on the left side. Near the end of the canal, continue straight to a grove of conifers where there is a campsite (18 mi).

A 1-mile section of quickwater begins a short distance below the pool by the campsite. In the first ½ mile there are several large trees, which partially block the channel. The fastwater continues under the ME-17/131 bridge (19 mi) to a sharp Class II rapid (19¼ mi) just above the bridge in Union. After 1½ miles of quickwater and flatwater, the Saint George River opens into Round Pond (20¾ mi).

The outlet of Round Pond is directly to the east, with flatwater the remaining ½ mile to the ME-235 bridge (21½ mi), at the edge of Seven Tree Pond where there is a public access ramp.

Seven Tree Pond—Warren   8¾ miles

Lakes, Flatwater, Class I, II
  High water: *recommended, early May*
  Medium water: *recommended, early June*
  Low water: *passable, some lining required*
  Forested, Rural, Towns
     USGS: Union, West Rockport, Thomaston

This section begins with a 2-mile paddle to the southern end of Seven Tree Pond, followed by flatwater most of the way to Warren. One-half mile past an old railroad trestle there is a road bridge (4¼ mi). Two miles beyond, the edge of a field on the right marks the beginning of ½ mile of Class I rapids. You pass under a powerline ¼ mile before·reaching the rapids (8¼ mi) just above Warren.

The rapids at Warren begin with a sharp, turbulent drop between a pair of old bridge abutments. There is a steep portage on the left. Beyond, there is ¼ mile of Class II rapids that end at a powerline. There is a good take-out point on the right above the ME-90 bridge (8¾ mi).

Except at high tide, there is a short rip under the bridge in the town of Warren (9 mi), with more easy rapids continuing beyond when the tide is out. In the spring, passage down these rapids is blocked by a fish weir.

At low tide there is a Class I rapid ¾ mile below Warren. The river passes under US-1 (12¼ mi), widens somewhat, then passes through a narrow, wooded valley before reaching the Wadsworth Street bridge in Thomaston, where there is a boat landing on the right (14½ mi).

OYSTER RIVER

The Oyster River rises in Rockport and crashes its way to tidewater on the St. George River.

West Rockport—Warren   **11½ miles**

Flatwater, Quickwater, Swamp, Class I, II, III, IV
  High water: *medium water if determined*
Wild, Forested
    USGS: Thomaston, W. Rockport
  Portages: Many e **Varying distances**
               5 mi R **Falls**
               8 mi R **Falls**
             (or portage 6 miles down ME-90
             and bag the whole thing)

From the start at Mill Street in West Rockport, the Oyster River is a tiny stream with more blowdowns than water. Two miles below an old dam site and ford (3 mi) is "Dan's

Demise," a narrow gorge and falls best carried on the right. Just past East Warren Road (7¼ mi) there is a complicated set of ledges followed by a series of sharp drops ending at Great Falls, where there is good access. Below the falls the river mellows and is wider to the Saint George.

Although short, it is an intense run, frustrating in low water, hair-raising in high. Unlike most remote streams, it is conveniently located not more than a 30-minute drive from nice, warm bars in Camden.

MAINE COASTAL PADDLING

Maine has hundreds of miles of coastline, most of it quite suitable for canoeing. Coastal scenery is spectacular and bird and animal life plentiful. Water level is never a problem, as it can be on interior rivers and streams. The Indians of Maine and the nearby Maritime Provinces summered on the coast, where food was abundant and breezes kept off the bulk of pesky insects.

Coastal canoeing presents the paddler with a whole new set of potential hazards. Rapids and falls are rare, but they do exist in spots, due to tide change, and tidal rips are very common. Water height varies in Maine from approximately 6 feet to 28 feet, becoming more extreme as one moves from west to east toward the Bay of Fundy. Wind opposed to tide can raise erratic and dangerous seas. The wake of boats compounds the problem. Canoeists should stay to the edge of the channel in courtesy to deeper-draft boats.

Navigation is much more complicated. A nautical chart, and the ability to use it, is highly recommended. Sea temperatures are cold, warming to the low 60s at best in August or September. Fog is quite common, indeed the rule, in early summer.

Despite these hazards, coastal paddling in Maine can be a very rewarding experience, safe and enjoyable if one is properly prepared and cautious. Be willing to abort the trip if conditions are not suitable. Have a contingency plan if fog or wind arises later. Know how to navigate in less-than-perfect visibility.

A good, deep-sided river canoe is quite suitable for Maine's waters. Sea kayaking is a specialized sport, and beyond the scope of this book. Nautical charts, not topographical maps, should be used for all but the most trivial trips. A good compass in each boat is mandatory. Fresh water is found on many islands, but often not in drinkable amounts or quality: bring much more fresh water than you can imagine using. Sea spray is hard on cameras and binoculars.

Some popular areas for coastal canoeing are Casco Bay, near Portland; Muscongus and Penobscot bays on the mid-coast; and Great Wass and Englishman Bay on the east coast.

Good places to avoid are Passamaquoddy and Cobscook Bay, because of high tides and extensive mudflats, Grand Manan Channel (just plain dangerous) the Boothbay region (tacky) and the sand areas south of Portland.

DOWN EAST COASTAL CANOE TRAIL

Various people have been working to establish a relatively safe tidewater-canoeing route with supporting campsites to make a week-long trip from Portland to Pemaquid feasible. This is a brief excerpt from their material.

The recommended route starts from Spring Point, in South Portland. It goes between Peaks and Diamond islands and west of Long Island. The first campsite is Little Chebeague Island (6 mi).

The route then passes south and east of Great Chebeague Island and west of Hope, Bangs, and Stockman islands. Turning east, it passes south of Basin and Potts Points to a campsite in Harpswell Sound (12 mi).

Continue north up Harpswell Sound, proceed through Erwin Narrows, Long Reach, and the Gurnet Strait, turning southeast into the New Meadows River. The portage to the Kennebec is made from Winnegance Bay to Winnegance Creek (Winnegance is an Indian word meaning "small portage"). Meadowbrook, a commercial campground, is near the portage trail (12 mi).

The portage starts at a boat-launching ramp at the east end of Brighams Cove. Continue over the ridge and along the trees beyond to the trail down to the water. A short portage must be made at the ME-209 bridge. Go up the Kennebec to Bath and turn east into the Sasanoa River (qv) to Beal Island (advance reservations required for camping)

(10 mi). Access at AMC Knubble Bay Camp ¾ mile to the southwest.

From Beal Island continue south down the Sasanoa River, cross the Sheepscot River to Townsend Gut, continue across Boothbay Harbor, round south of Spruce Point and north to East Boothbay. Portage from the boat ramp across the road into a pool and then through a culvert (when tide conditions permit). Go north up the Damariscotta River to Fort Island (12 mi).

Return to South Bristol, go through the Gut to the finish at the boat ramp just north of Fort William Henry (5 mi).

Wind, weather, and fog conditions make it highly likely that the trip will be delayed at some point. Allow for rest days or an alternate take-out when making plans.

The entire route is on National Ocean Survey Chart #13288 (Monhegan Island to Cape Elizabeth). Greater detail is found on #13293 (Damariscotta, Sheepscot, and Kennebec rivers) and #13290 (Casco Bay).

Further information may be obtained from the AMC Beal Island Committee or Bill Gerber, 16 Princess Ave., Chelmsford, MA 01863 (617-251-4971).

CHAPTER 8

Eastern Coastal Watersheds

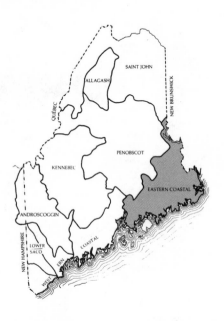

EASTERN COASTAL WATERSHEDS

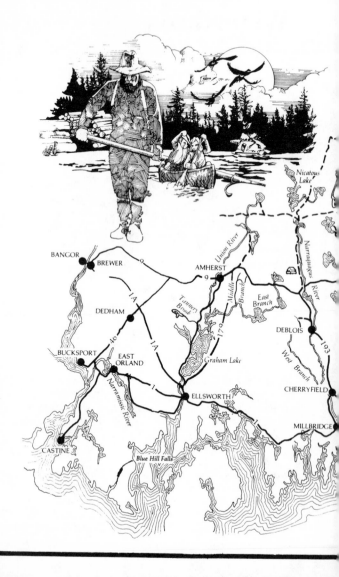

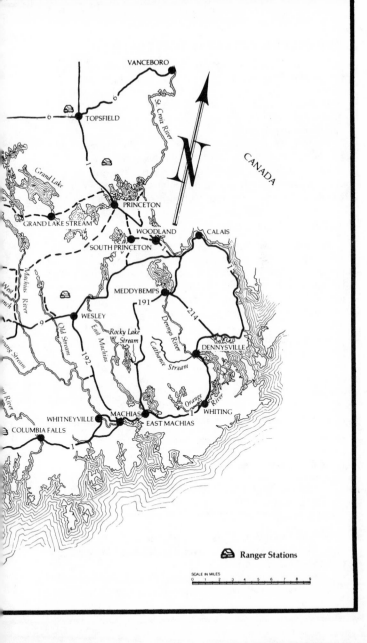

Ranger Stations

BLUE HILL FALLS

Blue Hill Falls is a tidal rip that is a good place for practice in handling rough water. There is approximately 100 yards of rugged whitewater that can be traversed over and over again. Conditions are excellent for approximately 3 hours. It can be run anytime the tide is right, although late summer is the warmest.

The falls is located by ME-175 where the bridge crosses the entrance to Salt Pond 3 miles southeast of Blue Hill.

The falls is best run starting 3 hours after low tide. It starts slowly and within 3 hours builds up to Class IV. It can be run and re-run using the large eddy on the right.

NARRAMISSIC RIVER

The Narramissic River is the outlet of Alamoosook Lake, and is the last freshwater section of a collection of lakes and ponds that flow into the Penobscot river at its mouth. The tidal section below Orland is called the Orland River for the last few miles to the Penobscot.

The largest lake that drains into Alamoosook Pond is Toddy Pond, which is pretty and somewhat wild at the southern end, but its outlet is not canoeable. The furthest upstream starting point is on Mill Dam Brook near Denham. This flows into Long Pond, the outlet of which is Moosehorn Stream, which flows through Dead River to Alamoosook Lake.

Denham—Alamoosook Lake   10¼ miles

Lake, Flatwater, Quickwater, **Swamp,** Class I, II
  Medium water, lakes anytime
  Forested
      USGS: Orland 15, Bucksport 15
    Portage: (10¼ mi   **dam at outlet)**

Several brooks join just below Denham. The going is heavy through a swamp and over deadfalls and beaver dams to Long Pond (2¾ mi).

Continuing on Moosehorn Stream from Long Pond (4¾ mi), the river flows over a beaver dam and a short rapid.

There is quickwater and Class I down to the ME-4 bridge, which is too low to pass under in high water. The stream slows for a while, and then drops over the most difficult rapids on the trip where the stream is small and full of sharp turns, under a small bridge on a dirt track. Soon it slows down and widens out, passing through a marshy area with beaver dams into the Dead River (7½ mi), really a northward arm of the lake now that the dam has flooded back up into it. It is 2 miles down Dead River to the narrows and another mile down the lake and around the corner to the dam.

Alamoosuk Lake—Orland   3 miles

Flatwater, Quickwater
  Passable at all levels
  Forested, Rural
    USGS: Orland 15
  Portage: (3 mi   **dam at Orland)**

This is a pleasant run through fields and woods that can be done as a return trip.

UNION RIVER

The confluence of the East and West branches of the Union River is now flooded out at the northern end of Graham lake.

Graham Lake   14¾ miles

From the last bridge on the West Branch it is 2¾ miles to the confluence with the East Branch, and another mile to a boat ramp on the west bank. Beyond a large island the lake opens up, narrowing again toward the south end and the dam.

Graham Lake—Ellsworth   4½ miles

Below the dam the river is mostly smooth for the next 4 miles to Ellsworth, except for a bit of quickwater at Ellsworth Falls halfway down. Below the high dam at Ellsworth the river is tidal.

UNION RIVER, West Branch

The West Branch of the Union River is formed by a collection of brooks south of Passadumkeag Mountain and flows south to meet the sea south of Ellsworth, where it feeds into the complex of bays around Mount Desert on the eastern side of Penobscot Bay. When the water is high, it offers relatively easy canoeing with easy rapids. It should generally be run before the black fly season.

The "Union River canoe trip" starts at Brandy Pond, follows Brandy Stream to Main River, and thence to Great Pond. The West Branch of the Union is the outlet of Great Pond.

Brandy Pond—Great Pond   8½ miles

Flatwater, Quickwater
   High water
   Forested
      USGS: Saponic 15
      Portage: 6½ mi   **short carry**

Brandy Pond can be reached from the private road, open to the public, which runs north from the ranger's cabin on ME-9 at Beddington. The outlet, Brandy Stream, is at the middle of the south shore. It is a small stream but in 1 mile it is joined by Buffalo Stream, bringing the drainage from Passadumkeag Mountain. These two streams join to form Main Stream, which for the next 3 miles meanders westward until it turns south. About 1½ miles below this turn it passes under the bridge of the logging road, and ½ mile below this bridge fastwater begins and continues for 1 mile to Great Pond. A half-mile below the junction with Alligator Stream there is a short, but difficult, carry over a 6-foot pitch. Main Stream enters Great Pond near the middle of the north shore. From here it is 2 miles across the pond to the outlet at the southeastern end.

Great Pond (Dow Pines)—Amherst   11 miles

Quickwater, Class III, IV (can be lined or portaged)
  High water: *early spring*
  Forested, Blueberry barrens
    USGS: Saponac 15, Great Pond 15

Great Pond and its adjacent region are a U.S. Air Force Recreation Area and can be reached by a road that leaves ME-9 at Aurora.

From Dow Pines to the dam is 1 mile along the lake. The washed-out dam at the outlet marks the beginning of the Union River. The quickwater in the vicinity of the dam flattens out for 2 miles. The banks steepen near a sharp 3-foot drop; then there are 200 yards of Class II water to a left turn and the last pool before Hell's Gate (3¼ mi). Take out right. Hell's Gate is a 3-stage drop up to Class IV at high water. The next 6 miles are mostly smooth, but contain 3 significant ledge drops that should be carefully scouted. Then there is ¼ mile of interesting Class II to the Gauging Station, a popular take-out on Tannery Road (10¼ mi). Just beyond the Gauging station is a long, steep ledge drop. Scouting is mandatory. The river passes under the bridge at the Tannery Road and continues with interesting riffles to ME-9.

Amherst—Graham Lake   6 miles

Quickwater, Class II
  Run any water level
  Forested
    USGS: Great Pond 15, Ellsworth 15
  Portage: 3 mi R **waterfall**

The next 3 miles are meandering quickwater to a 10-foot waterfall, followed by 100 yards of Class II. Following this the backwaters of Graham Lake are reached. Take out at Goodwin Bridge on ME-181 (6 mi).

UNION RIVER, East Branch

The East Branch of the Union River drains a number of ponds east of Beddington, and flows west and then south into the upper end of Graham Lake north of Ellsworth to join the main river.

Steep Landing—ME-179   14¼ miles

Lake, Flatwater, Quickwater, Marsh, Class I, II
  High or medium water: *until mid-June; after heavy rain*
  Wild, Forested
     USGS: Great Pond, Lead Mountain 15

Portages:	7½ mi	R	**Ledge Falls** (optional)
	10½ mi	R	**Island Rips** head of island (optional)
Campsites:	3 mi		**Spectacle Pond**

Steep Landing is where the esker crosses the river 2 miles below Rocky Pond. Do not try to drive down the hill the last 100 yards to the put-in.

The East Branch is half the size of the West Branch, twice as much fun, and three times as pretty. The crossing of Spectacle Pond and the 2½ mile flat paddle at the end tend to discourage the whitewater enthusiast, but the paddler with an appreciation for diversity will find the East Branch delightful.

From Steep Landing to Spectacle Pond the river is small and flows through alternating forests and bogs. There is a short Class I rip just before the entrance to the pond (2¾ mi). Spectacle Pond has few camps, little boat traffic in spring, as well as good sand beaches and campsites.

A 3-mile paddle across the lake through the Narrows brings one to "Poison Ivy Pitch" (5¾ mi), a short, sharp drop, Class II in high water. In a mile the Bog River (alternate start) comes in on the left bringing a substantial volume of water. The bog section ends at Ledge Falls (7½ mi). Look for granite ledge on left. Portage right if desired. Ledge Falls is the site of an old timber dam, the logs of which sometimes tear free and complicate the lower end of this Class II–III drop.

Shortly after begins "the Ramp," a delightful 2-mile section of narrow, snaky river loaded with blind bends and boulders. **Caution!** Although no drop here is greater than Class II in high water, you can come upon downed trees with awful suddenness. The ramp ends at the junction with the Middle Branch, where it is possible to take out (9½ mi).

More rips are just below. A quarter mile beyond a bridge you will find Island Rip (10¼ mi). A small channel of the river cuts right (not passable) forming a small island and a large island just beyond. The optional portage is on the right at the head of the large island—very easy to miss. Island Rip is 100 yards long, Class II-III, with many boulders and holes. The worst part is at the start. Below are two small Class I rips. The "Stanmoddar" (11¾ mi) is a huge, erratic boulder. Local Saxon legend has it that "Stanmoddar" gave birth to the myriads of boulders in this area.

The next 2½ miles are smooth with little current. Take out at the large sawdust pile on the left, or below the bridge on the right in the pool.

ME-179—West Branch   5 miles

Flatwater, Quickwater, Class I, II
    High or medium water: *until mid-June; after heavy rains*
    Wild
        USGS: Great Pond, Ellsworth 15
        Portage: 2¼ mi   R   **waterfall**   50–300 yds

This section is seldom paddled. About ½ mile below ME-179 is a ledge drop that should be looked at. Pleasant paddling takes one in a mile to a bouldery bend, Class I-II (1½ mi). Use caution on sharp bends here, as they blend together.

Get out before two stone bridge abutments (the jaws of death), and scout rapids below. Class II-III rips begin and continue right to the brink of Siltstone Falls (2¼ mi), a definite portage. As there are no good eddies, rescue spots, etc., before the falls, this is one place where "going for it" may result in "getting it." Portage right. Below the falls is another short drop of changing difficulty as the level of Graham Lake rises and falls.

There is no take-out at the confluence. Persons going upstream on the West Branch should use the drag-over (4½ mi) to the right to the West Branch, and paddle 2 miles up to ME-181. From the confluence it is 12 miles south to Graham Lake dam. Take-out may be possible at a boat ramp on the west shore (6¼ mi).

UNION RIVER, Middle Branch

This smallest branch of the Union River is the least used. The heaviest use is by fishermen who usually put in at ME-9 and paddle upstream into the large bog paralleling the Whaleback.

ME-9—East Branch   6½ miles

Flatwater, **Quickwater,** Swamp, Class I
  High or medium water: *spring*
  Wild
      USGS: Great Pond 15

Below ME-9 the Middle Branch flows through a swamp with occasional beaver dams. Swamp gives way to forest, and soon the first of two rough spots occurs (Class I), followed in 1½ miles by the other rough spot. Access is available at an old bridge crossing just before the East Branch.

TANNERY BROOK

Tannery Brook has its source in Burnt Pond on the border of Dedham and Otis. It flows eastward through Otis and Mariaville to Graham Lake. The river drops 195 feet in 5 miles, but much of it is in the first ¼ mile.

ME-180—Graham Lake   4½ miles

Class I, II, III
  High water
  Wild
      USGS: Orland 15, Ellsworth 15

Put in at the ME-180 bridge. The river is small, and most of the way is Class I, interspersed with ledge drops, Class II and III. Shortly below the ME-181 bridge it flows into Graham Lake.

NARRAGUAGUS RIVER

The Narraguagus flows from Deer Lake to tidewater at Cherryfield, and in the 40 miles described here it drops 391 feet, more than any coastal stream east of the Penobscot, except for the Saint Croix, which is appreciably longer. It also has more access points than the rivers to the east, because a road of some kind parallels it, more or less, all the way. Fortunately, the attractiveness of the river is scarcely affected, and it appears as wild as any in Maine.

Deer Lake—Deblois   **25 miles**

Lakes, Quickwater, Class I, II
   Highwater: *May*
  Forested
       USGS: Tunk Lake 15, Lead Mountain 15
Campsites: 0 mi   **Deer Lake**   MFS $ car
           11¼ mi L **Twenty-eight Pond**
                          permit
           19½ mi L **Beddington Lake**
                          Outlet permit

The drop in this section is 230 feet, virtually all of which is runnable in season. The rapids are Class I and II, except near the end at Rock Dam Rips, a Class III pitch.

The first 4 miles are flat, and should be avoided by someone pressed for time or unwilling to cope with windfalls and beaver dams. It is worth doing, but it will take 2–3 hours to paddle from Deer Lake through the Oxbow to the outlet of Haycock Pond, where the river approaches the road for the first time. Below the Oxbow, where the river flows slowly through a large meadow, there is a good current with many interesting rapids.

Lead Mountain, located north of the Airline (ME-9) and just west of the river, is a 1475-foot landmark that is visible from various points along the Narraguagus as far upstream as the Oxbow.

It is ¾ mile from the MFS campsite on Deer Lake to the outlet. En route you pass the road from Beddington, and if you can just squeeze a loaded canoe through the culvert, there will be plenty of water downstream. Below the dam for 1¼ miles the stream is flat, small, and occasionally blocked by deadfalls and choked with alders. After a log bridge (2 mi), the river, wider now, meanders for 2 miles through the Oxbow, where there are beaver dams and a few more trees across the water.

Below the Oxbow, the river approaches the road (4 mi) and the current picks up. As it passes Bracey Pond (out of sight to the west), there is a log bridge (6 mi), which is a good access point. In ¾ mile there is another bridge (6¾ mi), after which there is 1 mile of easy rapids that end just above a large dry-ki dam. The latter may be passable on the left if the water is high enough. There is quickwater to Third Pond, and below that more good current to Twenty-eight Pond (11 mi).

After Twenty-eight Pond, there is good current for 3 miles, followed by 1½ miles of intermittent Class I and II rapids to the Airline bridge (16¼ mi), and continuing for another ½ mile beyond. The paddle down Beddington Lake, beginning 1 mile past the Airline, may seem a little confusing if you follow the topographic map too closely, because the water level has dropped since it was made.

Below the old dam (19½ mi), there is good current for 1¾ miles to Bog Brook, where it picks up somewhat. Then, 1¾ miles later, below a huge boulder on the right and out of sight around a bend to the left, is Rock Dam Rips (23 mi), a nice Class III rapid less than 100 yards long that should be scouted from the left bank. Beyond the rapids a short distance, there is an abrupt 3-foot ledge drop, which is easily lined down on the left. Soon the current slackens to quickwater. There is a short, easy rapid a little way above Deblois (25 mi). Land right above the ME-193 bridge, because there is some very rough water below.

Deblois—Cherryfield   17¼ miles

Flatwater, Quickwater, Class I, II, III
   High or medium water: *May through June*
   Low water: *passable with some scraping above Stillwater*
   Dam
   Wild, Towns
      USGS: Tunk Lake 15, Cherryfield 15
   Portages: 0 mi   R   **Ledges at Deblois**   200
                                                   yds
               ¼ mi   R   **Ledges**   150 yds
             15¾ mi   L   **Stillwater Dam**   50 yds

The lower part of the Narraguagus is most easily characterized as a flatwater river that winds in a shallow, wooded
valley. In a few locations the blueberry barrens are visible
on the hills above. From the powerline crossing to Little
Falls, the banks are more open, with a thick growth of
bushes and small plants overlooked by numerous dead elms.

At the beginning are two sections that must be portaged.
Just north of the bridge in Deblois, there is a path along the
river that leads in ⅓ mile past a cabin to the flatwater below
the second impassable drop. In high or medium water, the
part between the drops can be run. Descend to the river
when you have reached the lower corner of the field, about
200 yards, and run easy Class II rapids to a pool. Take out a
little way below the pool on the right before a cabin, and
portage again about 150 yards around the falls.

In the first ¾ mile below the second portage, there are a
few short Class I-II rips. Then for approximately 9 miles
the river is quickwater, with a good current that lessens as
you continue downstream. The only landmarks are a powerline (4¼ mi) and Schoodic Brook (9¼ mi), which enters on
the left as the Narraguagus turns right.

A short distance below Schoodic Brook you reach the
first of two easy Class II rapids that precede Little Falls.
The falls are, in fact, a Class II rapid, about 100 yards long
with heavy waves in high water. There is a house on the left
bank.

Below Little Falls, there are three Class II rapids, the first
of which is almost flooded out in high water. Then flatwater

continues past the confluence of the West Branch (15¼ mi) to Stillwater Dam.

Below Stillwater Dam (15¾ mi), there are nearly continuous rapids for 1½ miles until you reach tidewater. The rapids are Class III, with three difficult pitches: just above and 50 yards below the railroad bridge, and just before the first road bridge. The other sections are easier, but here the Narraguagus is a big river. The rapids reach tidewater about 100 yards above the US-1 bridge (17¼ mi).

NARRAGUAGUS RIVER, West Branch

The West Branch of the Narraguagus River rises just west of Beddington in T22 MD, and flows southeast more or less parallel to the main river until it joins it a few miles above Cherryfield. The upper part of the river is too small for canoeing until it gets nearly to Deblois. It is possible to reach it here, and run down to the main stream with easy rapids and good fishing along the way.

Denbow Heath—Sprague Falls   14 miles

Flatwater, **Quickwater,** Swamp, Class I, II, III, IV
  High and medium water: *early June*
  Wild, Forested
        USGS: Lead Mountain, Tunk Lake 15, Tunk
              Mountain

Portages:	5 mi	L	**Rock Dam**	10 yd
	10 mi	R	**Long Falls**	½ mi
	(14 mi	R	**Sprague Falls**	150 yd)

This is a beautiful, little-used river, much like other east Maine streams. The rapids are granite ledges and piles of boulders.

Access to the put-in is through Denbow Heath Peat Mine. Inquire locally for permission and road conditions.

Rock Dam is a short ledge drop about 3 feet high that should be looked over. Spring River enters right at 7 mi. Long Falls definitely must be scouted. The first pitch should probably be carried. It is strong, complicated, and narrow.

There is a nice Class II–III pitch around the corner below. Optional portage on left.

There is a good take-out at Sprague Falls.

Sprague Falls—Narraguagus River　　　　4 miles

The last section to the Narraguagus River is mostly smooth.

PLEASANT RIVER

The Pleasant River flows from Pleasant River Lake, just south of ME-9 in Beddington, to Columbia Falls. It should be distinguished from the Pleasant River which is a tributary of the Piscataquis in the Penobscot watershed and others. The Pleasant has three distinct personalities: the upper portion is a fine wilderness trip with some whitewater; the middle portion meanders through an extensive marsh ending at Saco Falls; and the lower section is mostly smooth and settled to Columbia Falls, where it becomes tidal.

Pleasant River Lake—Columbia Falls　　　33½ miles

Flatwater, Quickwater, Class I, II, III
　High water: *early May*
　Wild, Towns
　　　USGS: Tug Mountain 15, Cherryfield 15,
　　　　　Columbia Falls
　Portages:　27½ mi　L　**Saco Falls**　2 mi
　　　　　　33½ mi　　　**Falls**

The Pleasant River starts at an outlet on the southern end of Pleasant River Lake. The river can be reached by taking a dirt road south from ME-9 at about the T30 MD Township line, which is marked. Drive straight on the dirt road for 2¾ miles. Keep to the left as several roads run off to the right to lakeside camps. The trip starts at a small wooden bridge and a broken dam at the southern end of the lake.

The Pleasant River drops over a series of narrow ledges to a pool 70 yards below. These ledges may be impassable in all but very high water. The best route is to the left. The river then passes through a number of marshes with numerous signs of beaver activity; lodges are scattered through the marshes, and dams block the river at several points.

After 5½ miles the river narrows and enters a stretch of Class III rapids west of Beech Hill at a point about ½ mile from the "Allison Worcester camp" on Tug Mountain quadrangle. The "hill" is almost indistinguishable in the rolling blueberry barrens. The most prominent landmark is a large boulder, which sits in the middle of the river.

Here the river narrows to about 20 feet. It cascades some 75 yards through Class II and III rapids. This section should be scouted, because it is rocky and there is little room to maneuver. **Caution!** Fallen trees may cross the river at this point forming "strainers." After these rapids, the river continues narrow and fast-moving for ¼ mile. After another 6½ miles there is a road access (12 mi) before entering an extended marsh. Canoeists wishing to take out here should spot a car on the dirt road, which can be reached by turning east off ME-192 almost directly opposite the Deblois airfield.

Pleasant River meanders for 14 miles through the marsh, following such a convoluted route that it requires almost a full day of paddling. After the marsh, the river passes through a forested area with low, alder-lined banks.

The approach of Saco Falls is indicated by several old farm buildings on the left (27½ mi). The river flows past islands and ledges composed of large rocks, and then narrows very sharply before dropping to the falls. Only the first 50 yards of the rapids can be run—on the left, but scout on the right. There is a take-out on the left in the pool below the rapid. Canoes can be carried 150 feet up a gravel path leading to a paved road. **Caution!** An unfinished dam stands below the pool, the footing of which causes a drop of several feet. The falls are 150 yards below, and the banks of the river are steep and the current fast.

The river thunders several hundred feet over a series of giant rock steps at Saco Falls. Since this would be a very long and difficult portage, it is better to end the trip here.

Putting in at Arty's Bridge, 2 miles downstream (29½ mi), the river is mostly smooth. Several hundred yards below the bridge is a short set of Class II rips, and another set of rips (31½ mi) where some dragging may be necessary in low water, about 2 miles above Columbia Falls. The river passes under a railroad bridge to the take-out on the right at the town hall, which looks like a church from the river (33½ mi). Below here the river passes over some falls to tidewater.

MACHIAS RIVER

The Machias River rates with the Allagash, the Penobscot, and the Saint John as one of Maine's most scenic waterways. It offers semi-wilderness travel with lakes, swamps, intermittent rapids up to Class III, ledges, a waterfall, and portages—all in a region that has much less use than the Allagash, and which is more accessible than the Saint John. When the last of the dams was removed in 1974, the Machias once again became a free-flowing river.

The route from Fifth Machias Lake to the sea offers one of the longest (76 miles) and most attractive semi-wilderness canoe trips in Maine. The three big lakes have only a few cabins on their shores, and above First Machias Lake there are none along the river.

Due to the ravages of the spruce bud worm there has been very extensive clear cutting of timber throughout the watershed of the Machias to salvage logs and pulpwood while it is still marketable. This has changed the characteristics of the river, causing a much more rapid run-off in the spring and a very definite response to rain.

Many years ago, there were two routes to the Machias River from Nicatous Lake. One went up Gassabias Stream, across Gassabias Lake, and over a long portage to Fourth Machias Lake. The other began with a portage into Upper Sabao Lake (sometimes called "Machias Lake"), and continued downstream to Lower Sabao Lake at the head of the West Branch. Although the first segments of each route, to Gassabias Lake and Upper Sabao Lake, respectively, are usable now, the remaining portions are impassable.

Fifth Machias Lake—ME-9   40 miles

Lakes, Flatwater, Class I, II, III
  High water: *May*
  Wild
        USGS: Nicatous Lake 15, Wabassus Lake 15,
              Tug Mountain 15

Campsites:			
3 mi		**5th Lake Outlet** (beach) permit
3¾ mi	R	**old damsite** permit
8¼ mi	R	**Knight Dam** permit
13¾ mi	L	**4th Lake** (N of Unknown Stream) MFS
15¼ mi	L	**4th Lake Outlet** permit—car
20½ mi		**3rd Lake Narrows** (island) permit
21 mi		**Getchel Lakes Outlet** (W side) permit
21¼ mi		**Prune Island** (S side) permit
23½ mi		**3rd Lake Outlet** permit—car
27¾ mi	R	**2nd Lake Outlet** (beach) permit—car
30¾ mi	L	**1st Lake Outlet** permit—car

Fifth Machias Lake can be reached from the Saint Regis Paper Company road that runs from Princeton to Costigan. A half-mile trail to Greenland Cove leaves that road 4½ miles west of the crossroads near the north end of First Machias Lake.

From the end of Greenland Cove it is 2½ miles across the lake to the beach at the outlet (3 mi). This point can be reached by car from the same road by turning north 3 miles west of Greenland Cove on road 42-00-0. This is the usual start for the river trip. From there, Fifth Lake Stream flows through a culvert and then a low, marshy area for 5¼ miles to Knight Dam (8¼ mi). Almost all the way there is quick-water, but there is a short, easy rapid less than 100 yards above the old washed-out dam. Then there are 1½ miles of Class I and II rapids, with five short sections to watch out for. The first three are ledge drops, the first and last of which are runnable. Unless the water is very high, the second one will have to be lined. After a little slackwater, you reach the fourth sharp drop; a narrow chute. The fifth tricky spot is just around the next corner. Soon thereafter the rapids end, and after 1¼ miles of flatwater Fifth Lake Stream empties into Fourth Machias Lake (11 mi).

In 1974 the dams on Fourth and Third Machias lakes were removed, exposing the land that was flooded many years ago. The shores now appear barren, particularly at the upper ends of each lake where the land is flatter, but in many areas grasses have already become established, and soon no doubt there will be bushes and trees.

Fourth Machias Lake is 4¼ miles long. At the outlet (15¼ mi), the remains of the old dam can be run in high water. Fourth Lake Stream begins with a short Class II rapid, followed by 1¼ miles of quickwater and smoothwater. Shoreline Rapids (16¾ mi), exposed when the dam on Third Machias Lake was removed, is a short Class II pitch that carries you below the old lake level. There is another Class I rapid before Third Machias Lake (17¾ mi) is reached.

It is a 5¾-mile paddle down Third Machias Lake to the outlet (23½ mi), where the remains of the old dam can be run. A good gravel road runs up the east side of the river from First Lake to this point.

The Machias River begins with ½ mile of Class I and II rapids, followed by another ½ mile of deadwater. Below the latter is Otter Rips, a ¼-mile set of Class II rapids that leads to a second deadwater, which is 1 mile long.

Long Falls (25¾ mi) begins at the boundary line between T43 MD and T37 MD; it is ¼-mile Class III pitch with some ledges and narrow channels. There is a portage on both sides that leads to a short stretch of quickwater below the rapids. In the remaining 1¼ miles to Second Machias Lake (27¼ mi), there are almost continuous Class I and II rapids. One-half mile of paddling on Second Machias Lake and 2 miles of flatwater on the river bring you to First Machias Lake (29¾ mi). Just before reaching the latter, the river flows under the logging road that connects Princeton and Costigan.

From the outlet of First Machias Lake (30¾ mi), the river is mostly smooth for 4 miles. Then, in the middle of an "S"-turn, there begin a few easy rapids that lead up to Carrot Rips, also called Karrick Pitch (35 mi), a short Class II–III drop that should be scouted or portaged on the right bank. One-half mile beyond, the West Branch enters on the right.

Below the confluence with the West Branch (35½ mi), there are 4½ miles of good current with occasional easy rapids. All of the latter, including the Class II rapids at Boot Rips (38¼ mi), are flooded out when the water is really high. As you approach ME-9, stop well before the bridge (40 mi), because the river above it has been channeled, and there are few good stopping places in the swift current. Airline Rapids, below the bridge, should be scouted.

ME-9—Machias   36½ miles

Flatwater, Quickwater, Class II, III
High water: *May*
Medium water: *June*
Wild
     USGS: Tug Mountain 15, Wesley 15,
            Whitneyville, Machias

Portages:	4½ mi	L	**Little Falls** ¼ mi
	8½ mi	R	**First pitch Wigwam Falls** ½ mi
	13½ mi	L	**Upper Holmes Falls** 200 yds
	14 mi	R	**Lower Holmes Falls** 150 yds
	25 mi	R	**Great Falls** ¼ mi
Campsites:	¼ mi	L	**Airline Rapids** MFS $ car
	4¾ mi	L	**Little Falls** (lower end) permit
	10 mi	L	**Wigwam Rapids, Third Pitch** (poor) permit
	13¾ mi	L	**Upper Holmes Falls** (lower end) permit
	23 mi	L	**Smith Landing** (poor) permit, car
	25½ mi	R	**Great Falls** (lower end) permit

The Machias from ME-9 to the sea is a large river with
many sections of flatwater separated by falls and, in high
water, heavy rapids. Depending on the water level and the
skill of the paddlers, Airline Rapids, Little Falls, the four
main pitches of Wigwam Rapids, and Great Falls require a
portage, are runnable, or can be lined.

The river banks approaching Whitneyville are in the
process of recovering from the disturbance of a fire and a
dam.

Below Smith Landing, the river passes through an area
burned in 1956. It is interesting to note the ease with which
the fire jumped the river, while at the same time leaving iso-

lated pockets of the forest unscathed. A good example of this is at Great Falls, where the island at the beginning was burned, but neither bank of the river at that point was touched. Little evidence of the fire remains. The old lake bed has gone to meadow and is very attractive.

The removal of the dam at Whitneyville, which backed up the water to Great Falls, has allowed the river to return to its original channel. When the old lake bottom was first exposed, it was covered with cords of sunken pulpwood, which has now been salvaged.

Airline Rapids, about ⅓ mile long, begins under the ME-9 bridge and should be scouted. It is Class III, can be run in two stages, and may have some heavy waves in high water. There is quickwater for 2¼ miles to two short Class II rapids followed by fast current to Little Falls (4½ mi). The upper section is Class IV, but the lower portion is Class II. The portage begins on the left, and ends at the campsite below the falls. Then there is more flatwater for 3¾ miles to Wigwam Rapids.

Wigwam Rapids (8½ mi) extends over a distance of 2 miles, with sections of varying difficulty depending on the water level. High water obliterates many riffles; when it does there remain four more or less distinct pitches. The first, upper Wigwam, begins ¼ mile below the mouth of Mopang Stream and should be scouted from the good portage, which begins in front of a cabin on the right bank. The upper section contains large boulders that make it Class III when the water is high, Class II when medium. The lower portion of the first pitch is much easier, and there are several places to put in partway down. The first pitch is ½ mile long, followed by half a mile of slackwater and then the last three pitches, which together make up Lower Wigwam. Within the next mile there are many small rapids, which are flooded out in high water; the one that is not is the second pitch, Class II. The approach to the third pitch (10 mi) is somewhat blind, and this rapid should be scouted from the portage on the left bank, as it is a short, tricky drop over a Class III ledge with an almost river-wide hydraulic; a sneak route on left. The fourth pitch, not far beyond, is a short Class II rapid.

After Wigwam Rapids there are 3 miles of slackwater to Upper Holmes Falls (13½ mi), a 15-foot waterfall with a portage on the left. One-third mile below is Lower Holmes Falls (Class III), which begins at Deadman's Island, on the northern end of which is a memorial to Obadiah Hill, a pioneer who died in 1786. The portage is on the right bank. The section of the rapids that is dangerous is at the end, and it cannot be seen from the trail.

Flatwater continues for 11 miles, passing the mouth of Old Stream (20¼ mi), and is interrupted only slightly by Getchell Riffles which are Class I (21 mi) and Bobsled Rips, hardly notable (24½ mi). At Smith Landing (23 mi) a good dirt road leads to ME-192. Great Falls (25 mi) is a long, continuous Class III rapid. The easiest route is on the left. Scout first. The portage is on the right bank.

There are 6¼ miles of quickwater to Whitneyville (31½ mi). The old lake bed forms a wide meadow with views of the surrounding hills, unusual on the lower river. Near Whitneyville are crumbling remains of cribs and piers from logging days. Almost nothing remains of the old dam. Within sight of the US-1A bridge the river splits around an island. The right is a straightforward Class II rapid; the left has a short Class III–IV ledge, which should be scouted.

Beyond the highway bridge in Whitneyville the river is flat for 1¾ mile except for a Class I rapid at the railroad bridge. Then comes Munson Pitch, a riverwide, Class II ledge run on the left.

The river flattens out for another 1¾ miles, then enters ¾ mile of easy Class I rapids between rocky bluffs. A short, flat stretch leads to an attractive little gorge with a nice Class II rapid. A final Class I rapid ends in a short slackwater behind the partly broken dam just below the bridge in Machias. Land on the right at the start of the pool or on the left at the bridge.

Beyond the bridge is the Machias Falls, the Indians' "bad little falls." They are easily carried on the left through town. The falls split around an island and drop about 15 feet at high tide. The left is unrunnable; the right has a big drop into a big hole, probably Class V.

MACHIAS RIVER, West Branch

The West Branch is small, wild, and seldom-traveled. It requires higher water than is needed on the Machias River below ME-9, so it must be run early in the spring. There is a convenient campsite halfway down—at Rolford Dam—if the trip is done in two days.

Upper Cranberry Lake—ME-9   19¾ miles

Lakes, **Flatwater,** Quickwater, Class I, II
  High water: *May*
  Wild
    USGS: Tug Mountain 15
Campsites: 0 mi   **Upper Cranberry Lakes**
                          MFS $ car
              9¾ mi   R   **Rolford Dam**   permit

As you follow the road to the Cranberry Lakes from ME-9, keep right at an intersection about 6 miles from the highway.

From the MFS campsite on Upper Cranberry Lake to the beginning of Cranberry Stream, there are 3½ miles of lake paddling, with a portage around a culvert connecting the two lakes. Cranberry Stream meanders sluggishly for 2 miles to its junction with the West Branch (5½ mi). [The West Branch flows for 1½ miles from Lower Sabao Lake to Cranberry Stream; it is flat and swampy.]

Beyond the mouth of Cranberry Stream, the current begins to pick up after ½ mile. Then there are 2¾ miles of intermittent, easy Class I and II rapids, with a low logging bridge near the end, before reaching Rolford Deadwater (8¾ mi). Rolford Dam (9¾ mi) is washed out and is runnable.

Between Rolford Dam and the bridge above the confluence with the Main Branch, there are 5¼ miles of mixed flatwater and Class I and II rapids, but there are also three ledges that must be lined. The first is reached only 150 yards below the dam and around the corner to the right. It is best lined empty from the left bank. The second, several miles beyond, consists of a broad ledge with water spilling over it the full width of the river, as if it were a mill dam. Like the first, it should be lined empty from or close to the left bank. The third, near the end, is narrower and can be lined along the right bank.

Under the bridge (15 mi) is a fourth ledge, which, if it

cannot be run, is more easily portaged beginning on the
left bank. The West Branch soon joins the Main Branch
(15¼ mi).

Below the confluence, the Machias River flows with good
current and occasional easy rapids for 4½ miles to ME-9
(19¾ mi). Stop well before the bridge, because the river
above it has been channeled, with the result that there are
few good stopping places in the swift current. Airline Rapids, below the bridge, should be scouted.

MOPANG STREAM

The trip from the boat landing on Mopang Lake to the
Machias River above Wigwam Rapids is a semi-wilderness
run of 32 miles, with only an occasional cabin or dirt road
to suggest otherwise. Mopang Stream flows through the
blueberry barrens, so that the canoer gets a feeling of space
similar to what travel on lakes provides. The dominant
groundcover of sheep laurel and lowbush blueberries, sprin-
kled with isolated red pines and stands of poplar and gray
birch, provides a distinct contrast to most other rivers in
Maine.

Below the end of Mopang Stream at Machias Eddy, the
nearest take-out is at Smith Landing, an additional 14¾
miles down the Machias River.

The water of Mopang Lake and Mopang Second Lake is
clear, but before it flows very far downstream it becomes
discolored by organic matter from swamps. The river below
Second Lake is small, and its banks are forested as far as
the meadow at First Lake. Beyond, it is mostly open.

Mopang Lake—ME-9   8¼ miles

Lakes, **Flatwater,** Class I–II
  High water: *May*
  Wild
       USGS: Lead Mountain 15, Tug Mountain 15
  Portage: 3½ mi   **Mopang Lake Dam**   15
                        yds
  Campsite: 5¾ mi   L **First Lake Outlet**
                        permit

Mopang Lake is reached by a dirt road that leaves ME-9 (the Airline) at a gravel pit 1.8 miles west of the bridge over Mopang Stream. Keep left at each of two forks. It is 3½ miles from the landing on Mopang Lake to the dam on Second Lake, which controls the water level on both bodies of water. The rapids below are barely passable at medium water. If the water is high, they should be scouted as far as the culvert ¾ mile downstream (road close by on left bank), for there is a sharp drop over a ledge and sometimes there are trees across the river.

Beyond the culvert (Road No. 5), the stream is Class I, with one or two blowdowns, becoming flat as it approaches Mopang First Lake. The latter is small, and below the old bridge at the outlet (5¾ mi) the river is wider and for the most part flat for 2½ miles to the ME-9 bridge (8¼ mi), although there are some Class I rips at and below the remains of an old log-driving dam just above the highway.

ME-9—Machias Eddy   23¾ miles

Flatwater, Class I, II
  High water: *May*
  Wild
        USGS: Tug Mountain 15
Campsites: 10¼ mi   R   **beside bridge** (poor)
                              permit
               15¼ mi   R   **Six Mile Dam**   permit

Most of the drop in elevation takes place in short pitches and at beaver dams. Only at Penman Rips are the rapids appreciably longer and more difficult. The rocks in the riverbed are coarse-grained, so they may scrape a canoe with unexpected authority in medium water. Much of the way the river traverses the blueberry barrens, but in the last three miles above the Machias River, it passes through conifer forests.

For several miles there are intermittent, easy rapids, after which the stream meanders through the barrens. Beech Hill Brook enters on the right 8 miles below ME-9 and, after winding for another 2¼ miles, the stream passes under a bridge (10¼ mi) near Duck Pond. For the next 5 miles to Six

Mile Dam (15¼ mi) the current is slow, with an occasional easy rip.

Six Mile Dam can be run, but there are some nasty spikes on the far left side. Below, the rapids are more difficult and more frequent, and there are also some rather high beaver dams. After 3½ miles you reach Penman Rips (18¾ mi), Class III, at least. **Caution!** These rapids begin just above a left turn, and at the top there are two ledges. Below the latter, the river is narrow with large boulders for about 50 yards, after which the gradient lessens. Below Penman Rips, ¾ mile, there is a short drop under a partially collapsed bridge (19¾ mi). The next 4 miles to the confluence with the Machias River (23¾ mi) are mostly flat, with occasional rips.

The next take-out, Smith Landing, is 14¾ miles down the Machias.

OLD STREAM

This river flows into the Machias River about 5 miles above Great Falls. It flows from a series of lakes in T37 MD. Third and First lakes are wild, and Second Lake has only a few cabins along its south shore. Since Canaan Dam no longer impounds water, a section of the river below First Lake is in the meadowland on the bottom of a once-larger lake.

Much of Old Stream above ME-9 is not far from a logging road. However, below the highway, the river is very isolated, and it meanders considerably, occasionally within a narrow valley bordered by steep banks.

As recently as the 1950s, long logs were driven down the river by the Saint Regis Paper Company.

Second Lake—Machias River   **25 miles**

Lakes, **Flatwater, Quickwater,** Class II
  High or medium water: *May*
  Forested, Wild
        USGS: Wabassus Lake 15, Tug Mountain 15,
            Wesley 15

Portages:	4 mi	L	**Canaan Dam** 20 yds
	11¾ mi	L	**Stinking Jam Rapids** 50 yds
	15½ mi	L	**Longfellow Pitch** 30 yds
Campsites:	11¾ mi	L	**Stinking Jam Rapids** permit
	14 mi	R	**head of rapids opposite wooded island** permit

Access: There is a roadside rest area on ME-9 beside Old Stream. Three-quarters of a mile to the east a logging road leads north past Canaan Dam and Second Lake.

Put in below the culvert at the outlet of Second Lake, where a portage is necessary if you begin farther along the road. The river here is very small and somewhat choked by alders, but it soon opens into a meadow. Just above First Lake there is a washed-out driving dam, followed by a shallow run-out.

Flatwater continues from the outlet of First Lake (1¾ mi) to just above Canaan Dam, where there is another washed-out driving dam. The remains of the dams above and below First Lake are almost unrecognizable in high water.

Canaan Dam (4 mi) cannot be run. There is flatwater to Glover Pitch, which can be recognized, in addition to the sound of it, by a large ledge on the right bank. These rapids begin with a low rock dam, which is followed by 50 yards of easy Class II. The flatwater and quickwater between Glover Pitch and ME-9 are broken by Hayward Dam, a series of ledges, which should be lined on the right.

Below ME-9 (8 mi) there is quickwater for about ½ mile, after which the river meanders in a narrow valley between conifer forests. There are a few rips. Stinking Jam Rapids (11¾ mi) is an unrunnable ledge drop followed by Class II rapids. (Take the ledge at the next left turn to the left of center.)

There is a ¼-mile Class II rapid around an island, and some distance later a runnable ledge before Longfellows Pitch (15½ mi), a 4-foot ledge, which must be lined or portaged on the left. From that point there is flatwater nearly all the way past New Stream (24½ mi), which enters on the left to the Machias River (25 mi).

The nearest take-out is 2¾ miles downstream at Smith Landing (27¾ mi).

EAST MACHIAS RIVER

The East Machias River is a pleasing mixture of easy rapids, expansive meadows, and lakes of varying sizes. Because of the rapids close to ME-9, the entire river is canoeable only in high water. However, the upper section from Pocomoonshine Lake to Crawford Lake is always canoeable when ice-free, and below Round Lake the river can be negotiated at low water with some occasional scraping. There are a few cabins, but most of them are on the lakes below ME-9.

In spring, the 45-mile trip takes three or four days. The island campsite on Crawford Lake and the one on Second Lake are among the nicest in eastern Maine.

Pocomoonshine Lake—Crawford (via Maine River)	**10 miles**

Lakes, Flatwater			
Passable at all water levels			
Wild			
USGS: Big Lake 15			
Campsite:	8 mi	L	**1st island close to East shore** (S end) permit

From Pokey Lake a wide, sluggish river winds through wide meadows and small ponds to Crawford Lake. In the summer, it seems as though you are paddling past seas of grass. Seldom do trees grow within fifty yards of the river, so easy access to dry ground is the exception. There is also little protection from a strong wind.

In the town of Alexander, follow the road from ME-9 that leads north 2½ miles to Pocomoonshine Lake Lodges, where there is a launching area. In 2 miles the Maine River flows from the lake. It heads generally south through Upper Mud Lake (3½ mi), and Lower Mud Lake (4¾ mi) to Crawford Lake (7¼ mi). The Crawford Public Landing (10 mi) is a short way below the cove, around which the few houses are located.

Crawford—East Machias   35 miles

Lakes, Flatwater, Quickwater, Class I, II
  High water above ME-9: *May*
  High or medium water below ME-9: *May or June*
  Low water: *passable with some scraping below Round Lake*
  Wild, Settled, Towns
     USGS: Big Lake 15, Wesley 15, Gardner Lake
            15, Machias

Portage:	2½ mi	L	**Pokey Dam** 20 yds
	(35 mi)		**dam at East Machias)**
Campsites:	2½ mi	L	**Pokey Dam** (poor) permit
	(21) mi	L	**Second Lake** (1st point S of outlet) permit

This portion of the East Machias River makes a nice two-day trip in the spring, when the water is high and the air is faintly scented with the smell of burned or burning blueberry fields. Since the rapids are not too difficult, this river is more suitable for people with limited whitewater skill and experience than is the Machias or Narraguagus.

Put in at the Crawford Public Landing, which is reached by a side road next to the cemetery. The East Machias River, by name, begins 2½ miles south of the landing at Pokey Dam, the outlet to Crawford Lake. After portaging the dam on the left, there are easy rapids and quickwater for 1¾ miles before reaching a deadwater (4¼ mi). After ¾ mile there are more rapids to the ME-9 bridge (5½ mi).

Below the Airline bridge, the current gradually slackens; in 3¾ miles the river enters Great Meadow (9¼ mi). The latter extends for 4¼ miles to Great Meadow Riffles (13½ mi), a Class II rapid about ¼ mile long. The remaining 3 miles to Round Lake (16¾ mi) is flat. Slow current continues for 3¼ miles from the outlet of Round Lake (17¾ mi) to Second Lake (21 mi), past the mouth of Rocky Lake Stream (18½ mi), which enters left in Oak Point Meadows, and is broken only slightly by Munson Rips (19½ mi).

From the outlet of Second Lake on the west shore, the river is flat for ¾ mile. Then, within 1½ miles, there are five rapids, which get progressively harder, from Class I to Class II. At Wigwam Riffles (22¼ mi) there is a low, runnable weir, and within ¼ mile there is another rapid.

Crooked Pitch (23 mi) is on both sides of an island, with the clearest channel on the right; and Smith Mill Pitch (23¼ mi) and Lower Riffles (23¾ mi) are straight chutes in high water. After 3½ miles of flatwater, including another large meadow, the river flows into Hadley Lake (27¼ mi). The outlet is 3¾ miles down the east shore. In the 1¼ miles between the lake and the ME-191 bridge, there are two easy rapids at low or washed-out dams.

There is a short Class II drop under the ME-9 bridge (32¼ mi), and another easier one past the next road bridge. The remaining 1¾ miles to East Machias are flatwater.

The dam at East Machias (34½ mi) no longer impounds water. **Caution!** Keep to the left, the inside of the turn, as you approach the town. Stop above the bridge to scout or portage. In medium and high water much of the debris and protruding steel is obscured. Caution is strongly advised. In low water, you can let down through the gates. Below the dam there are sporty Class II rapids, runnable at all water levels. At low tide they continue past the last bridge (35 mi), but the river fans out and the water gets noticeably shallower.

NORTHERN INLET & ROCKY LAKE STREAM

Northern Inlet, the tributary of Rocky Lake described here, is the beginning of an excellent summer trip that continues on the East Machias River below the mouth of Rocky Lake Stream. The lower East Machias is passable at all water levels, although sections of a few rapids, particularly Crooked Pitch, are bony in low water. This trip to the sea at the town of East Machias is 25¾ miles long, and it takes two full days when the water level is down.

Off ME-191—East Machias River 9¼ miles

Lake, **Flatwater,** Quickwater, Class I, II
  Passable at all water levels
  Wild
        USGS: Gardner Lake 15, *Wesley 15*
Campsites: 3½ mi   L   **Mud Landing**   permit,
                                 car
                 4½ mi   L   **Rocky Lake** (beach at S
                                 end)   permit, car

This trip begins at a bridge on a road that leads off ME-191 in T18 ED, just 1.9 miles north of the second railroad crossing from US-1 in East Machias. It is a dirt road; 2.8 miles from the highway it crosses Northern Inlet. It continues on to meet ME-9 at a sharp bend in Crawford, where a side road leads to Love Lake.

Begin on the right bank below the bridge. For most of the distance to Rocky Lake the stream is deep, wide, and flat. There are, however, about five very short, narrow sections with Class I–II rapids in high water; they must be lined or dragged in low water. At the last of these, an old log bridge blocks the stream at high water.

Mud Landing (3½ mi) is on the left just after the last rapid. It is another access point that can be reached via a dirt road, which leads off ME-191 about 1.5 miles north of the above-mentioned railroad crossing. One-half mile farther on, Northern Inlet opens into Rocky Lake (4 mi).

From the outlet (6½ mi) near the north end of the lake, Rocky Lake Stream, all flatwater, flows for 2¾ miles past the mouth of Northern Stream (8¼ mi) to the East Machias River (9¼ mi).

The first take-out downstream is at the ME-191 bridge below Hadley Lake, 13¾ miles to the left.

JOSH STREAM, GARDNER LAKE, and CHASE MILLS STREAM

Lakes and boggy streams combine for a beautiful 10-mile trip through surprisingly wild country. It runs from the isolated and remote Josh Pond to the East Machias River.

Access to Josh Pond via Sunken Lake   1 mile

From a wooded peninsula on the west shore of a marsh at the end of a shallow, winding channel off the southwest end of Sunken Lake, follow a trail first west along the peninsula, then southwest avoiding bogs to the left. The route is occasionally flagged by red tape. Cross a wet spot and ascend a low ridge. Turn right onto an old tote road a third of a mile from Sunken Lake. A ½ mile up the tote road turn left at a wooden boundary post. The trail descends south through open woods past a rock outcropping and a mossy green boulder on the left and then follows a dry ridge south. In sight of the lake it angles left off the ridge, reaching Josh Pond 300 feet east of the prominent point on the north shore of the pond. The route is dry and the grades gentle; not a hard carry for its length.

Josh Pond may also be reached by paddling upstream from Gardner Lake Road.

Josh Pond—East Machias   9½ miles

Lake, Flatwater, Class II
  All seasons if rapids are portages
  Wild, Rural
          USGS: Gardner Lake 15, Machias Bay

| Portage: | 7 mi | e | **Chase Mills** | 100 ft or ½ mi |
| Campsite: | 4 mi | L | **point between Second and Gardner lakes** | |

From the northwest corner of Josh Pond, beside a grassy bluff with scattered trees, Josh Stream winds slowly through a broad marsh. The channel is wide and deep; wild geese, ducks, and a bald eagle may be seen. Gardner Lake Road is 1½ miles from the pond; lift over the culvert and push over a log jam below. Just before Second Lake duck under a low bridge.

Paddle 1½ miles down Second Lake and turn left past a point and island into Gardner Lake. There is a campsite on the left opposite the island. Gardner Lake is beautiful, with forested bluffs and islands. Chase Mills is 3½ miles down the lake.

If Chase Mills Stream is high, there is ½ mile of Class II rapids to run. If it does not look high enough below the dam, carry ½ mile southwest down the road and carry 1000 feet northwest across a meadow to the stream.

After a few hundred feet of Class I rapids the stream flattens out, and after a mile it flows into the East Machias River. Another mile downstream is the village of East Machias on the right.

In Indian times this route, together with the Orange River, was an important route from Cobscook Bay to the Machias. This trip is still possible with 1¾ miles of carrying in three portages. It can be extended for miles by exploring Rocky Lake, Roaring Lake, Harmon or Clifford Streams, and the northern arms of Second Lake.

WHITING BAY and DENNYS BAY

Whiting Bay leads from the Orange River out to Dennys Bay and on out to Passamaquoddy Bay. Any canoeing on tidewater demands experience, consideration of the weather and wind direction, as well as the state of the tide.

Whiting—Reversing Falls   7½ miles

At low tide the head of Whiting Bay is just deep enough to float a loaded canoe. To Leighton Point (2½ mi) the Bay is narrow, often constricted by rocky points, very scenic. The tide runs at 3–5 knots. Where the bay widens beyond Freds Island there are mild currents down either shore. In the main channel down the center there may be 1- to 2-foot waves.

At Reversing Falls most of the tidal flow squeezes between Falls Island and Leighton Neck. A large reef exposed at all but high tide forms a big eddy with large wave trains along the eddy lines. The channel between the reef and Falls Island has a long line of 3-foot waves. The west channel has impressive boils and swirls. The mean tide range is 20 feet, and the rapids are probably Class III at midtide. At high tide, all this mayhem stops briefly for about 10 minutes.

ORANGE RIVER

Orange River is the outlet for a series of lakes, of which Rocky Lake is the largest, flowing east to Whiting Bay. It is an attractive, semi-wild flatwater trip available anytime. Rocky and Sunken lakes penetrate remote country.

Rocky and Sunken Lakes

Sunken Lake can be reached from Rocky Lake via a broad, shallow channel dotted with beaver lodges. Since the dam at Halls Mills burned, the lake has shrunk, and the northwest and southwest bays shown on the Gardner Lake 15 map have returned to marsh. Wildlife is common.

Rocky Lake extends 3 miles north, and Rocky Lake Stream is canoeable into the marshes nearly a mile more. Rocky Lake deserves its name: rugged bluffs and bare rock knobs grace every view.

Halls Mills—Whiting   6¼ miles

Flatwater, Class II
Passable most seasons with a little wading below US-1
Forested, Rural
    USGS: Gardner Lake 15, Whiting
Portages: 2½ mi L
             5¼ mi L **LLP Dam and falls at US-1** ¼ mi
       (6¼ mi L **Whiting Dam and rapids to tidewater)**

In high water the small connecting stream is runnable. Coming down Rocky Lake take the left channel and lift over the crumbling remains of a dam. The brook twists through alders to a culvert, which is runnable if not blocked by debris. Check first! A few hundred feet beyond is Dumpling Falls, a steep, straight flume dropping 4 feet (Class II) to the flatwater of Orange Lake. In low water this ¼ mile must be carried.

One-mile-long Orange Lake is pretty, but not as wild or rugged as Rocky Lake. One mile of marshy, gentle river with only one riffle under a bridge leads to the next lake, shaped like an X. One-half-mile down the lake a short carry at a house on the left connects to Roaring Lake, which wanders 1½ miles back into wild country.

Continuing down "Lake X," take the right channel, then the left in ¼ mile. After ¾ mile turn right again. At the old Lubec Light and Power dam, land on the left carefully. Beyond the dam is a Class III–IV chute under the old bridge and a Class IV falls under the new bridge.

To continue to Whiting, turn right and cross the old bridge. Cross US-1 and turn left at a closed-up house. Follow a dirt road 100 feet and turn left into the woods down a trail to the river below the bridges. The carry is ¼ mile long.

In the summer, the next ¼ mile will be low and require some wading. In the spring, there is a Class I–II rapid on the left-hand bend and beyond the next right-hand bend a Class II drop. The remaining ¾ mile to Whiting is flatwater. Land on the left along US-1 to finish an Orange River cruise or to portage to Whiting Bay. Below the dam at Whiting is a long series of Class II rapids that are normally too shallow to run even in the spring. Carry along US-1 and then cut right through a grassy area to the head of tide. The length of the carry is ⅓ mile at low tide, significantly less at high tide. Beyond is the rapid tidal river known as Whiting Bay.

HOBART STREAM

Hobart Stream rises on the western edge of Edmunds, flows into Hobart Lake and then east and finally north where it forms the western boundary of the Moose Horn Wildlife Refuge. It flows into Dennys Bay a few miles south of Dennysville.

The only access is by logging roads, which are overgrown at this time, or the North Trail, a gravel road of Moosehorn Refuge that is controlled by a gate and open only during hunting and fishing seasons.

Hobart Bog—Dennys Bay   7 miles

Most of the distance is smoothwater. Many obstructions block the upper part. There are frequent sharp drops, most of which are unrunnable and must be lined or carried. Not recommended.

The best approach would be to paddle upstream from US-1. See USGS Gardner Lake, Whiting, Pembroke.

DENNYS RIVER

The Dennys River flows out of Meddybemps Lake in the town of Meddybemps first southward, then southeast to Dennysville, where it flows into an arm of Passamaquoddy Bay. It is mixed smooth and rapid, with a good current and a number of rips, which provide a varied interest to the run.

Meddybumps—ME-86   18 miles

Flatwater, Quickwater, Class I, II
   Medium water: *rapids bony in low water*
   Wild
            USGS: Calais 15, Gardner Lake 15, Pembroke

Below the dam at Meddybumps Lake the quickwater soon slows down for the 7 miles of mostly smoothwater through swampy country to the site of Gilman Dam. This can be reached from the west by high-clearance vehicles via a rough logging road from East Ridge Road 2½ miles south of ME-191.

It is 1½ miles to Gardner Rips and another 1½ miles to Ayers Rips. Here the river becomes much more winding, and after passing around the north end of the Whaleback reaches Stoddard Rips in 2 miles. Little Falls, 2 miles below, is somewhat more of a rapid. Just below here the river turns south for a short bit and in 1½ miles reaches Camp Rips. Take out on the left above the railroad bridge 1 mile below Camp Rips, for there the river drops through a rough gorge.

ME-86—Dennysville   2¾ miles

Class I, II, III
  Medium water
  Forested
      USGS: Pembroke

Carefully look over the severe drop that is 200 feet beyond the bridge. It can be run by keeping as close as possible to the ledge along the right bank. Intermittent Class I-II rapids continue for the next half-mile. Soon Cathance Stream enters on the right (¾ mi). Tidewater begins just below the Dennys River Salmon Club (1½ mi). At midtide a Class II run can be made through Dennysville to take out on the left bank at the US-1 bridge where the river widens into Dennys Bay.

CATHANCE STREAM

Cathance Stream rises in Lake Cathance, which is located in Cooper and Township 14, and flows south and east to the Dennys River shortly above Dennysville.

Lake Cathance—ME-86   9 miles

Quickwater, Class I, II
  High water
  Wild
      USGS: Gardner Lake, Pembroke

Launch on the west side of Cathance Lake from ME-191. The outlet leaves from a long bay at the east southeast side of the lake.

Because the grade is unusually consistent, there are no rapids of special note—rather pleasant, mild, talking water. The rapids are steepest at the start, gradually moderating, with the last 2 miles quickwater.

A series of severe, unrunnable drops begins just above the ME-86 bridge, which is the usual terminus of the trip.

ME-86—Dennys River   9 miles

Little information is available on this section, and the information below is third-hand. Below the steep drop it is 4 miles to Great Works Pond, with slower going the remaining distance to the Dennys River. There are said to be many obstructions.

SAINT CROIX RIVER

The Saint Croix River flows from North Lake on the Maine-New Brunswick border and runs generally south forming the southern portion of the international boundary. The upper part is largely a succession of lakes, the middle section has a number of Class I and II rapids, which are runnable much of the year, and the lower portion also has some rapids, although it is more developed.

Report to customs in advance when planning to cross the border on your trip.

Orient—Vanceboro   36 miles

Lakes, Flatwater, Quickwater
    Anytime
    Forested, Cottages
        USGS: Amity 15, Danforth 15, Forest 15,
            Vanceboro 15
    Portages: 16 mi L **(Canadian side)**
              36 mi R **Vanceboro**

The highest point on the river that is easily accessible is at the north end of Grand Lake, where one can put in just below the U.S. Customs office on Boundary Road east of Orient. From here one can go eastward through the thoroughfare to North Lake if desired, but the more usual route is to proceed directly down Grand Lake, the first of the Chiputneticook Lakes. At the north end, Grand Lake is narrow, less than 1 mile wide, but after about 5 miles it opens out into a very large body of water. Although there are a few settled spots here and there, most of the lake is wild. After about 7 miles in the larger part of the lake, the canoeist approaches the southern end, where he or she should be careful to keep on the east side, where in 1 mile more he or she will arrive at the outlet. On the southwest side there is a long arm, some 4 miles long, which runs down to a dead end. This makes a pleasant paddle between high hills, if one wishes to make a side trip. At the outlet there is 1 mile of fast current past Forest City to the long deadwater below. This deadwater is followed 2 miles north to a steep drop, necessitating a long carry on the Canadian side (left). After 1 mile more of river Spednik Lake is reached. This is a long, narrow, and winding lake, which is followed 19 miles to Vanceboro, where the dam should be carried on the right, that is, on the American side.

There are alternate portages from Mud Lake to Spednik Lake (see USGS Forest 15). The first runs from west to east and reaches Spednik Lake ½ mile north of Forest City Landing. The second begins just before entering the narrows at the northern end of Mud Lake and runs northeast to Booming Ground Cove on Spednik Lake.

Vanceboro—Kellyland   33 miles

Lakes, Flatwater, Class I, II
  Dam-controlled: *good flow spring through fall*
  Wild
          USGS: Vanceboro 15, Kellyland 15, *Waite 15*
    Portage: 33 mi   R   **Kellyland Dam**   100 yds
  Campsites: 9½ mi   R   **Little Falls**   MFS
             19¾ mi   R   **Loon Bay**   MFS car
             29½ mi   R   **Spednic Falls**   permit

The Saint Croix has runnable rapids when most other streams in New England are too low. This is because the dam on Spednik Lake is used to regulate part of the flow of water to the generator at Grand Falls Dam. The other regulated drainage area that supplies water to the power plant is that of the Grand Lake chain, but it enters the Saint Croix at Grand Falls flowage, so it does not affect the river between Vanceboro and Kellyland.

The rapids below Vanceboro are all relatively easy, Class I and II, with Little Falls being the most difficult. Topographic maps name a dozen rapids in the first twenty miles to Loon Bay, but most of them are easy and some are apt to be flooded out in high water. For information on the water level, contact the Engineering Department, Georgia Pacific Corporation, Woodland, Maine 04694. If one gate at Vanceboro is open five feet, the river below it will be "high."

The best part of the river is the thirty miles between Vanceboro and Grand Falls flowage, and it can easily be run in two days. The middle portion of the river is accessible by car at Loon Bay, and there is another road that reaches Grand Falls flowage near Spednic Falls. Information on these roads is most easily obtained from the District Ranger in Topsfield (just east on ME-6).

As you begin the trip, you pass under a railroad bridge, which was the scene of an early act of sabotage prior to America's entry into World War II. The bridge was blown up to prevent the Canadian Pacific from hauling supplies destined for England.

Under the railroad bridge is the end of "kill me quick" rapids followed by 2 miles of flatwater to Wing Dam Island; run either side. At the end of Wing Dam Island (1 mile), the paddler will reach Elbow Rips (easy Class I). It is 1½ miles to Mile Rips (easy Class II) and another 2½ miles to Tunnel Rips (easy Class II). The trip to George's Rips (easy Class II) is ½ mile. It is 1 mile to Hall's Rips (easy Class II) and another 1½ miles to Little Falls (Class III). Little Falls may be run on either side; easier on the right, more technical on the left. Good portage trail on the right for those who wish to partake. Then it is 1 mile to Pork Rips (old-timers maintain that the original name was Pork Rips not Fork Rips as listed now. It was here that a barrel of salted pork was lost when a freight canoe carrying the Wangan upset in the logging days 100 years ago). Another mile brings the canoeist to Cedar Island Rips (easy Class II). After Cedar Island, watch for a clearing on the right with a large, white birch tree. Here is the grave of a baby found in the river by loggers, and it has been maintained by them since the late 1800s. It is then 1 mile to Tyler Rips (easy Class II), and 2 miles to Albee Rips (easy Class II). There is a large picnic and camping ground on the left (Canadian) side. It is 1 mile to Rocky Rips (easy Class II), with another Canadian campground on the left, 1½ miles to Split Rock Rips (Class II), 1 mile to Meetinghouse Rips (Class II), and 2½ miles to Hay-cock Rips (Class II), which empties into Loon Bay (2 miles long). One and a half miles below Loon Bay is Canoose Rips. **Caution!** Scout here; water level is the key to passage. If it is low, line on left; if medium, paddle chute on left; on the right is a rocky Class III; in the center a Class IV. Watch for obstructions at Canoose—logs and debris.

Below what is now called Canoose Rips there follows about 1 mile of easy Class I rapids called Canoose Rapids. On to Dog Falls, where there is a runnable ledge on either side of the island, easier on the left. There are about 5½ miles of flatwater to Kendricks Rips. From here on is open flatwater to Kellyland Dam. The flowage, an open body of water with many peninsulas, is crossed. Canoeists should have a topo with them or they could spend the day looking for Kellyland Dam.

Kellyland—Calais   21 miles

Quickwater, Flatwater, Class II
   Partly dam-controlled; *usually runnable spring through fall*
   Forested, Towns, Settled
      USGS: Kellyland 15, Calais 15

Portages:	9½ mi	L	**Woodland Dam and rapids** 1,000 ft. to ⅓ mi
	19½ mi	L	**St. Croix Rapids and Milltown Dam** ⅔ mi
	21	R	**Calais Falls** 0 to 500 ft. per tide level
Campsites:	3½ mi	R	**informal sites on islands**

The lower portion of the Saint Croix River is a mixture of complete isolation and heavy industry, flatwater and very difficult rapids, rural countryside and large towns. The former of each pair predominates. It is a very large river because it has picked up substantial drainage from the west. The flow is good all summer, but occasionally it is low if Georgia Pacific's generators are not running.

From the power plant in Kellyland the river races downstream but after an exuberant but easy Class I mile it settles down to a slow, deep coast through the forest. It is an attractive north woods setting, almost wild. If you look underwater in the shallows, sunken logs from the old river drives are visible. Keep to the right-hand side of the island at Ash Brook for the deep channel. The deadwater of Woodland Lake begins here. The narrow channel to the left of Mosquito Island is blocked by stranded logs. On the right shore is a boat landing, 6½ miles from Kellyland.

Beyond here, the wild character of the river is traded for a more settled but still attractive setting, at least once Woodland is passed. Where the lake narrows at Woodland Junction, slip over a log boom, near the left shore. Approaching the dam and pulp mill at Woodland stay left to pass another boom and land at the left end of the dam to portage.

If the river channel is dry below the dam, carry 1,000 feet down across the first dry channel, up to the powerline pylons, and down and along the major dry channel to where the flow is restored from the mill. The footing is loose and rocky on this carry.

If the river is not dry below the dam, carry ⅓ mile down the railroad tracks and then to the right down to the river at the head of a small rapid.

In the first ½ mile are two Class I rapids, then the river is flat but shallow to Bailey Rips, a slightly harder Class I-II rapids. Below the deadwater of Loon Bay is another riffle at Butler Island and another Class I where the river turns left. When the river narrows just below Haywood Island there is a little Class I-II rapid.

At Upper Mills the river runs through a curving Class II rapid ⅖ miles long, ending in a broad, shallow bay. The next 3½ miles to Milltown are flatwater curving through marshes and hardwood forest. Take out on the left (Canadian) shore to carry St. Croix Rapids and the Milltown dam. Carry ⅔ miles either along the railroad or the road paralleling it on the left to a landing below the dam on the left shore.

St. Croix Rapids are really a falls, Class IV-V. The pool behind the dam is very short and complicated by a boom, so the carry is not worth breaking into two carries (around the falls and dam separately).

Below Milltown is ½ mile of Class II rapids ending at Union Mills. At high tide this is the end of flowing river. At low tide a pool extends ½ mile to Calais Falls, which drops to tide. The low tide carry is on the right, 500 feet long. At midtide the rapids are a heavy Class II-III. At high tide the falls are drowned, not even a ripple left. Take out on the right just beyond the bridge in Calais (pronounced Cowlus).

GRAND LAKE STREAM

Grand Lake Stream flows from West Grand Lake to Big Lake, the first in a series of lakes that connects with Grand Falls flowage on the Saint Croix River. The flow is dam-controlled, with the drainage area being the entire Grand Lake chain. The heavy rapids would be dangerous in high water, but provide a possible run when there is no water elsewhere. The dam is reached over a public road from US-1 north of Princeton, and is owned by Georgia Pacific Corporation in Woodland, Maine.

West Grand Lake—Big Lake   3 miles

Flatwater, **Class I, II**
  Low water: *dam-controlled*
  Wooded
        USGS: Wabassus Lake 15, Big Lake 15
     Portage: ¾ mi   L   **Big Falls**

If the water is high enough to run the rapids below the bridge in town, and low enough to run Little Falls, reached by a road down the left bank 2 miles to a picnic area, the rapids will be Class II except for Big Falls, which should probably be lined or carried.

Put in below the dam from either bank. Class II rapids extend a mile to Big Falls, around a sharp "S"-curve starting to the right with a house on the left bank; line on the left. Rapids continue another mile to the picnic area at Little Falls. (Camping is no longer permitted.) After another mile the rapids end at a group of cottages, but the paddle through the marsh to Big Lake is very beautiful. A fishing access lies in a deep cove to the left on Big Lake.

APPENDIX

American Whitewater Safety Code

The following code was prepared by the American Whitewater Affiliation.

I. PERSONAL PREPAREDNESS AND RESPONSIBILITY

1. **Be a Competent Swimmer** with the ability to handle yourself underwater.

2. **WEAR a Lifejacket.**

3. **Keep Your Craft Under Control.** Control must be good enough at all times to stop or reach shore before you reach any danger. Do not enter a rapid unless you are reasonably sure you can safely navigate it or swim the entire rapid in event of capsize.

4. **BE AWARE OF RIVER HAZARDS AND AVOID THEM. Following are the most frequent KILLERS.**
    A. **HIGH WATER.** The river's power and danger and the difficulty of rescue increase tremendously as the flow rate increases. It is often misleading to judge river level at the put-in. Look at a narrow, critical passage. Could a *sudden* rise from sun on a snow pack, rain, or a dam release occur on your trip?
    B. **COLD.** Cold quickly robs one's strength, along with one's will and ability to save oneself. Dress to protect yourself from cold water and weather extremes. When the water temperature is less than 50 degrees F, a diver's wetsuit is essential for safety in event of an upset. Next best is wool clothing under a windproof outer garment such as a splash-proof nylon shell; in this case

one should also carry matches and a complete change of clothes in a waterproof package. If, after prolonged exposure, a person experiences uncontrollable shaking or has difficulty talking and moving, he must be warmed immediately by whatever means available.

C. STRAINERS: Brush, fallen trees, bridge pilings, or anything else that allows river current to sweep through but pins boat and boater against the obstacle. The water pressure on anything trapped this way is overwhelming, and there may be little or no whitewater to warn of danger.

D. WEIRS, REVERSALS, AND SOUSE HOLES. The water drops over an obstacle, then curls back on itself in a stationary wave, as is often seen at weirs and dams. The surface water is actually going UPSTREAM, and this action will trap any floating object between the drop and the wave. Once trapped, a swimmer's only hope is to dive below the surface where current is flowing downstream, or try to swim out the end of the wave.

5. **Boating Alone** is not recommended. The preferred minimum is three craft.

6. **Have a Frank Knowledge of Your Boating Ability.** Don't attempt waters beyond this ability. Learn paddling skills and teamwork, if in a multiple-manned craft, to match the river you plan to boat.

7. **Be in Good Physical Condition** consistent with the difficulties that may be expected.

8. **Be Practiced in Escape** from an overturned craft, in self rescue, in rescue, and in **Artificial Respiration.** Know first aid.

9. **The Eskimo Roll** should be mastered by kayakers and canoeists planning to run large rivers and/or rivers with continuous rapids where a swimmer would have trouble reaching shore.

10. **Wear a Crash Helmet** where an upset is likely. This is essential in a kayak or covered canoe.

11. **Be Suitably Equipped.** Wear shoes that will protect your feet during a bad swim or a walk for help, yet will not interfere with swimming (tennis shoes recommended). Carry a knife and waterproof matches. If you need eyeglasses, tie them on and carry a spare pair. Do not wear bulky clothing that will interfere with your swimming when water-logged.

II. BOAT AND EQUIPMENT PREPAREDNESS

1. **Test New and Unfamiliar Equipment** before relying on it for difficult runs.

2. **Be Sure Craft Is in Good Repair** before starting a trip. Eliminate sharp projections that could cause injury during a swim.

3. Inflatable crafts should have **Multiple Air Chambers** and should be test inflated before starting a trip.

4. **Have Strong, Adequately Sized Paddles or Oars** for controlling the craft and carry sufficient spares for the length of the trip.

5. **Install Flotation Devices** in noninflatable craft, securely fixed, and designed to displace as much water from the craft as possible.

6. **Be Certain There Is Absolutely Nothing to Cause Entanglement** when coming free from an upset craft; i.e., a spray skirt that won't release or tangles around legs; life jacket buckles, or clothing that might snag; canoe seats that lock on shoe heels, foot braces that fail or allow feet to jam under them; flexible decks that collapse on boater's legs when a kayak is trapped by water pressure; baggage that dangles in an upset; loose rope in the craft, or badly secured bow/stern lines.

7. **Provide Ropes to Allow You to Hold Onto Your Craft** in case of upset, and so that it may be rescued. Following are the recommended methods:

    A. **Kayaks and Covered Canoes** should have 6-inch-diameter grab loops of ¼-inch rope attached to bow and stern. A stern painter 7 or 8 feet long is optional and may be used if properly secured to prevent entanglement.

    B. **Open Canoes** should have bow and stern lines (painters) securely attached consisting of 8 to 10 feet of ¼- or ⅜-inch rope. These lines must be *secured* in a way that they will not come loose accidentally and entangle the boaters during a swim, yet they must be ready for immediate use during an emergency. Attached balls, floats, and knots are *not* recommended.

    C. **Rafts and Dories** should have taut perimeter grab lines threaded through the loops usually provided.

8. **Respect Rules for Craft Capacity** and know how these capacities should be reduced for whitewater use. (Life raft ratings must generally be halved.)

9. **Carry Appropriate Repair Materials:** tape (heating duct tape) for short trips, complete repair kit for wilderness trips.

10. **Car Top Racks Must Be Strong** and positively attached to the vehicle, and each boat must be tied to each rack. In addition, each end of each boat should be tied to car bumper. Suction cup racks are poor. The entire arrangement should be able to withstand all but the most violent vehicle accident.

III. LEADER'S PREPAREDNESS AND RESPONSIBILITY

1. **River Conditions.** Have a reasonable knowledge of the difficult parts of the run, or if an exploratory trip, examine maps to estimate the feasibility of the run. Be aware of possible rapid changes in river level, and how these changes can affect the difficulty of the run. If important, determine approximate flow rate or level. If trip involves important tidal currents, secure tide information.

2. **Participants.** Inform participants of expected river conditions and determine if the prospective boaters are qualified for the trip. All decisions should be based on group safety and comfort. Difficult decisions on the participation of marginal boaters must be based on total group strength.

3. **Equipment.** Plan so that all necessary group equipment is present on the trip: 50 to 100 foot throwing rope, first aid kit with fresh and adequate supplies, extra paddles, repair materials, and survival equipment if appropriate. Check equipment as necessary at the put-in, especially: life jackets, boat flotation, and any items that could prevent complete escape from the boat in case of an upset.

4. **Organization.** Remind each member of individual responsibility in keeping group compact and intact between leader and sweep (capable rear boater). If group is too large, divide into smaller groups, each of appropriate boating strength, and designate group leaders and sweeps.

5. **Float Plan.** If trip is into a wilderness area, or for an extended period, your plans should be filed with appropriate authorities, or left with someone who will contact them after a certain time. Establishment of checkpoints along the way at which civilization could be contacted if necessary should be considered. Knowing location of possible help could speed rescue in any case.

IV. IN CASE OF UPSET

1. **Evacuate Your Boat Immediately** if there is imminent danger of being trapped against logs, brush, or any other form of strainer.

2. **Recover With an Eskimo Roll if Possible.**

3. **If You Swim, Hold Onto Your Craft.** It has much flotation and is easy for rescuers to spot. Get to the upstream end so craft cannot crush you against obstacles.

4. **Release Your Craft if This Improves Your Safety.** If rescue is not imminent and water is numbing cold, or if worse rapids follow, then strike out for the nearest shore.

5. **Extend Your Feet Downstream** when swimming rapids to fend against rocks. **Look Ahead.** Avoid possible entrapment situations: rock wedges, fissures, strainers, brush, logs, weirs, reversals, and souse holes. Watch for eddies and slackwater so that you can be ready to use these when you approach. Use every opportunity to work your way toward shore.

6. If others spill, **Go After the Boaters.** Rescue boats and equipment only if this can be done safely.

INDEX

Index